White Middle-Class Identities and Urban Schooling

Identity Studies in the Social Sciences

Series Editors: **Margaret Wetherell**, Open University; **Valerie Hey**, Sussex University; **Stephen Reicher**, St Andrews University

Editorial Board: **Marta Augoustinos**, University of Adelaide, Australia; **Wendy Brown**, University of California, Berkeley, USA; **David McCrone**, University of Edinburgh, UK; **Angela McRobbie**, Goldsmiths College, University of London, UK; **Chandra Talpade Mohanty**, Syracuse University, USA; **Harriet B. Nielsen**, University of Oslo, Norway; **Ann Phoenix**, Institute of Education, University of London, UK; **Mike Savage**, University of Manchester, UK .

Titles include:

Will Atkinson
CLASS, INDIVIDUALIZATION AND LATE MODERNITY
In Search of the Reflexive Worker

John Kirk and Christine Wall
WORK AND IDENTITY
Historical and Cultural Contexts

Ben Rogaly and Becky Taylor
MOVING HISTORIES OF CLASS AND COMMUNITY
Identity, Place and Belonging in Contemporary England

Margaret Wetherell (*editor*)
IDENTITY IN THE 21ST CENTURY
New Trends in Changing Times

Margaret Wetherell (*editor*)
THEORIZING IDENTITIES AND SOCIAL ACTION

Diane Reay, Gill Crozier and David James
WHITE MIDDLE-CLASS IDENTITIES AND URBAN SCHOOLING

Identity Studies in the Social Sciences
Series Standing Order ISBN 978–0–230–20500–0
(*outside North America only*)

You can receive future titles in this series as they are published by placing a standing order. Please contact your bookseller or, in case of difficulty, write to us at the address below with your name and address, the title of the series and the ISBN quoted above.

Customer Services Department, Macmillan Distribution Ltd, Houndmills, Basingstoke, Hampshire RG21 6XS, England

White Middle-Class Identities and Urban Schooling

Diane Reay
University of Cambridge, UK

Gill Crozier
Roehampton University

and

David James
Professor and Director of the ESRC Wales Doctoral Training Centre,
Cardiff University, UK

First published 2011
First published in paperback 2013 by
PALGRAVE MACMILLAN

Palgrave Macmillan in the UK is an imprint of Macmillan Publishers Limited, registered in England, company number 785998, of Houndmills, Basingstoke, Hampshire RG21 6XS.

Palgrave Macmillan in the US is a division of St Martin's Press LLC, 175 Fifth Avenue, New York, NY 10010.

Palgrave Macmillan is the global academic imprint of the above companies and has companies and representatives throughout the world.

Palgrave® and Macmillan® are registered trademarks in the United States, the United Kingdom, Europe and other countries.

ISBN 978–0–230–22401–8 hardback
ISBN 978–1–137–35501–0 paperback

This book is printed on paper suitable for recycling and made from fully managed and sustained forest sources. Logging, pulping and manufacturing processes are expected to conform to the environmental regulations of the country of origin.

A catalogue record for this book is available from the British Library.

A catalog record for this book is available from the Library of Congress.

Transferred to Digital Printing in 2013

Contents

List of Tables

Preface to the Paperback Edition

It is a little over two years since the first publication of *White Middle-Class Identities and Urban Schooling* and we are delighted that it is now available in paperback. Two years is a long time in politics and in education, and for that reason we need to say something about the most important continuities and changes that have a bearing on the relevance of the book.

Firstly, processes of individualisation, marketisation and the dismantling of the welfare state in Britain, have accelerated alongside society becoming more and more unequal. Prolonged economic recession is met with austerity measures that are internationally contested. Austere times normally bring a sense of 'we're all in this together', but 21st century austerity has proved to be different, generating further divisiveness in relation to social class, race and ethnicity. Immigrants, alongside the putative 'benefit scroungers' and 'skivers', are seen to be simultaneously threatening and greedy. In this new neoliberal discursive landscape the working-classes, both white and minority ethnic, play an increasingly important symbolic and affective role in how the middle-classes understand themselves. Whilst poor and working-class people are pathologised, middle-class attitudes, behaviours and lifestyles are presented as normal and are valorized. This might be expected to provide a psychic bolstering of the middle-class self.

Things are not, however, that straightforward. Whilst inequalities deepen, there has also emerged what some have termed the 'squeezed middle': for many of this group, the near-certainties of middle-class life have gone, as welfare cuts bite, job security is non-existent and credential inflation – particularly for graduates – takes hold and is felt more keenly by more people. More of the middle-classes find themselves on uncertain ground, positioned between an extremely rich powerful elite and a growing number of struggling poor. For people like those in our study, this economic and social in-between-ness is lived out, practically and psychologically, in a struggle with a contradiction between wanting the best educationally for their own children, yet at the same time desiring a fair educational system for all children. Such tensions generate anxiety, insecurity and ambivalence.

One key area of insecurity is in relation to social reproduction. While the notion of 'an aspiration nation' encapsulates empty promises for the vast majority of working-class people, we also need to ask what it represents for the middle-classes, especially those using state schools, when so few of their children are upwardly socially mobile and increasing numbers are at risk of downward mobility.

Linked to stalling social mobility is the current state of the labour market. At a time when opportunities for the elite appear to continue unabated, the ordinary middle-classes are anxiously seeking ways to gain their child at least a chance of a competitive edge. We see this clearly in these white middle-class families sending their children to multi-ethnic state comprehensives and the pervasive rationale that doing so gives access to particular forms of capital, ranging from a multicultural awareness, ease or fluency, to exposure to a mix of social classes, to being 'streetwise' and avoiding the social narrowness that parents often reported characterized their own schooling. Yet the choice of school is a multi-layered and uneasy one in which the contradictions and psychic dilemmas that arise in trying to act ethically in an unethical situation remain serious, troubling and persistent.

It remains crucial to distinguish between the 'against the grain choosers' in this study, and what we might term 'mainstream choosing', whilst also appreciating the overlaps between the two. By 'mainstream choosing' we mean the more excluding and exclusive white middle-classes using conventional measures of academic examination results, league tables and school reputations, and of course the independent sector, to secure advantage and avoid whole swathes of school provision. (In England at least, Government policy has recently revalued the main currency here, so that a wide range of qualifications that are vocational or skills-focused, hitherto accepted as equivalent to the academic qualifications, will no longer 'count' when schools are compared). Those choosing ordinary urban comprehensive secondary schools make a very different choice to most of their middle-class peers, often dismissing conventional indicators and comparisons that would portray their choice is a 'bad' one. However, they do so under conditions of anxious rather than accepting proximity. They share, with the traditional middle-class, some of the fears of the working-class 'other', yet still make a decision that could be deemed more inclusive.

As well as being psychologically difficult, the situation is also sociologically complex. Contrary to what might be expected, the choice of an ordinary urban comprehensive secondary school does not seem to undermine the educational advantages associated with a middle-class background. Rather, there appear to be strong affinities between the parents' wish for an environment in which their child is highly nurtured, and the school's need to maximize its measurable outcomes in a currency that will be more widely recognized. Parental and school perceptions of academic prowess and potential appear largely in alignment. The attribution of 'brightness' (and similar characteristics), highly prevalent across our interviews, denotes a confidence that high achievement was likely, and this was bound up with a sense of entitlement. A range of mechanisms (e.g. being a governor, having personal contacts with teachers) and extra resources (e.g. the Gifted and Talented scheme) found their way to supporting the educational project of the white middle-class child, and help explain why these young people did so well in conventional academic terms.

The book offers a detailed account of these intricate social processes, and has generated some interest amongst educational researchers. But it is also our intention that by understanding these processes, this might be of some help to parents, teachers, head-teachers, governors, and the many other groups with a stake in education. For education to work towards social justice requires that we first understand how it works to confirm or generate social inequality, and we would argue that parents like those we interviewed, are in a particularly strong position to make a difference in this regard.

Diane Reay, Gill Crozier and David James, April 2013

Series Editors' Preface

The concept of identity has had a long and chequered history in the social sciences – many chafe at its ambiguity and frustrating complexity – yet it remains the pivotal site for exploring the relations between social life and subjectivity. Who we are is always complicated – a matter of social classifications, shifting social categorisations and group memberships, and a matter, too, of the ways in which social and cultural materials are organised as psychology and taken on as personal projects. Identity draws attention to 'names' and 'looks'. It is lived out in grand narratives and performances which construct sometimes passionately invested 'imagined' routes and destinies as well as in the more mundane arenas of everyday interaction, inter-subjective relations and in social institutions. Identity guides and predicts social action. It highlights positions and intelligibility defining what is possible and liveable and what is unthinkable and excessively troubled.

We suggest, in short, that identity is one of the most interesting points at which the trajectories of post-colonial societies, globalisation and assumptions about 'liquid modernity' come into focus along with new formations of social class, gender relations and issues of inequality, rights and social justice. Identity is at the heart of some of the most intractable and troubling contemporary social problems – community conflict, racism, discrimination, xenophobia and marginalisation.

It is the key laboratory, too, for any social psychologist focused on the interface of personal lives and social lives.

Identity Studies in the Social Sciences brings together psychologists, sociologists, anthropologists, geographers, social policy researchers, education researchers and political scientists to address this territory. The interdisciplinary reach of the series is matched by the degree of theoretical diversity. The books reflect on and take inspiration from the many 'theory wars' in the social sciences which have used identity as their hinge and also develop new theory and critique for current times, including new ontologies and new politics to do justice to contemporary amalgams of practices and subjectivities. The series includes empirical work, scholarly debate and research reviews on the core social categories and the intersections of these including 'race', ethnicity, social class, gender, generation, disability, nationality and sexuality along with less easily nameable social and institutional categorisations and affiliations. *Identity Studies in the Social Sciences* highlights the ways in which identities are formed, managed and mobilised in contexts and spaces such as schools, workplaces, clinics, homes, communities and streets. We welcome you to this rich collection of accounts from the various front-lines of identity studies.

Margaret Wetherell, Valerie Hey and Stephen Reicher

Acknowledgements

We would like to thank the other members of the team with whom we conducted the research project *Identities, Educational Choice and the White Urban Middle Classes* on which this book is based – namely Phoebe Beedell, Sumi Hollingworth, Fiona Jamieson and Katya Williams. We are also very grateful to Margie Wetherell for her excellent leadership of the Economic and Social Research Council-funded Programme *Identities and Social Action*, which we found offered support and challenge in exactly the right balance. As series editor, Margie also provided very helpful comments on an earlier draft of the book. We are indebted to the parents and young people who were so generous with their time and so willing to share their views and experiences during our fieldwork, and to the school head teachers who helped us to make contact with some of our participants.

We also wish to acknowledge the Economic and Social Research Council whose grant (ref. RES-148-25-0023) made this work possible.

Diane Reay, Gill Crozier, David James

Introduction: The White Middle-Classes in the Twenty-First Century – Identities Under Siege?

Mike Savage (2003 p. 536) argues that 'the unacknowledged normality of the middle-class needs to be carefully unpicked and exposed.' This book unpicks the unacknowledged normality of both whiteness and middle-classness. It does so through an analysis of white middle-class identities and privilege and the importance of personal and family histories in this. We take the globally topical and salient issue of school choice as the central lens through which we examine the 'normality' and identity formations of the middle-classes. School choice is a particularly apposite lens for examining contemporary white middle-class life. Choice and the ability to make choices across a wide range of areas lies at the heart of white middle-class identity. And as social reproduction becomes a more risky and uncertain process for the middle-classes, greater psychological, social and economic resources are invested in making the 'right' school choice. School choice then is used here as an analytical tool for understanding white middle-class identities and identity formation in a global age characterised by uncertainty, financial crises and the hegemony of self-interest.

Our analysis looks back to the twentieth century for the antecedents of middle-classness becoming an ideal social identity, and at developed countries across the globe, in particular the United States (Brantlinger 2003; Lareau 2003; Weis 2008), the United Kingdom (Ball 2003, 2008) and Australia (McLeod and Yates 2008), in order to interrogate the continuing hegemony of white middle-class privilege. Throughout we engage with dominant discourses of neoliberalism, arguing that these have changed the landscape, reduced the spaces for mutuality and respect in Western society and had powerful consequences for white middle-class identities in the twenty-first century. Despite the advent of the 'age of anxiety', the emergence of the 'super-rich', and economic

1

upheavals (Apple 2010), it appears that the white middle-classes continue to thrive, their social position strengthened and consolidated. However, there are also growing signs of unease, the exacerbation of anxiety and a lack of ontological security, 'the sense of continuity and order in events, including those not directly within the perceptual environment of the individual' (Giddens 1991 p. 243). These insecurities are particularly evident in regard to their children's education, and the book's main focus is white middle-class relationships to education.

In both the United States (Lareau 2003; Van Galen and Noblit 2007; Weis 2008) and the United Kingdom (Savage 2000; Ball 2003; Skeggs 2004; Sayer 2005), scholars have also begun to focus on the lived experience of class, and this is a central concern of our book. As Weis (2004) asserts, with the growing ascendancy of neoliberalism accompanied by an intensification of social inequalities in the United States (Apple 2003, 2010), the United Kingdom (Blanden et al. 2007; Seager and Milner, 2006) and more widely (Freeman-Moir and Scott 2003; McLeod and Yates 2006), the need for serious class-based analyses could not be more pressing. However, the focus of much social justice work has traditionally been on the working-classes (Sennett and Cobb 1973; Willis 1977; Weis 1990; Skeggs 1997), and this has also been our focus in the past. We have written about both the white and black working-classes (Reay 1998b; Crozier 2000), but as Curry-Stevens (2008) argues, it is increasingly necessary to shift our gaze from the margins to the centre. So this book is different because it is about 'people like us', the white middle-classes, and more specifically, public sector liberals committed to the welfare state and to ebbing notions of collectivity. As such it generates difficult, uncomfortable feelings. Driven by the data, the analysis that it develops undermines the integrity of the 'we' that in optimistic moments the authors and people we know like to think we belong to, a particular fraction of the white middle-classes who both pride themselves on their liberal values and are still basking in the glow of cosmopolitan multiculturalism. Our findings question any easy, comfortable sort of belonging along these lines. In part, this is because of the wider social and economic context in which the white middle-classes in the global north find themselves (Connell 2007). It is a context that generates troubled and uneasy white middle-class identities that are far removed from earlier depictions of a complacent and comfortable white middle-class that dominated research in the last century. As Jacob Hacker (2006) asserts in relation to the United States, 'the insecurities that were once limited to the working poor have increasingly crept into the lives of middle-class.' In particular, the stable, middle-class, emotional economy, in which satisfactions, entitlements and a sense of ease balance fears and anxieties is now beginning to topple, as risks threaten to outweigh familiar securities (Kalleberg 2009). The sense of being right and being secure that permeated perceptions of the white middle-classes in the last half of the twentieth century, including those of the white middle-classes themselves, is increasingly questionable.

At the beginning of the twenty-first century research points to a growing class polarisation within the most economically advanced societies (Blanden and Machin 2007; Foster and Wolfson 2010). This growth in inequalities is seen to be underpinned by two major trends. Firstly, the disappearance of collective institutions capable of mitigating the effects of global capitalism, a process involving the repositioning of the universal values associated with the idea of the public realm (Ben-Ner and Putterman 1998). Secondly, processes of individualisation (Beck 1992) which it is argued have developed directly out of the disintegration of welfarism (Dobbernack 2010). As Graham Crow contends, while in the past the welfare state used to institutionalise commonality of fate, currently 'the sense of all citizens engaged in a collective endeavour and enjoying common entitlements has broken down as individuals have come increasingly to calculate whether they are winners or losers in such arrangements' (Crow 2002 p. 35). For some sociologists this has led to the imposition of 'a sort of moral Darwinism' that 'institutes the struggle of all against all and cynicism as the norm of all action and behaviour' (Bourdieu 1998 p. 4), resulting in cultures that stress individual choice and responsibility, and which promote high levels of competitiveness. One consequence, according to Ulrich Beck (1992 p. 141), is that 'community is dissolved in the acid bath of competition.' As Berking (1996) argues, processes of privatisation and social protectionism appear to have generated a society where accrual and acquisitiveness are prioritised, and assets in solidarity have been exhausted. The irony is that current debates have moved from an earlier view of the family as the bedrock of society and a haven from competitive individualism, greed and the rampant consumerism that characterised both the workplace and the wider social world (Lasch 1978) to progressively positioning the family as central in the making of a selfish, acquisitive, uncaring, hyper-performance culture (James 2008). Recent moral panics focus not on the traditional object of moral concerns, the working-classes, but on parenting more generally, while a national survey of contemporary UK childhood singles out selfish parents and excessive individualism as contributing to high levels of unhappiness among children (Layard and Dunn 2009). The very qualities that, in the past, secured white middle-class privilege are now seen to be destabilising the white middle-class sense of security and equilibrium. It could be argued that Barbara Ehrenreich's (1990) prescient commentary on the America of the 1980s is even more valid today. Ehrenreich presents an analysis of a white middle-class in retreat from values of democracy and fairness as they struggle to protect their class and ethnic privilege. This may be a viable explanation of contemporary English white middle-class practices in the field of education.

Such trends seem to be pervasive. One possible way of countering them lies in revitalising notions of 'the common good' in particular through a continuing commitment to, and defence of, the public sector by the middle-classes who are not its main intended beneficiaries. Tony Crosland, a prominent champion of the Welfare State, saw universality of provision as a vital stepping stone in achieving social equality and commitment to the common good (Crosland 1962). The study upon which we draw in the book gives particular consideration to this possibility through its focus on middle-class choice of ordinary public sector schools. However, Sayer (2005) stresses the need to recognise the conundrum the middle-classes are caught up in, forced to address the troubling issue of how to balance ideals against social privilege and tactical imperatives for social reproduction. This is particularly difficult as the new century moves into its second decade, and the fragility and volatility of national economies in a still largely unregulated global free market becomes evident (Hutton 2010). Economic commentators (Mishel et al. 2009) view the economic downturn affecting both North America and Europe as greatly undermining the security and stability of the white middle-classes (Behreandt 2007; MacWhirter 2008). One of the US President Barack Obama's first White House economic briefings predicted that job losses would double in 2009 from their already high 2008 levels and that many of these losses would be white-collar jobs (*New York Times* 2010).

The majority view emerging from these debates is white middle-class identities are increasingly under threat, subject to economic forces beyond their control and sharing in a growing sense of insecurity that was once the preserve of the working-classes but now permeates almost the whole of society. If this is the case it could be further argued that just as the integrity and value of the working-classes was undermined over the last decades of the twentieth century (Skeggs 2004), the beginning of the twenty-first century may herald the unravelling of white middle-class identity. The view of Pearmain (2008) and many experts on the left is that we are indeed now witnessing an equivalent disintegration of the comfortable, complacent, settled middle-classes. The contemporary moment then can be seen as a pivotal one for the white middle-classes. The current crisis could result in retrenchment and a culture of protectionism and safeguarding of white middle-class privileges or it could produce a more creative and generative questioning of the status quo; one that might lead to more openness, reflexivity and fairness. The irony has been that throughout our recent 'age of reflexivity' there has been a lack of reflexivity, especially with regard to degrees of privilege, social inequalities and the consequences of class.

Historically the academic and political consensus around white middle-class identity constructed it as an idealised one held up for the lower classes to aspire to. Currently, in the 2010s the white middle-classes, and in particular the images of them as they are inscribed in policy discourses, best fit the traditional notions of the democratic citizen – individualistic, responsible, participatory, the active chooser. However, more and more research on social class and whiteness both in the United Kingdom and in the United States is disrupting such comfortable notions of the white middle-classes. It points to particularly disquieting aspects of this normative white middle-class identity. We can glimpse the ways in which neoliberalism has seeped into the middle-class soul, via Tony Giddens' excluding and exclusive white middle-classes (Giddens 2000), Tim Butler and Gary Robson's isolationist non-mixers (Butler with Robson 2003), and Stephen Ball's strategic, self-interested profit maximisers (Ball 2003). In the United States, there are Barbara Ehrenreich's anxious paranoid middle-classes with their fear of falling socially (Ehrenreich 1990) and Elaine Brantlinger's selfish white middle-class parents hell-bent on their children outperforming their peers (2003).

It increasingly appears that the still idealised norm of the successful white middle-class as 'go-getting', high-flying, winners take – all no longer works against a backdrop of excessive greed, political rapaciousness, financial irresponsibility, deception and mismanagement on a global scale. Competitive individualism and self-interest, middle-class qualities that have been particularly valorised over the last 30 years, are argued to be the very ones that have led to economic and political implosion (James 2008). This book engages with, but also attempts to move beyond, this social and conceptual terrain. Butler and Hamnett (2010) distinguish between the *urban-seeking* and the *urban-fleeing* white middle-classes. The parents we have studied epitomise the urban seeking. Not only are they living at the heart of three urban conurbations, but they are also sending their children to schools which encapsulate the rich cultural diversity of the cities they live in. Our focus then is on middle-class identities that appear to be grounded in sociality and an openness to difference. We want to understand how these might work against, and disrupt, normative views of what it means to be 'middle-class' in the twenty-first century, though we are also interested to see whether, and if so, how they might continue to re-inscribe class and 'race' privilege.

The workings of identity-making are particularly visible within the educational system. Traditional notions of 'the bourgeois self' have prioritised individuality, self-interest and self-sufficiency, alongside civic commitments. However, it has been argued that developing market forms in education and the wider public sphere are producing new kinds of moral subjects (Rose 1998; Miller and Rose 2008). The contemporary educational market also draws upon 'classical liberal views underpinned by a political and economic liberalism which is deeply embedded in modern Western societies' (Ball 2003 p. 112). The individualised, self-interested and self-sufficient self remains the ideal, in which the centring of rational choice and a capacity for transcendence both occludes group-based harms of systemic oppression and conceals the complicity of individuals in the perpetuation of systemic injustices (Applebaum 2005). It appears that what is being progressively marginalised in white middle-class identity formation is civic commitment and a sense of communal responsibility, the commitment to 'the common good' that we mentioned earlier. This is not really surprising when contextualised within a contemporary 'post-politics' culture. As Chantel Mouffe asserts, 'our present Zeitgeist is characterized by a profound aversion to the political' (Mouffe 2005 p. 110). For Zizek (2006) politics has not only become 'a dirty word' but the language of political intervention no longer appears to make sense of, and in, the contemporary. Similarly within the field of education leading sociologists such as Stephen Ball have argued that values of the market, choice and individualism have stood out and triumphed over those of the fragile discourse of welfare (Ball 2003). One of the main points of continuity between Conservative–Liberal coalition and both the Labour and Conservative administrations which preceded it has been a growing disenchantment with the public sector and the welfare state. Successive administrations have presided over the destruction of the system of meanings and values which founded the welfare state and rendered it coherent as a project, and over its replacement by doctrines and rituals of instrumental rationality (Cooper 2000). While this process has been evident across all sectors of the public sphere, it could be argued that it is particularly apparent within contemporary educational systems. For sociologists ranging from Ulrich Beck to Richard Sennett the dominance of neoliberal doctrines of instrumental rationality and untrammelled choice can be seen to have been at enormous costs for all sections of society. Beck (1992), Melucci (1996) and more recently Bradley (2010) emphasise the link between the growth of choices and escalating social anxiety. More specifically within the field of education, research increasingly shows that contemporary education policies promoting parental choice, competitive school enrolment, performance league tables and school specialisms generate an ethical framework that encourages and legitimates self-interest in the pursuit of competitive familial advantage (Oria et al. 2007; Martin 2010). Increasingly, winning has become the 'be-all and end-all' of education which has, to an extent, degenerated into an obsessive race for credentials.

There are, then, plenty of reasons to focus on those white middle-classes who do not fit traditional mainstream notions of what it is to be middle-class, and to focus on how their identities as middle-class and white are played out within the sphere of socially divided urban state schooling. The white middle-class families we studied (both parents and children) constitute a particularly interesting case study for two principal reasons. First, in sending their children to urban, socially diverse, state comprehensives, they are managing far higher levels of risk in relation to education than the majority of white middle-classes tolerate. Second, in doing so, they are active at the boundaries of both class and ethnic difference at a time when class and ethnic segregation and polarisation are growing (Webber and Butler 2007; Butler and Hamnett 2010). So while they share much in common with the white majority middle-classes who continue 'to put their children first' (Jordan et al. 1994) by seeking more exclusivist educational choices, they also represent a bolder, more risk-taking white middle-class cohort, and simultaneously, perhaps a more hopeful, open one. The rest of this chapter provides a summary of the book followed by a brief overview of the research which is described in more detail in Appendix 1.

Chapter 1 explores white middle-class identities as they have traditionally been, and currently are, theorised. It examines representations of the white middle-classes both historically and in the present, and attempts to delineate the specificity of English middle-classness by contrasting it with images of the middle-classes more widely, in the United States, Australia and Europe. Chapter 2, 'Family History, Class Practices and Habitus', looks at our white middle-class sample through a focus on family histories. Family narratives are drawn on to demonstrate the power of restructurings and reactivations of the habitus as some parents deliberately chose social and educational trajectories for their children that were very different to their own. Chapter 3 focuses on the ways in which the spatial and thus locality is crucial in middle-class identity formation. The chapter assesses data from interviews across three very different urban locales to generate insight about whether different urban spaces are repositories of distinct middle-class sets of values, or share more commonalities than differences when it comes to white middle-class attitudes and practices.

Chapter 4 draws out the contrast between dominant models of choice, couched in terms of individuals engaged in rational action based on available information (such as league tables and other proxies for educational quality), and the subtleties of the cultural facets of school choice as revealed in our analysis. It addresses the less-than-expected incidence of moral and political orientations in white middle-classes choosing socially diverse urban schooling, and explores the more prevalent instrumental and pragmatic considerations of many parents, and, additionally, the *provisional* nature of choices that are seen as reversible. Chapter 5 then interrogates whiteness as integral to white middle-class identity. For many parents and children, there are very positive gains to be had from a socially diverse school, and ethnic diversity is often valued for its educative potential. Nevertheless, we show that even these white middle-classes committed to multi-ethnic schooling face the perils of middle-class acquisitiveness, extracting value from, as they find value in, their multi-ethnic 'other'. The chapter examines these processes of generating use and exchange value in which the 'multi-ethnic other' becomes a source of multicultural capital.

The main focus of Chapter 6 is the frequently overlooked anxieties, conflicts, desires and tensions within middle-class identities created by operating within contemporary education choice policy. The chapter explores the psychic costs and tensions for these parents of having different notions of 'the best' for their child to those normative within white middle-class culture. Chapter 7 focuses on the impact on children of parents' choice of socially diverse urban schooling. We look at how their views and attitudes echo or diverge from those of their parents, examining the complex dynamic between echoing parents' views and asserting independence and difference. The chapter also looks at the difference between social mix and social mixing, drawing on both children's and parents' interviews.

Chapter 8 emphasises the democratic possibilities that emanate from middle-class identities that are grounded in sociality and an openness to difference and the ways in which these might work against, and disrupt, normative views of what it means to be 'middle-class' at the beginning of the twenty-first century. The chapter explores discourses and practices of civic engagement and democratic citizenship, and an important focus is the significant minority of white middle-class families who still possess a strong 'vocabulary of association' (Jordan et al. 1994 p. 43). However, the chapter also describes the difficulties of converting these commitments and investments into more equitable interactions with class and ethnic others.

The final concluding chapter comes back to issues of wider structural inequalities, arguing that the white middle-class parents in the study are negotiating an impossible situation that individually they can do little to improve. It discusses the ways in which the wider social context of structural injustices throws up impossible moral dilemmas and leads to all sorts of morally inconsistent behaviour. It goes on to outline the challenges for democratic citizenry and the importance of developing critiques which, whilst recognising how people negotiate inequitable situations, also constantly keeps in play the structural injustices within which they are situated. The final section synthesises the new ways of thinking and understanding white middle-class identity that emerge from the findings, before outlining the challenges the data present for education and wider social policy.

The research study involved in-depth interviews with 125 white middle-class families (181 parent and 68 children interviews in total) who had chosen inner city comprehensive schooling in three UK cities in three different geographical areas. These were London, Riverton in the South West and Norton in the North East of England. 'Riverton' and 'Norton' are pseudonyms. Strictly speaking Norton data is not confined to one city as we involved a few participants from beyond the city limits. We interviewed 63 families in London, 30 in Riverton and 32 in Norton. All names of people, places and institutions have been anonymised and disguised where necessary and as much as possible, except for London and London boroughs.

We strove to include a number of fathers as well as mothers in our sample, also ensuring that there was a balance between families with daughters and those with sons. Those middle-class parents who 'work the educational system' by choosing and getting high-status comprehensive schools at the top of league tables were only a tiny minority in our sample. At the time we carried out the fieldwork, three quarters of the comprehensives the families sent their children to were performing at or below the national average. This is because our main target group was middle-class parents that appeared committed to comprehensive schooling as an educational principle; those who deliberately eschew 'working the system to their advantage'. We also collected rigorous demographic data. The interviews with 68 middle-class young people were composed of 39 interviews with young women and 29 with young men (28 in London, 20 in Norton and 20 in Riverton). A majority (41) of these were 18 years or over at the time of the interview. They were interviewed in order to find out about their school experiences, but also to explore their identities and identifications and the extent to which these were constructed in accord with, or against, the orientations, commitments and dispositions of their parents.

In the next chapter on white middle-class identities we outline wider sociological understandings of middle-class identity in order to be able to specify what distinguishes the middle-classes who have been the focus of our study, and position them within a complex diffuse landscape of middle-class heterogeneity.

1
White Middle-Class Identity Formation: Theory and Practice

Introduction

> Contemporary theorizations of class, unlike many of their predecessors, are less concerned with class as a form of socio-economic classification, a position in the labour market or as a relationship to the means of production, and more concerned with the ways class as an identity is forged and experienced.
>
> (Dowling 2009 p. 2)

> Identity continues to be the place where collective action, social movements, and issues of inequality, rights and social justice come into focus and demand attention.
>
> (Wetherell 2010 p. 1)

In this chapter we are examining both the history and geography of white middle-class identity formation, as well as normative understandings of what it means to be middle-class, both historically and currently. In a later chapter we focus on whiteness as a powerful aspect of identity, but here it is 'middle-classness' that is scrutinised. Our intention is to map out the broader landscape of middle-class identity in order to be able to specify what distinguishes the particular section of the middle-classes who have been the focus of our study, and draw out their similarities and differences with normative 'middle-classness'. This means that heterogeneity within middle-class identities is an important focus. We ask to what extent the middle-classes share a common relationship to each other, despite this diversity, that is largely exclusive of everyone else? We also ask about the role that education plays in middle-class identity formation and identifications. Can we view education as central in understanding what sort of middle-class person an individual is?

11

However, first we need to define and position the middle-classes as a social grouping, outlining how they came to be central in English society and their changing character over time. Historical accounts for the most part agree that the term 'middle-class' came into usage in the mid- to late eighteenth century (Seed 1992). According to John Seed, the middle-classes:

> were distinguished from the landed aristocracy and the gentry by their need to generate an income from some kind of active occupation. And they were distinguished from the labouring majority by their possession of property … and by their exemption from manual labour.
>
> (Seed 1992 p. 36)

Implicit rather than spelt out in this definition of the middle-classes of the eighteenth century is a presumption of power. One of the key enduring attributes of middle-class status was, and still is, the ability to wield power over others (Gunn and Bell 2002). Absent is a further defining characteristic of the middle-classes, namely their values. Perhaps above all the distinguishing feature of the middle-classes is a particular set of values, commitments and moral stances. Yet, while these have inevitably shifted and changed over time, certain attitudes have remained constant. As we have argued in the introductory chapter, the hallmark of both contemporary and past middle-class identity is a sense of responsibility, underpinned by individualism combined with agentic citizenship and a propensity for choice. Middle-classness is seen to be embedded in a range of virtues and positive attributes such as ambition, sense of entitlement, educational excellence, confidence, competitiveness, hard work and deferred gratification. In this way the perpetuation of middle-class privilege works in and through what are seen to be individual qualities within the control of the individual. But a further consequence is that the middle-classes have now replaced the working-classes as 'the moral identifier' (Butler with Robson 2003 p. 17) that lies at the heart of English society.

Another significant attribute of the middle-classes is the ability to erect boundaries, both geographically and symbolically. In the twentieth century such boundary building was visibly manifest in the suburbs. Suburbanisation, a process that began in the 1920s and continued into the 1980s, was primarily about creating social as well as geographical distance from others, about constructing a different, distinctly middle-class way of life. As Thompson asserted:

It was only in the setting of this sort of house, where the family could distance itself from the outside world in its own private fortress behind its own garden fence and privet hedge and yet could make a show of outward appearances that was sure to be noticed by the neighbours that the suburban lifestyle of individual domesticity and group-monitored respectability could take hold.

(Thompson 1982 p. 8)

The suburbs are associated with both the rise and the sprawl of the middle-classes. As Willmott and Young (1967 p. 15) pointed out, 'the move outward was also a move upwards'. Suburbanisation was a powerful process of middle-class formation in which the suburbs gained meanings and resonances that were deeply socialising of those who lived there. Traditionally, research has focused on the relationships between distinctly middle-class ideals of home and family and suburban residential space (Duncan and Duncan 2004; Knox 2005). There has been a veritable cocktail of evocative and nostalgic images, from the poet Stevie Smith's homage to Potter's Green in 1949 to the Conservative Prime Minister John Major's paean to 'invincible green suburbs' in the 1980s. For Stevie Smith:

We are not only this healthy suburb where babies may flourish but we are also to be envied and congratulated because we have our rich community life and are not existing in a bored box-like existence that is what most people think of suburb life.

(Smith 1981 p. 97)

For most of the twentieth century suburbia represented a powerful image of the middle-class 'good life' (Watt 2009). But underneath a normalising, and at times idealising, of 'the middle-class suburbs', lay, as we glimpse in the Stevie Smith quote, a less attractive snobbery and petty class-consciousness, an implicit sense of superiority and a mapping out of social difference. Describing the inter-war years Gunn and Bell (2002) point out that anti-working-class feeling was an essential ingredient of what it meant to be middle-class at the time.

It is through their association with the suburbs that the middle-classes came to be depicted as 'middle England' in policy and the media, a label that also assumed a degree of homogeneity. In reality the middle-classes are striated by a proliferation of cross-cutting differences. The most researched differences are occupational ones that operate either horizontally, dividing the middle-classes into professionals, managers and the self-employed, or vertically, conceiving key differences amongst the middle-classes according to levels of income and status (Bottero 2004). However, less researched but also important are divisions that emerge out of geography and political persuasion. In the next section we explore these intra-middle-class differences in order to further engage with middle-class heterogeneity.

Differences within the middle-class

Horizonal differences

It is horizontal differences between the middle-classes that have attracted the most attention from sociologists over the last 30 years. Since the late 1970s Basil Bernstein and others have argued that one of the main cleavages within the middle-classes is the divide between public and private sectors of employment (Bernstein 1977; Dunleavy 1980; Perkin 1989). However, as Sally Power and her colleagues demonstrate through their empirical study of the middle-classes and education (Power et al. 2003), the old twentieth-century distinctions between managers and professionals, private and public sector workers have become blurred. The old binaries no longer work in a contemporary world where there are tensions and increasingly complex differentiations within intra-middle-class categories. Divisions have opened up within divisions. In particular, public sector workers are divided into those who continue to espouse a public sector ethic and those who have developed as entrepreneurs, while the growing privatisation of the public sector has resulted in private sector workers working in public sector settings (Ball 2008). Sectoral differences have diminished considerably as 'the opportunity to hide from capitalism' (Bagguley 1995 p. 298) is rapidly vanishing in the professions generally and the public sector specifically (Vincent and Ball 2006). This inability to any longer escape the logics of capitalism and the reach of neoliberalism impacts on all middle-class groupings but particularly those in our sample who traditionally come from middle-class groups who have espoused anti-capitalist sentiments and oppositional attitudes to neoliberalism or to right-wing political beliefs.

One generative approach to recognising the blurring and messiness of differences within the middle-classes is that of Mike Savage and his colleagues. Their (1992 pp. 127–128) 'assets plus lifestyle' approach to intra-middle-class differences is not based simply on occupational differences but attempts to incorporate lifestyle differences as well, connecting lifestyle categories with types of occupation. They distinguish between three groups: (1) the ascetic public sector welfare professionals, a group reliant on cultural assets rather than money; (2) the post-modern private sector professionals and managers, who are equally at home consuming both high and low culture; (3) and the corporate undistinctives, managers and government bureaucrats with indistinctive patterns of consumption. However, they also recognise that these three categories are cross-cut by differences of age and location. Together with those of other leading analysts in the field (Ball 2003; Vincent and Ball 2006), the analysis of Savage and colleagues draws upon Bourdieu's concepts of capital. In *Distinction* Bourdieu (1984) saw the main divide among the middle-classes in the late twentieth century as one between intellectuals on the one hand and entrepreneurs and industrialists on the other. Bourdieu's 'field maps' of French society in the same work recognise more nuanced and refined intra-middle-class differences defined by both the volume and composition of capital possessed by individuals. However, despite the extensive academic interest in horizontal divisions, it is probably vertical divisions that are currently most pronounced.

Vertical differences

Fissures among the middle-classes have been forced apart recently by the ongoing banking crisis. It is increasingly evident that a rich exclusive coterie of upper middle-classes heavily invested in moneymaking and profiteering now has a tenuous connection with the vast majority of middle-classes who are middle-ranking employees on average salaries. Giddens (1998) argues that the upper echelons of the middle-classes are separating themselves off from the rest of society and that this poses new problems for democracy and social inclusion. He uses the term 'disembedding' to describe the processes whereby the upper middle-classes create a regime of power without responsibility, generating new forms of exclusivity.

Alongside this focus on the top echelons of the middle-classes, Vincent et al. (2008) have led a renewed interest in the intermediate classes, once described as the lower middle-classes (Mayer 1975; Halsey et al. 1980). In doing so, they problematise the boundaries of what constitutes the middle-classes. Other contemporary research also focuses as much if not more on vertical as opposed to horizontal differences within the middle-classes. Bennett et al.'s (2009) impressive study mapping British cultural taste divides the middle-classes into two: (1) a smaller upper-middle-class grouping of executive professionals and managers and (2) a larger intermediate-middle-class grouping which includes lower managers and higher supervisory staff. In their work on the middle-classes choosing higher education Reay et al. (2005) developed conceptions of established and novitiate middle-class groupings, characterised by intra-class differences based on family history, dispositions and the type and quantity of capitals they possessed. In this study we have developed more tightly specified vertical fractions in order to help make sense of the intra-middle-class differences that emerged from the data. As we describe in more detail in Chapter 2, 20 per cent of the parents were first-generation middle-class, a larger group (40 per cent of the parents) were second-generation middle-class, while the remaining 36 per cent of the parents could be described as established middle-class. However, muddying an already complex picture, such vertical and horizontal differences can oppose and confound each other as in the case of composite families where the partners work in different vertical strata and/or occupational sectors of the labour market.

Geographical differences

We have touched on the impact of geography on middle-class formation in the earlier discussion of suburbanisation but more recent research by social geographers has revealed that contemporary white middle-class formation is associated more strongly with the urban than the suburban. As Butler with Robson (2003 p. 29) point out, 'today's middle-class does not want to live in the safe suburbs in which it was mostly brought up; after university it wants the excitement and difference of living in socially mixed areas with a cultural infrastructure.' One consequence is that complex middle-class differences exist within the urban as well as between the rural, suburban and urban middle-classes. In particular, Butler with Robson (2003) argue that although the London middle-classes can be differentiated in terms of locality, what they share dwarfs their differences and makes them a distinct middle-class characterised by a metropolitan habitus which sets them apart from both the middle-classes in rural areas, suburbs and county towns, and their 'sisters and brothers in provincial cities'. The reason, in part, for their distinctiveness lies in the opportunities different urban fields provide. By including provincial cities in our sample alongside London we are able to examine the extent to which white middle-class families differ according to geographical location, and ascertain the extent to which London both attracts and sustains a metropolitan habitus that is distinctive from those of our two provincial cities, Norton and Riverton. Like Vincent and Ball's (2006) research on the London middle-classes, Butler with Robson found different 'metropolitan habituses' in different city locations. What both studies conclude in the context of London is that the metropolitan white middle-classes share a common relationship with each other that is predominantly exclusive of everyone else. Vincent and Ball (2007) describe a taste for enriching educational activities (that are clearly distinguishable from working-class practices) as a commonality binding their urban middle-classes together, while Butler with Robson (2003 p. 2) conclude that they 'huddle together into essentially white settlements in the inner city' and that both they and their children, for the most part, have friends just like themselves. Our anticipation (and, to some extent, our hope) in conducting this research was that those white middle-classes making a positive choice in favour of social mix in their children's schooling would have a more open and inclusive outlook.

Political persuasion

There has been a longstanding link between middle-class radicalism and public sector employment. In both the United Kingdom and the United States there is a sociological tradition that associates well-educated professionals (Parkin 1968; Gouldner 1979; Lash and Urry 1987) with challenge to the established order and radical potential. Gouldner's (1979) theory of 'the new class' held that highly educated professionals, especially those employed in public and non-profit organisations, shared a culture of critical discourse engendering anti-authoritarian and oppositional political beliefs. This tradition, fuelled by middle-class involvement in new social movements over the second half of the twentieth century (Bagguley 1995), has portrayed sections of the middle-class across the Global North (Connell 2007) as 'dynamic change-makers, key actors in social transformation' (Bennett et al. 2009 p. 178). In the 1970s US theorists linked the rise of left-wing ideas in sections of the middle-class (Bruce-Biggs 1979; Brint 1984) to increasing levels of education. They suggested 'a struggle for power and status in American society between a rising "new class" of "knowledge workers" and a still dominant "old class" of business owners and executives' (Brint 1984 p. 31). This new liberal left-leaning middle-class was seen to be related to two labour market developments, the growth of occupational groups such as service sector and social-cultural professionals, and the decline of the industrial sector in the economy. For Brint, the radical attitudes of some middle-class occupational groups (for example, those that are not directly instrumental to profit maximisation like arts, education, social and other services) were largely due to higher education. Lamont (1987) however disagreed with this conclusion, arguing that such liberal attitudes can be explained by the common class situation of the 'relatively autonomous cultural capital workers' (Lamont 1987 p. 1505). In her words:

> The common interests of relatively autonomous cultural capital workers are to maintain and increase their autonomy and to expand the non-profit realm by encouraging the development of the public sector, promoting policies to increase business taxation, and supporting values and political ideologies that favour non-economic aspects of social life, such as post-materialist values, environmentalism, or New Left politics.
>
> (Lamont 1987 p. 1504)

More recently a scepticism has set in as to the radical inclinations of the middle-classes and, in particular, their ability to disorganise capitalism. While once university education and employment in the cultural and service sectors appeared to generate radical dispositions, their power to do so seems to have waned considerably in the present. Recent UK survey findings (Bamfield and Horton 2009) indicate that while the highly educated middle-classes continue to hold permissive views in relation to race and homosexuality, their views in relation to social class are less tolerant. According to Goldthorpe (2007), the middle-classes, despite intra-class differences, will always protect the status quo, and in the twenty-first-century act as bastions of the social order just as much as they did in the past. As Vincent and Ball (2006 p. 164) point out, 'values and attitudes cannot easily be read off from occupational categories' and, certainly in relation to the middle-classes, historical evidence from the last 50 years supports their reservations.

A common class?

However, as well as trying to distinguish the differences within the middle-classes it is important to focus on the commonalities that exist across difference. Most of these are rooted in the privilege and relative power that comes with middle-class identity. What is shared to varying degrees is class power and dominance, infused, as Butler with Robson (2003 p. 28) wryly comment, 'with a good dose of moral superiority'. Regardless of all the complex differentiations the negative connotations placed on working-class practices, values and aspirations across the middle-classes appear to remain intact (Maxwell and Aggleton 2010). As Vincent et al. (2004 p. 242) conclude, 'despite differences, there are also important and maybe overwhelming similarities, an internal homogeneity'. Power (2000 p. 142), drawing on the findings from her study of the middle-classes 'Destined for Success?', argues that 'the differences within the middle-classes may be only superficial rather than deeply secured.' A quality that the middle-classes share across difference is a strong commitment to education as key to middle-class cultural reproduction, and we turn to middle-class relationships to education in the next section.

Education, education, education

The middle-classes have a very long history of successfully securing their cultural reproduction by ensuring that their children got the best kind of education. As David Lockwood (1995 p. 10) pointed out, 'they have always used their superior moral and material resources to full effect, above all by giving their children a competitive edge in the main site of social selection, the educational system'. While we may wish to dispute whether occupying 'the moral high ground' is the same as possessing superior moral resources, what is incontrovertible is the middle-class propensity for capitalising on their capitals in order to guarantee educational success. The educational system has become a central mechanism of white middle-class identity formation.

Historically speaking, the assumption or pretence that education is primarily a level playing field in which anyone could succeed is quite a recent viewpoint or position. Tomlinson reminds us that:

> In the nineteenth and early twentieth centuries, education was openly intended to reinforce a class structure based on ascription by birth and wealth. 'The different classes of society, the different occupations, require different teaching', as a major Schools Inquiry Report put it in 1886 (Taunton Commission 1886). This translated into 'public' schools for the aristocracy and upper classes, minor public schools and a hierarchy of grammar schools for the middle classes, and an elementary education for the masses.
>
> (Tomlinson 2005b p. 164)

Eighteen years earlier, in 1864, the Clarendon Commission had reported on the state of the 'nine leading schools', the 'public' schools that are still regarded by many as representing excellence in secondary education. But as Tomlinson goes on to point out, the Taunton Commission's report reflected the demands of an expanding middle-class who desired that academic education and credentials should replace ascription. The report alludes to 'a great body of professional men who have nothing but education to keep their sons on a high social level' (Taunton Commission 1886 p. 93). We might understand this in Bourdieusian terms as a transparent demand for the opportunity to convert comfortable incomes into cultural capital, all the better to sustain a social advantage. It contributed to the social elevation of an academic curriculum, and the relegation of more practical forms of craft and technical education to lower classes, which in turn 'set the scene for the twentieth century two-tier system persistently associated with social class' (Tomlinson 2005b p. 164). One point to take from this is the relatively simple one that the growth of secondary schooling (to become 'universal' following the 1944 Education Act) had social class differentiation in its very foundations. The middle-class to some extent defined, and was then defined by, the extension of secondary schooling in forms that continue to be celebrated, emulated and in many cases, revered.

In this research project we have been concerned with what we can learn about white middle-class identity formation from a particular kind of school choice and relationships to schooling and education. But it is worth pointing out that there are two ways of thinking about the social world, and identities within it, that we find unhelpful and seek to avoid. The first is the idea that a social position in terms of (say) class and ethnicity somehow determines everything that is important about identity, that we can predict or 'read off' people's beliefs and actions from a category like 'white urban middle-class'. Hence we use the concept of habitus, discussed in more detail in the next chapter, because it captures in a much more subtle way the dynamic relationship between social structures and selves. Social structures and situations do indeed normally establish a sense of reality, a sense of limits, or dispositions: It is important to find out what these are like and what they seem to influence without falling into the trap of determinism.

The second way of thinking that we avoid is in a sense the opposite of this first one, and is one that is quite close to much common-sense thinking. It posits that categories like ethnicity and class are of little consequence in a modern age of individualisation in which identity itself has lost its class and community moorings. A helpful summary of this 'individualisation thesis' describes how it argues that people

...must now develop their own life worlds, unanchored by tradition, constructing identities that are more negotiable, looser, reflexive
and autonomous. People's senses of self are thought to be more provisional as a consequence, less firmly rooted in the ethics of duty,
responsibility and self-sacrifice, dominated instead by the 'religion of
me'. Life as a result is said to have become more risky and uncertain,
although exposure to this risk remains highly unevenly distributed.

(Wetherell 2009a p. 5)

Collectively, the larger programme of research of which our project was
a part supports critics of the individualisation thesis (e.g. Savage 2000;
Skeggs 2004) in showing that whilst there are examples to be seen, these
are characteristically over-generalised, with individualisation being 'a
"now you see it, now you don't" phenomenon' (Wetherell 2009a p. 8).

So is it possible to talk about social class and identity whilst avoiding
the extremes of social determinism and individualisation? The answer
is yes, provided care is taken to focus on those practices, actions and
experiences that are about identity formation. An important part of the
formation of identity is the laying down of dispositions in social settings and social structures. Education is particularly important in the
development of the habitus. As Bourdieu puts it:

> The habitus acquired in the family underlines the structuring of
> school experiences...and the habitus transformed by schooling,
> itself diversified, in turn underlies the structuring of all subsequent
> experiences (e.g. the reception and assimilation of the message of the
> culture industry or work experiences) and so on, from restructuring
> to restructuring.
>
> (Bourdieu 1977 p. 87)

Schooling is, then, a high-stakes business in the formation of identities. It is 'diversified' (increasingly so – see Chapter 4), and the choice
of a school appears as the one real chance that parents get to structure
a significant slice of socialisation beyond the home. There is plenty of
evidence of the correspondingly vast emphasis, effort and anxiety surrounding school choice, especially (though of course, not exclusively)
in middle-class families (Ball 2003).

As we reached the end of our research project, we were able to say with
some confidence that 'against the grain' school choices led to a confir-
mation of the white middle-class identities of the young people. Yet
these identities had been forged whilst participating in a schooling that

differed markedly from mainstream white middle-class practices, and also differed from that experienced by most of the parents themselves.

There are several quite different ways in which one might theorise the question of the relationship between identity and social action (see Wetherell 2009b). Our primary interest is in social practices of identity-work, and we acknowledge that this leaves some classic concerns in the study of identity untouched. In taking a mainly Bourdieusian approach, we attempt to do more than simply study sets of individuals and then draw parallels between them. Of course we are interested in individuals, but we are just as interested in what they show us about social practices, spaces, positions and relations. Our data and analysis show that whatever else it is, identity is always both a reflection and an enactment of these social dimensions. This is firstly because people cannot simply choose to ignore the 'steer' that their own habitus gives them, or simply choose to act without recourse to the various forms of capital at their disposal: As Bourdieu put it, though we might 'dream of social flying', we cannot 'defy the gravity of the social field' (Bourdieu 1984 p. 370). Secondly, and equally important, participating in social spaces always changes things for other people. In attending a particular school, a young person and a family are not simply choosers and recipients of a 'service' with particular 'qualities': the act of participation itself changes the nature of what is on offer, in various and sometimes contradictory ways. Recognising such things requires a 'break with common sense', and we have commented elsewhere that this can be likened to shift in perspective from a Newtonian to an Einsteinian physics: Whilst the former concentrates on individual items and their interactions, the latter treats positions and the spaces between them, that is the field, as just as important (see James et al. 2009). To put this another way, people are always embodying and enacting the social world, and understanding something of how this works is an important task. In the next chapter we continue to explore the idea of segmentation within the middle-classes, drawing on the concept of habitus to link intra-middle-class differences with family histories.

2
Family History, Class Practices and Habitus

Introduction

Given the dominance of ideas like 'choice', 'diversity' and 'the market' in educational policy and implementation, it is perhaps tempting to see secondary school choice through the most apparently simplistic of economic perspectives, as if it was best understood through choices made by rational, calculating individuals in an increasingly information-rich environment. Yet even the most casual of conversations with parents making such choices, or with school head teachers, or with young people, will quickly expose other kinds of consideration, and indicate that school choice is much more than a sum of intelligent use of market data and the odd pragmatic consideration. For this reason, we cannot begin to understand it unless we bring to bear some appropriate tools.

Habitus is one such tool. It is variously defined and characterised, though perhaps most usefully as a set of 'durable, transposable dispositions' (Bourdieu 1977 p. 72) or 'the active presence of past experiences... in the form of schemes of perception, thought and action' (Harker 1992 p. 16). There is a strong sense of *embodiment* too, so that a person's habitus is a taking on board of various elements of the social positions they occupy and have occupied. In addition, it is meaningful to speak of habitus as 'the amalgam of accumulated history, both personal and collective' (Adams 2006). We are concerned to explore something of what Pat Allatt describes as 'relational aspects of schooling choice which reverberate within and down the generations' (Allatt 1996 p. 170). The family can be said to have a habitus, and rich patterns emerged from the family histories of our sample, patterns that were textured not only according to location and type of schooling but also by the extent to which the families were established within the middle-classes.

In this chapter we begin by setting out some basic details of the parents in the 125 families we studied. We then offer a brief discussion of the concept of habitus and the idea of segmentation of the middle-class, before presenting some of the patterns in practices that link against-the-grain school choice and family backgrounds.

Parental educational backgrounds

The 250 parents were a highly educated group. At 58 per cent, the proportion of parents in the sample who had attended either private or selective state grammar schools was very high (26 per cent and 32 per cent respectively). Some 5 per cent had attended secondary modern schools, and 18 per cent had attended comprehensive schools. If we set aside the category 'other schools' for a moment, 163 parents were wholly or mainly educated in the state sector (71 per cent) and 66 of the parents were wholly or mainly educated in the private sector (29 per cent). The latter figure is more than four times the national average rate of private secondary schooling (see Table 2.1). It is also notable that the proportion of those who had attended Grammar (selective state secondary) schooling is considerably higher than national averages. Whilst private school attendance was high in the sample, in the majority of families there were strong intergenerational associations with state

Table 2.1 Secondary schools attended[a] by parents in the study – to nearest whole percentages (actual numbers in parentheses)

	Mothers	Fathers	Parents
Secondary Modern	5 (6)	5 (6)	5 (12)
Grammar	36 (45)	28 (35)	32 (80)
Comprehensive	22 (27)	14 (17)	18 (44)
Other state schools[b]	9 (11)	13 (16)	11 (27)
Private schools	26 (33)	26 (33)	26 (66)
Other schools[c]	2 (3)	14 (18)	8 (21)
Totals	100 (125)	100 (125)	100 (250)

Note:
[a] Where parents attended more than one type of school they have been allocated to the category representing the greatest portion of their schooling.
[b] This category includes five fathers who attended State Boarding schools.
[c] The cases in this row include schooling overseas.

Table 2.2 Parents' highest qualifications – to nearest whole percentages (numbers in parentheses)

	Mothers	Fathers	Parents
Degree level	54 (68)	59 (74)	57 (142)
Degree plus postgraduate	34 (42)	19 (23)	26 (65)
Qualifications 'below' degree and others where not known	12 (15)	22 (28)	17 (43)
Total	100 (125)	100 (125)	100 (250)

schooling. In terms of social reproduction, almost all of those schooled privately came from the established or second-generation middle-classes where private schooling was already common.

As Table 2.2 shows, the parents in the study were also very highly qualified indeed – 83 per cent to degree level, with over a quarter also holding some form of postgraduate qualification as well (and with mothers holding nearly twice the number of postgraduate qualifications as fathers, making them front-runners in a marked shift from the male dominance in postgraduate qualifications up to the 1960s – see House of Commons 1999).

Many of the largest single group by schooling – the grammar school attendees – were the first in their family to go to University, a highly visible marker of the role education played in their class mobility. However, a more detailed look at the parents' schooling also revealed considerable variety and movement, including various faith and secular schools, schools overseas, boarding and different systems within the collective experience, and in some cases, as indicated above, of individual experience. There were no clear-cut associations between the type of school attended and the quality of the experience, although many of the parents did report a sense of loss at being separated from their friends at transition from primary to secondary schools (usually after passing the 11+); or feeling barely rich/clever/good enough at private schools. Across the sample, negative school experiences were most often associated with an old-fashioned school ethos, including highly gendered expectations or environments, or with strict religious teaching. A liberal or progressive ethos, whether at private or state institutions, was more commonly valued.

The school careers of this group of parents had often been profoundly affected by changes to the status quo including job insecurity, relocation, divorce or other parental absences. This drew our attention to the importance of a range of life events in terms of the impact they can have on schooling. However, we have no way of knowing whether our participants had experienced particularly high levels of turbulence in these respects. What we can say is that with very few exceptions, the adults we interviewed were at secondary school between 1965 and 1975 and were either the last of the school cohorts to take the 11+ or amongst the first of the cohorts to avoid it. Some had personal experience of the transition from one system (selective) to another (comprehensive). Thus, during their own periods of adolescence, our respondents were as a whole subject to the formative effects of segregation by class and ability to pay for private education; class-related re-segregation according to academic ability in grammar schools (or though personal circumstances in state boarding); and of desegregation through the introduction of comprehensive schooling.

As we will see, family history, and especially parental and previous generations' experiences of schooling, appeared to function as key points of reference for contemporary and recent choices of school.

The concept of habitus

There is a lot of misunderstanding about the concept *habitus*. Probably the most common error is to regard the term as more or less equivalent to 'personality', then find it wanting as a predictive category. Also common is the suggestion that the term brings with it an underlying determinism in Bourdieu's whole position. However, we do not find habitus to be deterministic in the ways that some (e.g. Jenkins 1992, 2002) have suggested. We would agree with Harker (1984) and Harker and May (1993) that such a view is based on a misconception of the nature and purposes of the approach within which it is located. We would also suggest that the view arises because a great deal of Anglo-Saxon common-sense thinking gives primacy to *the individual* – conceived as fundamentally a free agent – in any explanation of social phenomena (Robbins 2006). Bourdieu's theoretical tools are helpful in many ways, one of which is that they facilitate units of analysis *other than* the individual. This is particularly important in dealing with something as multiply-defined as social class. It is also a specific help if one is trying to understand how sets of habits, attitudes, assumptions, expectations and practices come to the surface in *families*, all of whom have *histories*. The question is – categorically – *not* one of 'what is a middle-class habitus and what set of behaviours does it produce'. Rather it is a question of using a theoretical tool which helps us understand practices for what they are, namely complex, situated actions with a range of precursors and a range of consequences, anticipated, unanticipated, highly visible or less visible.

None of this is to deny that the concept comes with difficulties and challenges. One concern is how it is that the dispositions that go to make up the habitus are acquired or laid down in the first place. Sayer notes that in much of Bourdieu's writing, dispositions seem to be acquired '...though a process of osmosis and shaping, through accommodation to material circumstances and social relations, like living in crowded housing or being accustomed to hard manual labour or serving others' (Sayer 2005 p. 27). These are indeed important examples of the sorts of mechanisms through which 'a sense of reality' or 'a sense of limits' could be established. However, drawing upon a discussion in Bourdieu's *Distinction*, Sayer also reminds us that the habitus generates not only meaningful practices but perceptions that give meaning as well:

> Ways of thinking can become habitual. Once learned they change from something we struggle to grasp to something we can think *with*, without thinking *about* them. In other words, for much of the time our conceptual apparatus is not itself the subject of reflection. One can therefore acknowledge the conceptual and concept-dependent dimensions of social practices without assuming that this necessarily takes the form of an ongoing rational discussion ... Orientations and behaviours such as condescension and deference involve habit, feeling and comportment but they also imply tacit understandings and evaluations: they involve 'intelligent dispositions'.
>
> (Wood 1990 p. 214)
> (Sayer 2005 p. 27, emphasis in original)

To this we would add that habitus is also a dynamic concept, in that it is subject to continuous re-adjustment, a point we illustrate with examples from our fieldwork below. As we mentioned in the previous chapter, perhaps the main reason that school choice is such an important and emotive topic is that it represents (or at least *appears to represent* or is *presented as if it was*) the *only* real opportunity outside the family and immediate home environment where parents might exert a major influence on the habitus of the child. But the main reason we need the concept of habitus is that, put together with *field*, it helps us to understand practices, and also the generative principles underlying practices...Particular practices should not be seen, then, as simply the product of habitus, but as 'the product of the *relation between* the habitus, on the one hand, and the specific social contexts or "fields" within which individuals act, on the other'.

(Thompson 1991 pp. 13–14; original emphasis)
(Mills 2008 p. 85)

Thus it was that in a study of interactions between parents and primary schools, Reay (1998b) pointed out that parents' engagements with the primary school differed in ways attributable to differences in habitus and the different kinds of capital held – and some of them did not have the right 'currency' in the particular field. Similarly, in a study of teaching and learning in Further Education, James and Diment (2003) showed how a set of professional dispositions and capitals generated and celebrated in one set of circumstances could quickly become devalued and driven 'underground' in the face of powerful shifts in definitions of learning and assessment which changed the social space of work (that is, the field) (see also James and Biesta 2007).

The families in our sample are a good example of how social class and the structures of educational opportunity are *not* deterministic in any simple sense. Here we have middle-class families making choices which appear to go against self-interest, to be counter-intuitive. Yet, as far as we can tell, the experiences and outcomes of this process do not appear damaging to position or prospects: on the contrary, they appear to represent the generation of new forms of capital, and to secure identity and opportunity. We are, therefore, as much concerned with *choice, agency* and *strategy* as we are with notions of how such things are constrained or framed or determined.

School choice and middle-class segmentation

In Gouldner's (1979) terms the parents in our study would be defined mainly as New Middle-Class, in that most worked in the public sector. However, our interviewees' responses to some of the early questions in our interview schedule alerted us to the need to develop a classification along the lines of historical class location. Around a quarter (24 per cent) of the parents were from aspiring working-class backgrounds and were the first in their family history to be in a professional occupation: We term these *first-generation middle-class*. Some 40 per cent of the parents in our sample were themselves children of people who were first-generation middle-class, and we term these *second-generation middle-class*. Finally, 36 per cent of the parents could be best described as *established middle-class* (the old middle-class in Gouldner's 1979 terms or 'inheritors' in Bourdieu's: see Bourdieu and Passeron, 1979). Most of this latter group attended private schools as well as university and their own parents and grandparents often went to private schools and university, including elite universities, at a time when very few people in the United Kingdom went to university. In such families there were often clear markers of wealth and positions of power, status and influence (see Crozier et al. 2008).

We use these 'generation' terms where it helps us describe themes in the data, and occasionally there are glimpses of how the classification suggests further hypotheses. One example of this would be how some parts of our data suggest that 'against the grain' secondary schooling may be more anxiety-ridden (and more closely managed and monitored) amongst *first generation* than amongst *established* middle-class families. Yet whilst there are some powerful examples of this, there are sufficient counter-examples to prevent us declaring it as a general tendency.

In their study of education and the middle-classes, Power et al. (2003) show that whilst a majority of the parents saw educational success as crucially important, and the choice of the 'right' school as pivotal, there were nevertheless '... wide differences ... about what the "right kind" of school looked like that can be related to tensions between the old and new middle-class' (Power et al. 2003 p. 32). This 'horizontal' distinction drew upon a development of Durkheim's concept of organic solidarity, the 'social glue' that keeps societies more or less integrated but which is not reliant on the more explicit contractual arrangements of mechanical solidarity. Bernstein proposed that organic solidarity could itself take two forms in contemporary society. The first was based on radical individualism, corresponding to values of enterprise and professional control developed in the nineteenth century, and this form still underpins the actions of the old middle-class. In families, this leads to an emphasis on positions, unambiguous roles, hierarchy and reproduction. The second form of organic solidarity rose quickly alongside the twentieth-century emphasis on culture and communication, and was more person-centred. New middle-class families are person-focused, have weaker 'boundaries' and authority relationships that are less defined by position held. Having earlier classified the schools in their sample on Bernstein's (related) 'instrumental' and 'expressive' orders, Power et al. argue that whilst

...the most 'elite' members of the middle class chose the most elite schools, and...those in the lower socio-economic groups tended towards the lower end of the prestige hierarchy...there was no simple linear relationship between socio-economic and school status. Horizontal divisions reflected different orientations towards learning and school organisation which Bernstein's distinction between old and new middle class helps us to understand. In general, the former tended to favour schools with the more hierarchical ethos found in state grammar schools and the 'respectable' private sector. New middle-class parents, more likely to favour more differentiation and openness, could find this both in elite schools and in some comprehensives. They were also more likely to have given weight to their child's preference.

(Power et al. 2003 p. 41)

This is a helpful analysis, and it is worth mentioning that in the few cases where it occurred, a liberal or progressive ethos was a celebrated facet of the earlier schooling of the parents we interviewed. However, as discussed in Chapter 1, the new middle-class is itself far from homogeneous. Bernstein's own sub-divisions of it denote quite disparate – even contradicting – interests and orientations.

Our study did not set out to produce generalisations about these kinds of class categorisations, and in any case our sample size would not support such an endeavour. We do not see this as a significant weakness: Like Ball's study (Ball 2003) our research is not directly concerned with the refinement of class categories or indeed with class theory, but takes *class practices* as its core concern. Ball points out that '...there is relatively little empirical or conceptual development around middle-class practices apart from the important work done by Savage and Butler and their colleagues and one of two others....' Like Ball we are '...attempting to return to an emphasis on the lived realities, the situated realizations, of class and class reproduction' (Ball 2003 p. 6).

This focus led us to look at parental biographies across the sample, and to note two recurrent themes within them. Firstly, there was a high valuing of education *per se*. The vast majority reported that their own parents (and often previous generations) had a keen sense of the value of education, although there was wide variation in what particular actions this appeared to justify, and in whether particular aspirations for educational achievement had been fulfilled or thwarted. Secondly, there was a high incidence of what we might term a 'sociological' perspective on the relationships between education and social class, and with this a marked awareness of the historical development of parts of the education system. In particular, the emergence of comprehensive secondary schooling was a frequent historical point of reference in parents' accounts.

As we examined our data, it became clear that recent and contemporary school choices were frequently understood, expressed and explained with reference to durable (though adaptable) dispositions. However, these were not purely *individual* dispositions, but collectively-held family educational histories, or *family habitus*. The 'generational' intra-middle-class groupings discussed earlier were significant aspects of this habitus. We now explore some examples of the relationship between family habitus and contemporary secondary school choice.

Reactions to family habitus

A number of the parents shared in some detail their wish to avoid certain features of their own schooling being repeated in that experienced by their children. Negative experiences of private schooling were the most frequently cited feature of this kind. John Levy (London, established middle-class), who described his own parents as upper middle-class, had attended a well-known public school for boys:

> My own experience of education has had an enormous effect on me not just in terms of my views about my children's education but I'd say just about everything, my outlook on life, how I view the world. I think I could trace it all back to what happened or rather started to happen to me at seven. At seven I got sent away to a prep boarding school. That was bad enough, the sense of being exiled. I missed my family, my mother in particular, terribly. But you know that was what families like ours did and it was bruising.

John's account gives us a strong glimpse of a particular habitus formation, including the ways in which earlier experiences are internalised, becoming layers of dispositions onto which later layers are melded:

> I took on the ethos, absorbed it to the extent I began to think it was normal and I suppose that isn't unsurprising because alongside the brutality there was friendship, support, you know, a whole lot of nurture. You bought into the package and to an extent just got on with it but in retrospect a lot of it was horrific, as I said brutal and brutalising. But there was another aspect I found deeply troubling

when I looked back that we all just took for granted at the time, that it was incredibly limited socially, a sort of complacent sameness.

Whilst habitus reflects the social position in which it was constructed, it also carries within it the genesis of new creative responses which are capable of transcending the social conditions in which it was produced (Bourdieu 2000). John, speaking of his brother who became very ill during schooling, reflects 'public school was supposed to make upper middle-class men of us but it crushed my brother'. A strong family tradition is therefore challenged by his experiences and those of his brother, leading John to declare that private schooling is 'something I just would not contemplate for my own children':

> I knew I never wanted that for my own children. Pat [his partner] must have told you about my parents' trust fund for the children. Well I knew despite any trust fund that I didn't want either private or selective schooling for my own children. But then it was so difficult because that was the accepted behaviour in my family, that's just what everybody did in my family, go to private school. And I think the seminal moment came when I read that Daniel Day Lewis had been to an urban comprehensive. I remember thinking that's alright then. I don't know how many qualms his father had but he's come out creative and fairly sussed so you can choose that for your kids and they can survive. And I do remember thinking when I read it – and the children were very young at the time – this is good.

John worked as a criminal lawyer, a job that needed empathy with a wide range of people and a capacity to deal quickly with difficult situations. He was adamant that it was not his schooling *per se*, but the witnessing of his brother's illness and some subsequent voluntary work (translating benefit claim forms and rules for claimants) that had equipped him for this work: 'People just know. They can see...if you are some middle-class kid with no depth, or you have got a sympathetic approach, you know, someone who is going to listen.' Despite his established middle-class background, John's assessment is that private schooling, and even the more selective kinds of state schooling, were to be avoided. As he put it, 'I wanted (my own)...kids not to be detached from society really.'

This last point, rather than specifically negative experiences of the sort outlined by John, was the most common reason for parents to react against their own schooling as part of the making of choices and decisions for the education of their children. Ella Rosen (Norton, established middle-class) spoke of the narrowness of the social group in most private schools, and the worrying tendency for those in power in government and civil service to have been to those schools themselves, making them detached from the lives of everyone else. In another family, Libby Greensit (Norton, established middle-class), a GP, argued that both schools and the health service needed to 'work for everyone'. Sarah Rhymes (London, established middle-class) described a lengthy and intricate process of considering several schools for her daughter Naomi, but ruled out private schooling 'on principle'. The privilege she herself experienced whilst still in her teens now appeared distasteful, and she described her dismay when at 19 years old she found that her chosen university was

> ...full of public school children! I took a gap year and just as I thought I'd escaped those kind of people I ended up being right in the middle of them again. So actually my closest friends were from State schools. I did get on with those from private schools, but I just couldn't believe that I'd ended up in a university that was full of them, full of the types I thought I'd escaped. That put me off even more. I just couldn't bear their arrogance, just their whole attitude to life just turned me off.

One of our cases illustrates the tenacity of family habitus in that a father's own experiences and views of secondary schooling continued to have a strong impact even after his death several years earlier. Audrey Caisey (Norton – established middle-class) described how Neil, her (second-generation middle-class) partner, had passed the 11+ examination and attended a selective boy's Grammar school. However, he had hated being at the school, for its academic emphasis, the fact it was single-sex, and for how it separated him from his friends who 'all went to a local secondary modern school'. This experience had reverberated through their discussions about where their own son should go:

> we had sort of slight arguments all through [the time of] Christopher at primary school because Christopher's a very bright child and Neil often thought, is he being pushed enough or should we maybe have sent him off somewhere else?... [we discussed] do you think you know, Christopher would do better in a private school?

Christopher went to The Park, the local state comprehensive, partly because the experiences and wishes of his father had a continued presence. However, there were other factors. Audrey also talked at length about the 'security' or reassurance that she and other parents gained from a critical mass of middle-class young people going to the nearby state comprehensive. Following this, a strong perception of private schools (based in part on her experience as one of six children in a totally privately educated family) provided a compelling rationale:

...he'll get more introverted and more shy if he goes to a little boys school, than getting out into the world. And I just think you know, okay Christopher mixes with the same old people and he doesn't bring Darren White and all these children who go [to the school] home...but he knows they're there, and he meets them in school, and I know when he grows up and he's going to be a lawyer or teacher or whatever, at least he knows where people have come from, what people are like and he's not going be like the people I see who are barristers and doctors who never actually met anyone in the world at all except for their narrow little band, and yes we still exist within our nice narrow little middle class environments. I'm not saying that I go out having tea with my patients [she is a GP]...but I know they are there and I know what they are about and I know what lives they lead and it gives you a slightly greater understanding of different people.

Audrey's apparent certainty about Christopher's occupational future was a widely shared feature of parent interviews, and one we return to later in the book. Meanwhile, she went on to suggest that in some cases the choice of a private school is made with an element of 'snob value'. She also thought that some of the children in a particular private school nearby were 'not bright enough to exist anywhere else', and contrasted them to 'the top stream at The Park School (who) are much brighter, more with it, more alert'. Audrey wanted her own children to be exposed to a breadth of people:

I don't want my children to think you know, that everybody's got a holiday house in Sardinia, and everyone's daddy drives a four by four and you know and everyone, you know, can go to tennis club and squash club and blah, blah, blah, have holidays skiing and this that and the other...they've got to realise that not everyone does that, we're not all the same...and I just think god if everybody would just go to state schools it would be so much better, but a lot of people don't.

In a few families there was a firm decision not to choose private secondary schooling despite (a) a long familial tradition of private education, (b) the clear availability of funds from other family members and (c) parents themselves having had a positive personal experience of it. Josie and Jimmy Baker (London, established middle-class) had both been privately educated up to age 18. Both now worked in jobs with a 'political' dimension and described themselves as having friends in the 'left spectrum'. Jimmy described how they wished to avoid private education if they could. For both of them, the exposure to a breadth of different kinds of people was fundamental:

> ...I think for me definitely I felt that the thing I missed out on in growing up was being able to get on with, you know, all sorts of people. As time has gone on that is less of a problem [for me]...when she [Angela, their daughter] hits teenage years we want her to get on with pretty much anyone. And then also because the local secondary school...was a good one. I think it might have been different if the local school was really rubbish, I think it might have been different, but to us at the time it was...well it's not *brilliant* but it is going to be fine.
>
> (Jimmy)

> I think it (private education) just goes against our politics very, very strongly. Having said that if Angela was deeply unhappy ...I do know someone in Manchester whose child was being bullied and you know was having a horrible time, and he decided to send him to private school and I don't have a problem with that actually. For me what it's about is doing the best thing for your child, and I currently believe that the best thing for my child and for most children on the whole is to go to a school where they meet a whole range of people. If that stops being best thing for her then yes I would consider it. It would hurt – but I would do it.
>
> (Josie)

The theme of schools providing the opportunity to meet 'a whole range of people' was a strong one in Ball's research amongst parents choosing state over private schools (see Ball 2003 p. 138), and for some of the new middle-class families in the study by Power et al. (2003) who sought out secondary schools with a wide social mix. Amongst the parents we interviewed, it was, additionally, a reason given for the choice of 'ordinary' state schools over more selective or higher-achieving state schools. We will return to the effects of this social mix in later chapters.

It is however worth noting that for most of the parents in families we have referred to as 'established middle-class', and for many others, private schooling remained a kind of safety-net, something that could be activated if things went wrong with the choices that had been made. Furthermore, the negative assessment of social narrowness did not mean that the private sector was seen as homogeneous: there was recognition that private schools themselves differed greatly (c.f. Edwards et al. 1989).

Re-creations of family habitus

As we have described, several established middle-class families used against-the-grain school choice to counter or disrupt parts of an historical familial habitus. By contrast, for others who were mainly amongst the first-generation middle-class families, against-the-grain school choice seemed part of a deliberate re-creation of elements of the parental trajectory.

Despite some pressure to 'go private' from parts of the extended family, Angela and Anthony Smith (Riverton, first-generation middle-class) were keen not to 'buy privilege' for their children, and wanted them to have to work hard for what they achieved. Angela attributed this to her own working-class background, saying 'I feel very much on my kind of background tramlines here, you know, you've got to do it and that's what you're going to stick at.' However, at the same time she acknowledged the experimental nature of the undertaking, pointing to the presence of relative privilege as a safety-net:

> ... if we had to, we could sell the house and move, or if we really had to, we could just about afford private education ... but we don't want to, but we thought, well, we could ... if we really think it's not working for Sadie, there is a choice

> *Interviewer: Why is it something you wouldn't want to do?*

> Just politically ... a principle ... really, it's just that thing of buying privilege and all that ... but it's also about wanting her to be able to participate in the wider world and understand, in that actually we're very lucky as it is ... life is good, we've got a comfortable house, we have an income ... you know, there is nothing ... we don't go hungry,

we don't do any of that stuff, by a long way, and wanting her to experience a bit what it was like for us both when we were growing up. You know that there is a bit more of a range there and you have to be able to get on with other people.

Interviewer: Would it be true to say that for you schooling should be about learning to relate to a very wide range of people?

Yes, absolutely, definitely ... and also I think even more ... you know, Anthony works at Oldstone University and they have a huge intake of kids from very privileged backgrounds. He says they are clueless, they just haven't kind of woken up to the world, a lot of the time in the seminars he was doing with first years, he was really teaching them to open their eyes to the kind of social structure of Britain even. You know, they're just not ... a lot of them just aren't tuned in yet, as I was saying. And I just don't want, we don't want our children to be like that.

Here and in some other families we noted that against-the-grain school choice was part of an educational project with a much wider remit than schooling (though schooling always remained central). For example, the Smiths put considerable effort into broadening the range of young people with whom their children had social contact, and their efforts here included running a youth group. They held fast with their choice of the local state comprehensive school despite their daughter Sadie wanting desperately to go to a private secondary school along with her best friends from primary school, and despite a protracted episode of bullying during the first year. In addition, the Smiths closely managed many aspects of schooling and this included using personal contacts in the school (see James and Beedell 2009). But whatever the level of such intervention, many first-generation middle-class parents, like the second-generation and established middle-class parents, valued exposure to social diversity. They also shared a view that those schools described as most successful in conventional terms would be less likely to provide it. Christine and Robert Locke (Norton, first-generation and second-generation middle-class respectively) had a daughter, Amy, who was about to transfer from a largely middle-class primary school, characterised by 'some cultural diversity', to a more socially mixed secondary school. There she would 'probably meet people who don't have as much as she does, which she might hopefully learn from that ... that she can't just have everything she wants all the time' (Robert). As Christine put it, Amy would be alongside

…children from disadvantaged backgrounds. I don't think that's a bad thing at all. I don't think that the children should grow up feeling that what *they've* got *everyone* has, is not a good thing, that's not something I want my children to grow up with. I want them to realise that they do have some advantages in life and that all people don't have that.

(Christine)

Christine also mentioned that her children had 'friends from other backgrounds' and that for them this was simply 'part of life'. She mentioned that the family had employed au-pairs since the children were small, and explained that this provided exposure to other countries and languages. This familiarity with diversity was closely coupled with a general view of education as a 'life-changing experience'. Christine herself had grown up living on a council estate and had attended a comprehensive school which at the time had just ceased being a secondary modern school, and which she now regarded as having had low standards and low expectations. She nevertheless did well academically, and following 'A' levels had attended a redbrick university and also completed a postgraduate teaching qualification. This (in the context, unusual) trajectory remained an explicit reference-point when it came to her own children:

I think education is still the one thing that can genuinely give you a life changing experience, that can give you access to opportunities and experiences that you would otherwise struggle to find, and that's still the case. So I do believe in education in that respect. I think I'm living proof of that, so that in terms of my experience, my upbringing compared to the kind of opportunities that my children now have are because of my education really.

In these and similar cases there are middle-class families making similar kinds of school choice but with differing underpinning rationales: put most simply, for some families the choice of an ordinary state school might amount to an opportunity to *avoid* history repeating itself, whilst for others the same choice can provide an opportunity for *making* history repeat itself. Yet in both sets of cases, there is also a strong common feature – the desire for contact with social diversity. Examples like these illustrate the importance of background social class locations in shaping current practices, but they also suggest that even with something as specific as against-the-grain secondary school choice, it is much too simplistic to think of 'the middle classes' in an undifferentiated way.

Against-the-grain school choice to meet specific needs

The choice of an ordinary secondary school was usually characterised by difficulty and anxiety in most of the families we studied, at least in the initial stages. But in a small number of cases, the choice of such a school was such a great departure from the family habitus that it deserves closer attention. One such example was in the Denton family in Riverton. Annie and her husband were both from established middle-class backgrounds, and like their own parents, both had been privately educated. The discovery that two of their three children had learning difficulties led to the Dentons seeing educational processes in a new light:

> I suppose we sort of thought that we might educate them privately in a very abstract way, because that's what our experience was. So I think that obviously became a non starter, so I think it (the identification of special educational needs) made us rethink everything really. It made us re think a lot of our own attitudes to things and it liberates you from that whole middle class thing actually.

By 'that whole middle-class thing' Annie was referring to the difficulties faced by some of her friends of choosing between private schools and high-performing state schools, and also to the assumption that all their children would go to university after an increasingly pressurised and narrowly academic process. She had taken her son Ralph to look at the special needs provision in Mountstevens, a high-performing, ex-grammar state secondary school, and had come away very disappointed. The provision seemed poor, the school seemed overly concerned about its league-table position, and a teacher had surreptitiously advised her 'don't send him here'. Annie then recounted what happened when Redwood, a secondary school located in a white working-class area and with well below the national average level for GCSE results, came into contention:

> I was beginning to think... and I said 'Redwood School's our next [option]... but no child of mine is ever going to go to Redwood, you know, dreadful place.' And all my middle class prejudices came back. We went to see a solicitor who specialises in that sort of family law and child admissions and she said 'If you want to put him into Waterford, you're going to have to prove to a committee or whoever sits and decides these things, that (the local authority) can't meet your needs, so you're going to have to go and have a look at

Redwood.' So I thought – it was a complete, you know, dragging myself through the gates with my nose in the air, I'll be brutally honest. Went in, met the special needs lady and thought 'She's really nice.' Really nice room, nice feel to it, nice atmosphere, you know, gut instinct really. And I just thought wherever he goes, he's not going to find it easy, but I think the support mechanism is here. So I came out and thought well for better or worse, we haven't got a lot of choice, we'll send him here. And then I thought 'Well, I'm not going to think about it because it's too scary and it's going to be too hideous … the first day he's there and it's going to be like primary school, but about a million times worse.' So I just put that thought on hold because I just thought we haven't got anywhere else to go really. So, yes, I spent all the summer holidays trying not to worry about it. He's gone there, I'm not sure academically he's doing great things, but he's incredibly happy for the first time ever.

Later in the interview, Annie talked more about the kind of environment that the school offered, and the potential benefits. Here she refers to avoiding her son being 'cocooned', a point with a direct connection to her own educational background in which she had become isolated in small private provision that felt removed from the real world:

What I didn't want was that he went somewhere where he was sort of cocooned, because I thought at the end of the day he's going to have to go out to the outside world and I think actually, subconsciously I suppose, I thought, well actually throw him in somewhere like that, which is a pretty full on city comprehensive … it can't be any worse than the environment he's been in, in primary school really. He's either going to sink or swim actually.

So Ralph attended Redwood, a below-average-performing state comprehensive school, not because it is his 'catchment' school (which it was at the time) but because it had a very good special needs provision compared to Mountstevens, the ex-grammar, high-performing state comprehensive in another part of Riverton. Redwood is seen as 'a pretty full on city comprehensive'. His two sisters went to Mountstevens and Hammerton (an above-average-performing, out-of-town state school) respectively. The one at Hammerton went to the induction day at Redwood, and the experience speaks strongly of the family habitus and how, if it is sufficiently adrift of *field*, the habitus finds itself as a 'fish out of water':

I went for Redwood because we'd been lulled I think, by Ralph's experience. It's not a popular school, it's not the school of choice for parents around here, Redwood just isn't. So we didn't even look at another school for her, she was going to go to Redwood and she was fine about it, but no girl was going from her (primary) school and she went to the induction day, I just dropped her off – fine, but how wrong I was... I picked her up and she was practically hysterical, which is unlike her, she's very straightforward, and she just looked at me in that way that you think 'I can't actually ignore this...' She said 'Please don't send me there'... So she went down for a day, absolutely, absolutely hated it.

Interviewer: What did she dislike most or did you not get to the bottom of it?

No, I absolutely got to the bottom of it and I knew the minute she said 'Please don't send me there.' I knew she's too middle class... she didn't see anybody there that... she didn't know anybody which I think is a disadvantage for any child. And I think it does come down to identity really. [I said] 'well you can't tell me that everybody in your tutor group was horrible.' She said 'they weren't horrible, but nearly everybody came up to me and said, you're really posh aren't you?'

Interviewer: And her friends had gone elsewhere?

All gone elsewhere. There were a lot going to the private sector.

Annie described to us how, following this episode, she realised that she could not 'fight for all three' of her children and how she 'took the easy option', securing a place at Hammerton. Her daughter had a friend already going to Hammerton, and appeared to be 'really happy there'. But reflecting on this, Annie told us:

It's worked out really well, but it went against all my judgement to do that really. I found it really hard... I wrote a long letter to the school (Redwood) saying our feelings for the school hadn't changed, we still felt it was doing a fantastic job, Ralph was still very happy there, but at the end of the day, my sanity and her happiness just had to come above all other worthy principles... I think sometimes, you have to make a decision that... at the end you have to go against your principles because actually I thought by sticking to them, I'm actually not doing what's right for her as an individual.

We will return to the theme of a tension between 'principles' and 'doing what's right for the child' in Chapter 4 and subsequently. Annie describes her engagement with school choice as having taken her 'slightly outside the general soup of what parents... our social group, looks at'. Whilst it may be going too far to call this an 'out of habitus experience', it does seem to have given her a distance that is generally unavailable to other parents in her geographical, economic and social location. It generated new forms of reflection, which she articulated when we asked her what she hoped her children might be doing as adults:

> Now almost without a shadow of a doubt, most of my contemporaries see academic success, university... as absolutely the norm. And actually as not just the norm, its food and drink, there's almost nothing outside that. And within that... I am quite concerned that... our generation of children are becoming very narrow in our view of what a human being is. Maybe having Ralph has allowed me to broaden my thoughts on that. I think I would have been just like that had we had three very able children who went to private school – I would have absolutely been on that same escalator going up. Because I haven't been able to, it's a very liberating thing because you can stand back and look at it.

We came across several examples of families finding state comprehensive schools to be particularly responsive to the special needs of particular children, and this responsiveness was highly valued.

Conclusion

We would argue that the concept of habitus provides a helpful lens through which to view against-the-grain secondary school choices. Habitus is not only 'a sense of place' (Hillier and Rooksby 2005), it can also be 'a sense of the past' (Reay 2004). A high proportion of the parents in our sample had themselves attended either selective state or private schools for their secondary education, and they were also a highly qualified, geographically mobile group. In the course of our research we found that against-the-grain secondary school choices for their children could be understood as expressions of elements of family habitus. However, this did not operate in a uniform direction or manner. Several of the established and second-generation middle-class families made school choices that were a conscious reaction to the perceived narrowness (socially and/or academically) of the parents' own schooling. On the other hand, particularly amongst the 'first generation' middle-class families, the choice of an ordinary state school sometimes reflected a wish to reproduce in microcosm the trajectories of the parents: there was a desire on the part of those parents that their children should have to compete in ordinary circumstances for their success and should experience something of the same climb they had themselves made as part of their own upward mobility. In other cases, against-the-grain school choices are both the product and expression of a disdain for conventional views of school quality or educational success, or a 'sociological' confidence that characterises family habitus. We have used the example of the Denton family to illustrate some of this because it provides particularly clear examples of practices in which middle-class habitus and school choice interact. Later, in Chapter 6, we return to the link between habitus and the psycho-social.

In the next chapter we consider how 'place' and locality interact with habitus in relation to choices of schooling.

3
Habitus as a Sense of Place

Introduction

The parents in our study reside in three urban locales which differ in a variety of complex ways. These include size of city, ethnic diversity and global links. London is the key global, cosmopolitan city which in turn offers a rich variety of resources and experiences to those in a position to exploit them, leading Butler with Robson (2003) to describe the London middle-classes as embodying a 'metropolitan habitus'. Whilst we do not set out to explore the existence of a 'metropolitan habitus' in Riverton and Norton, we draw on this idea to compare and contrast the similarities and differences for the families in our study, extant across the three sites. In particular we explore how different geographical spaces impact on the parents' choice of school. We look at the ways that geography gives rise to differential distribution of goods and resources which in turn exacerbates the competitiveness between social classes and class fractions. This aspect is particularly salient for our parents in terms of the availability of the 'acceptable' local school and the supplementary educational support they often felt they needed to provide for their children.

Therefore the main purposes of this chapter are to demonstrate pertinent similarities and differences amongst the parents in the three locales; the similarities and differences in the three locales themselves; and to identify the salience of these similarities and differences in terms of school choice and identity formations. We discuss data from interviews across these three urban locales and consider the implications these spatial differences make to white middle-class identities and as part of that their choices for their children's school. We build on the concept of habitus as outlined in the previous chapter, though with a particular emphasis on 'habitus as a sense of place' (Hillier and Rooksby 2005).

Local landscapes – Geographical Differences: the significance of local educational and socio-economic and cultural contexts

As seen in Chapter 2, it is possible to subdivide the middle-class families in our study in terms of classed generations. In this respect we analyse what Bourdieu (2005) refers to as the 'dialectical confrontation between habitus, as a structured structure, and objective structures' (p. 46). All of the parents are encountering conditions different to those upon which their own habitus/dispositions were constructed, whether this is in terms of their new or relatively new class locations, or within the context of the urban comprehensive school itself. Both the school and the home locality are spaces where these tensions and possibilities for identity generation are played out. Moreover, socio-economic and political contexts impact on parents' perceptions and actions; for example, in Norton only 8 per cent of the inner city population was middle-class and there were far fewer ethnic minorities than in London where over a quarter of the population was middle-class and in some areas ethnic minorities made up the majority. As we will show in later chapters these aspects influenced parents' responses and attitudes to the schools and their children's school experiences.

Amongst the families studied within and across the three locales there were considerable areas of overlap in terms of cosmopolitan dispositions and left-leaning, pro-welfare tendencies. There were also differences such as in terms of occupation: London had the largest percentage of parents working in the private sector, 43 per cent, compared to 17 per cent and 12 per cent in Norton and Riverton respectively. London also had the highest number working in creative industries (London 19 per cent; Norton 6 per cent; Riverton 7 per cent). Riverton had the largest number of educational professionals, at 37 per cent, with 29 per cent in London and 21 per cent in Norton. The largest professional group in Norton were health workers with 38 per cent (mainly doctors) (see Appendix 2 for more details). Given these profiles it is perhaps not surprising that the majority of our participants were highly committed to the welfare state. As indicated earlier, there were also class differences in terms of their family histories. In London 40 per cent of parents were established middle-class with the majority of these having attended private schools as children and most having parents who had been to university. Norton had the highest percentage, at almost 40 per cent, of first generation middle-class, whose own parents were working-class; the second-generation middle-class grouping was more evenly spread across the three locales although there was a slightly higher percentage in Riverton. Although we cannot read too much into such data we would suggest that these class locations have some impact on self-concept of class and possibly on confidence and a sense of class in/security.

There were also discernible spatial differences between the parents in relation to political activism and civic engagement. Whilst most had at some time been on political demonstrations, such as anti-Iraq war demonstrations, few were politically active in terms of current trade union activity or party political activity. Most of these were in London with almost 25 per cent of the parents claiming to be involved in something of this kind. Whilst this is substantially higher than the other two areas, Butler with Robson's (2003) survey of London parents showed that political interest was a 'low scoring prime activity' and even those who were members of a political party tended to be largely passive (p. 134). However, over a third of our London parents demonstrated their active citizenship in terms of their role as school governors, although almost a quarter of Riverton parents had been school governors too.

In terms of wealth as indicated by the ACORN[1] categories of location of residence, our families occupied similar types of residence indicating similar income levels. Our research ranged across all areas of inner and greater London, Riverton and Norton, although the majority of participating Norton parents resided in predominantly white areas which were largely middle-class. Across all areas a substantial proportion of the parents (London 48 per cent, Norton 47 per cent and Riverton 33 per cent) lived in high-income areas. Almost a quarter of those in London lived in ACORN category 15 areas, where only 1.17 per cent of the UK population live. Just over a third of the Riverton parents, and a fifth of those in Norton, lived in ACORN category 13, where only 0.87 per cent of the UK live (ACORN 2006). These high-income areas are characterised by large houses, with four or more bedrooms, often in Georgian and Victorian terraces, or detached, owner-occupied by professional couples and families. Of the other parents across the three locales, 29 per cent lived in medium-income areas most of which are areas that have been or are in the process of being gentrified; and only 4 per cent lived in poor-income and multi-ethnic areas (one in Norton and four in London). (See Appendix 3 for further details.)

As a global and cosmopolitan city, London has the scope and capacity to offer the white, middle-classes immense opportunities. Living in London is thus in itself potentially advantaging but even more so for the already privileged. But living there is also highly risky, for example in terms of the quality of education and the anxieties of social and ethnic mix (Butler with Robson 2003): indeed some Norton and Riverton parents had moved out of London precisely in order to reduce such risks. Arguably the relative wealth and social and cultural opportunities offered in London mediate these risks, making them worth taking. Specifically for these parents, if the school experience didn't work out there were plenty of alternatives.

Place and time are important elements in influencing and impacting on the parents' attitudes and behaviours with respect to school choice. In all three areas the majority of parents in our sample sent their children to a local comprehensive school even though by conventional measures the general quality of state education in Riverton and London was particularly poor, thus limiting the landscape of choice for even the advantaged. In Table 3.1 we present data on the participating children's schools in terms of the Office of Standards in Education (Ofsted) performance indicators and demographic indicators for 2004 and 2005.[2] The key measurement that Ofsted and other agencies use for secondary school academic achievement is the percentage of five A*–C GCSEs; at the time of our research the national average was 57 per cent of pupils gaining five A*–C GCSEs. In Riverton and Norton some of the data were particularly difficult to access, therefore some of this is incomplete. However, the table below provides an indication of the types of schools attended by the children in our study and the similarities and differences across the three locales.

Although the choice of schools in Riverton and London may appear to represent a challenge to middle-class expectations for class reproduction, with respect to London at least, Bridge (2006) argues that the scale of the metropolitan area means that the range of strategies middle-class parents employ can be accommodated within their desired neighbourhoods. As he says: 'The size of London enables middle-class residents to keep all social fields (in the Bourdieusian sense) in play at the same time' (p. 725). Hence whilst risk of school choice is prevalent, if it doesn't work out there are alternatives. In Riverton the only real alternative was the private sector, though for most families in the sample this was not a real option on either ideological or financial grounds which suggests that other considerations became part of the location decision-making process for these parents.

Table 3.1 School performance indicators and demographic details

	Number of schools participating children attended	% of the schools performing at or below the national average of (57%) A*–C × 5 GCSEs	% of the schools with Black and Minority Ethnic pupils	% of the schools with over 10% on free school meals	% of the schools with 10% of children with SEN	% of the schools with between 10% and 28% of children with SEN	% of the schools with 50% or more of children with SEN
London	40	80	95 with 50 or more BME	92 (60% had over 25%)	13		8
Riverton	12	83	17 with over 50 BME	75		75	
Norton	12	50	25 with 10–17% BME	42 (33% had between 20% and 28%; the other schools had less than 13% i.e. the national average)		67	

Note: Percentages have been rounded up.

As others have found (e.g., Butler with Robson 2003; Bridge 2006) there are indeed a range of reasons for families' choice of location. For many of our parents choice of location was based less on considerations of local schools and more on the 'ready-made aesthetic product' (Bridge 2006 p. 725) such as those who bought into high-income areas (for example, Mountvale in Norton or Hillside in Riverton) or those gentrifiers who sought aesthetic satisfaction from characterful Victorian houses and vibrant, diverse and/or ideologically conducive locales.

As Abby and Stuart Spedding explained in describing their area of St Marks in Riverton:

It's kind of middle class, I mean there's a small... a certain diversity in the ethnicity but not very large, so it's what I would call kind of more successful Afro-Caribbean... And a lot of white middle class public sector professionals I think... Fairtrade coffee and that kind of thing. Yeah, it's the reason why certain shops we buy from in Whittington Road... there's a greengrocers where people serve you and... I mean it's actually, I think it's just managed to survive from people who used to have it like that but kind of buoyed [by] the new people coming in... I mean Whittington Road's just got an amazing array of little shops hasn't it? Most of the shops have been replaced by coffee bars now but as I say.... they were talking about Fairtrade this and organic veg box that... but people, I mean recently well to do, so there are a lot of cars out on the street as you saw, you know two car families and things and what we've seen is, we've been here 11 years, is more and more families... fewer student houses or... it's become more of a residential area which we're probably part of.

(Abby and Stuart Spedding, Riverton)

These are Savage's (2010) 'elective belongers' for whom the aesthetics of their home and the green credentials of the locality or colourful 'ethnic' shops are attractive. Similarly privately educated teacher Ella Rosen and her family chose Marchfield in Norton for similar reasons, though in addition to the local aesthetics of place she also indicated the desire to experience difference: a different kind of world; a factor which was more generally and explicitly articulated in relation to choice of the urban school:

And that's also why we chose City Road Primary, or I suppose why we are living in Marchfield as opposed to Mountvale or Barchester, because obviously we could afford to live in those places, is because I wanted them to grow up and have friends who came from all different kinds of background and just think that was the norm. Which they have done, or they are doing. Now what will be interesting is, to see if they kind of revert to type as they get older, to sort of you know be quite choosy, you know seek out people who are you know, people like George[her husband] and I. I don't know if they will or not really, but, I just feel it's a much more balanced experience of life for them.

(Ellen Rosen, Norton)

In London Julie Hextell talked in similar terms about the local diversity or 'mix' as she put it, influencing their choice:

...we went to a local estate agent for somewhere to live and he said 'I know where would suit you, Manor Park' and it did. I mean he described it as a Liquorice Allsorts area, that was his description of it, for which I think he meant you know its racially mixed and 'you will like that'...I like it here, yeah I like the mixture and I like the sort of vibrant...there is lots happening; there are lots of different things going on lots of different people...You know it is probably the most racially mixed place you can find. I mean there are lots of places where there are high numbers of non British, non British born here, but it is the mixture here and yeah it's fascinating.

Here we see active choosers of locality driven by particular desires of how they wish to construct their and their families' lives. For these families, this is a lifestyle choice, driven by notions of community or getting close to 'real people', 'real experiences', and possibly by elements of romanticism or nostalgia (Savage 2010). This point about 'mix' is important since it also emerged as a key driver in the choice of school. However, it can be a misleading term since in practice it may not actually refer to social mixing *per se* but rather to the social backdrop, the context for living: the nature of the place without the realisation or actualisation of the space (De Certeau 1984). The white middle-class parents interacted little with these diverse surroundings and as Savage describes they bracket out what doesn't fit or work for them:

The landscape is one which is also defined by physical, rather than social markers. Visual and other sensory perceptions are crucial, whereas the values, attitudes and interests of other local residents seem less important, unless they intrude.

(Savage 2010 p. 6)

The relationship to place for these 'elective belongers' and 'gentrifiers' is fragile, and it 'oscillates between belonging and not belonging' (Savage 2010).

For some, choice of place was though very specifically about belonging and identification with the other residents like themselves:

> We found while we started looking further afield than Barchester and into Mountvale, that we liked the people whose houses we were looking at in Mountvale, more than we did the type of person that was living in Barchester. It was an odd thing, so that's how we ended up being ... We concluded that the kind of people who lived in Mountvale were probably more like us than the kind of people who lived in Barchester, just by judging the type of people whose houses we were looking at.
>
> (Carolyn and Fred Drummond, Norton)

Mountvale in particular is an example of a middle-class enclave. It offered a village-like, safe space for the parents and their children within an urban context. As Sheila Moss explained:

> I've always been able to say to the kids if they were out and something happened there would be a hundred doors they could knock on, really. You know, people [who] would even know their mum by sight or that know them, I think that's really quite important for children.
>
> (Shelia Moss, Norton)

For these parents Mountvale evoked a strong sense of place and belonging. It provided a community of support and safety. It was a place to locate their identities – 'a place called home' (Massey 1994).

Not surprisingly, there were fewer such choices for some of the new first-generation middle-class families. Aspirant and reluctant to live where they had come from, they sought affordable suburban enclaves:

> It's not town life ... we couldn't afford town life when we first moved in, but it's become a lot more affluent, over the last 7–8 years house prices have rocketed. I mean we bought this house 12 years ago for

£45,000. It's worth over 200,000 now and I think it's the overspill from Rivermouth that's moved here so you've got lots of professional people ... I was just saying to [Mike] the other night there's three convertible cars in the street now and we never had convertibles, lots of new cars, er, you know, it is quite an affluent area.

(Sarah Potts, Norton)

Geography and the impact on choice

Although all the parents in our study sent at least one, and in most cases all, of their children to comprehensive schools, they do appear to some extent, to have exercised their 'choice'. In London, whilst a number of parents sent their children to schools performing at well below the national average, a number of others were clearly active choosers, 'playing the market' in terms of assessing the league tables, the distance from home, putting their children in for 'entrance exams' or an interview and going to appeal if they weren't allocated their choice of school. In Riverton the Booths sent one daughter to a low-performing comprehensive (Rivermead, then with GCSE results of 29 per cent A*−C) but then 'worked up' their Roman Catholic credentials for the younger, non-statemented dyslexic daughter to get into Faithdown (46 per cent A*−C). Riverton had experienced a prolonged period of white flight into the private sector and to neighbouring local authority areas, arguably helping to depress the average state school performance of 35 per cent five GCSE A*−Cs across the Local Authority area (2004) – at the time amongst the lowest in the country. The parents committed to the urban schools were highly exercised to find a school they considered acceptable.

In London also many families sent their children to different comprehensives according, in their view, to their children's differing personalities and needs: another aspect of playing the market and a key feature of New Labour's rationale for the right of parents to 'choose' their child's school. In making this choice London parents frequently weighed up the nature of the comprehensive school and whether their child could cope with what they perceived as the challenges of class and ethnic diversity.

In Norton only three families sent their children to those schools performing well below the national average; one of these was a lone parent living in one of the low-income areas who sent one of her daughters to the local comprehensive in that area. Her older daughter went to a high-performing Catholic school. In her case the choice was more to do with her limited options and resources given that her younger daughter failed the entrance exam to the Catholic secondary school. Parents living in the gentrified area we call Castlewall, where their local school had the largest minority ethnic population in the city, is predominantly working-class and in 2004, when we began the research, gained 32 per cent on the GCSE 'economy', preferred to send their children across the city to the more 'acceptable', 'good enough' comprehensive schools. Parents living in another gentrified area, Marchfield, also favoured the Park Comprehensive over closer, more working-class schools which included a Sports Academy.

Geography in terms of space and place of city and locale is clearly an issue here. This includes: the size of the middle-class group (SEC 1–2); the housing patterns of the middle-classes; whether or not there is social integration or segregation and/or middle-class white flight altogether from the inner city. In all three cities, we came across a number of low-performing comprehensive schools in which, according to head teachers and other contacts, there were no middle-class children at all.

Most of our Norton parents, as we have indicated, lived in the affluent Mountvale area. Therefore, for most parents their nearest primary school (Mountvale Primary) had a majority of middle-class children. Mountvale, like the majority of primary schools attended by children in the study, was high performing, above the national average.[3] As it happens for the Mountvale residents, their nearest comprehensive school is The Park and whilst at the time most of our participants' children started there it was achieving below the national average; at the time of writing it is achieving well above this (at 63 per cent), compared to the national average of 59 per cent. The Park given its location and proximity to Mountvale is a, if not the, feeder secondary school and is therefore patronised by a significant minority of middle-class children who had known each other at Mountvale Primary School.

In starting our research we anticipated that sections of the middle-classes engaged in a form of resistance in choosing not to play the educational market and in sending their children to their local urban comprehensive. Yet the reality is more subtle and complex, and shaped by location. There is clearly less need for middle-class parents in Norton to work the market. In Riverton many schools were immediately discounted either because of geography, attainment or reputation. The few schools regarded as acceptable were so regularly oversubscribed they were not seen as worth applying for. Hence there were fewer 'acceptable' comprehensive school alternatives. House prices in Riverton were high and were rising just as fast as in London. We can see a mutually reinforcing situation developing in Riverton between the housing and education markets: for example, the low house prices in the Broadway area in the 1980s led to a cohort of white middle-class children into City Wall Primary School feeding in to Redwood Comprehensive School, the school where the largest number of our Riverton families sent their children (13 families: 43 per cent).

In London urban comprehensives are more socially and ethnically diverse and as such are considered to be challenging and generate anxiety. Whilst some parents settled for the local school many employed their privileged knowledge to try and find the best possible acceptable option. Where they lived, either by choice or otherwise, did impose risks in terms of school choice. There is in a sense a tension between being an active gentrifier and the consequences of this for the future of their children's education. Although many parents seemed to have considered the potential consequences for schooling when choosing their homes, others had not thought this through. In a few cases there was the happy discovery that the local comprehensive school was, after all, acceptable. In Julie Hextell's case, for example, she found they were 'lucky' with their children's school:

I think that I have been lucky enough to live near a school where I can practice what I believe... I believe in state education, I believe in people being taught. I believe in the comprehensive system, I believe in the comprehensive educational system, if done properly it works. But we've just had too much tinkering around. But I was lucky in as much as I lived in an area where I could send my child to the local comprehensive school in Hackney. If I'd had a boy and my nearest school was Hazelmere I'm quite sure I would have done what my friends did who work at Friends of the Earth and are social workers and are bang on socialists, they moved for a year to get their child into Denisford. And they are much more, far more moral than I am. I was lucky so where – so my financial ability to be able to live in a house like this has enabled me to live by my moral choice, if that makes sense. These things are never cut and dried. I got lucky. To be able to say, 'oh yes I sent my child to a comprehensive school in Hackney, aren't I good, look how well they're doing'. But really I just got lucky.

(Julie Hextell, London)

Maureen Evercroft, in Eastvale Park, London, said something similar but in her case was saved by the critical mass of people like her:

I feel extremely lucky in this area because one of the things that made the choice of schools relatively easy is there are a lot of normal wealthy middle class people as teachers, and social workers. I have got a friend who lives in Chiswick whose daughter has also gone to a local comprehensive on a point of principle but because there is so much more money in Chiswick she felt she was almost the only person in her street whose child was at a state school let alone a local comprehensive... The fact that (here) there is a mix and so there is a mix of classes in the area but there is this sort of nexus of people that I feel comfortable with as well as a bigger variety that my kids feel comfortable with, made it a lot easier.

Feeling 'lucky' signals the parents' relief at being able to act out their principles with a less angst ridden and risky choice in sending their children to these schools. However, it may also be a reminder that such matters can rarely be cleanly categorised into 'conscious decisions' and 'lucky outcomes'. For Bourdieu, social practices often entail factors that are neither particularly conscious nor unconscious and which are 'misrecognised' (i.e. attributed to other realms of meaning) as they occur (see for example Grenfell and James 1998).

Relationship to the local – rooted in or routed through?

Just under 70 per cent of all parents (for whom we have information) were 'incomers' to the area in which they were living. If we look at this in terms of family units, more than 50 per cent of families were incomers in London, Norton and Riverton. In London and Riverton, just less than 10 per cent of families (that is, both parents) are from that area, but the figure is almost double in Norton, with 18 per cent of families where both parents grew up and have remained in the area. The rest of the family units are a mixture of one parent from the area and one parent an incomer. Many of the incomers came to the area for university and stayed or came for graduate jobs. In Norton and Riverton there was a very small number of families (two in Norton and one in Riverton) who moved there (out of London) specifically for a better quality of life and cited the desire for better schooling as one of the motivating factors.

Although the families tend to live in ethnically diverse and gentrified areas, particularly in London and Riverton, as we have said, there was very little social mixing between the families and their local communities, in any of the three locales. There was very little social mixing amongst the children in their secondary schools (which we discuss further in Chapter 7) and their primary schools are often predominantly white with majority middle-class intakes, although there is more evidence of social mixing at primary school level.

Social geographers have written extensively on the significance of place. In our study the significance of place plays out differently across the three locales. Drawing on May's (1996) analysis, the work of Harvey, Massey, as well as May, can help us glimpse some understanding as to the parents' relationship to their localities. Harvey (1989, 1993), for example, has argued that in contemporary society the urban dweller frequently becomes defensive, territorial and competitive about their urban space, creating spatial barriers or 'bounded space'. Massey (e.g. 1994) suggests a more optimistic view of (urban) space and the relationship between place and identity. She argues that space should be understood as multi-dimensional and comprising the 'simultaneous coexistence of social interrelations at all geographical scales', and therefore that place can be conceived of in this way too (p. 168). Following on from this she argues that the 'identity of place' is therefore more provisional than is most often acknowledged, and the identity of place is actually formed through juxtaposition and interrelationships and interactions outside of that particular space. Massey therefore sees greater possibilities for more progressive and harmonious engagement with space and place. May (1996) as he says himself, takes a third view: one that is less polarised and which aims to acknowledge greater complexity of 'contemporary place identities' (p. 195). In his analysis (of Stoke Newington) he argues that there is evidence to show that people are likely to draw on what he calls 'multiple place identities' (p. 210). In his case study he demonstrates an instrumentalism amongst sections of the community (the 'new cultural class') in their desire to accumulate life-enhancing, aesthetically desirable opportunities and experiences as defined by them, and what seems to have 'cultural' currency. In other words, he argues, these residents have the control (over their locale) to enable them to construct their locale as a space in which they 'can have it all' (p. 210): perhaps this is akin to Butler's 'metropolitan habitus' (Butler with Robson 2003). Although there is some evidence of all of these types in all three of our locales, we could say that in areas of Norton and the Mountvale area in particular, the middle-class inhabitants tended to relate to their locale in terms of Harvey's 'bounded space' (1993). This can in part be attributed to the desire for a critical mass of 'people like us' particularly for those Norton white middle-classes living in the inner city where they constituted a tiny percentage (8 per cent) of the urban population. In Riverton the relationship can be categorised as 'a more progressive sense of place' (Massey 1994), whereby local attachment is less constrained to a bounded area of the city or indeed the city itself. It is a more provisional aspect of identity influenced by 'the readymade aesthetic product' (Bridge 2006) or ethos of the region as well as areas of the city. In London the relationship is more akin to May's (1996) 'multiple place identity' in the sense of taking on different identifications and moving in and out or between different milieu and cultural experiences but not necessarily being wholly captured by or committed to anything in particular. However, separateness between the classed and 'raced' groups dominates relationships to the local across all areas.

Community has always been a morally charged concept because it is about the obligations to, and expectations of, the individuals one lives closest to (Williams 1976; Revill 1993). It links personal responsibility, commitment and identification with people other than the family. However, within dominant, including political, discourses on both the right and left, and social policy theorists (Putnam 2000), there is seen to have been a demise of community dating from the 1980s. In the twenty-first century we still have powerful imagined communities, but there is scant empirical evidence that communities, rooted in the local and with the power to reach across class and ethnic boundaries, actually exist. People may share neighbourhoods as a living space but this does not mean they will interact together as a community (Lee and Newby 1983). Rather in relation to social class, as we have indicated and as other research has found, the 'new' professional middle-classes tend to be positive about living in close proximity with working-class families within inner cities without either wanting or having any social interaction with them (Ley 1996; Butler 1997; Savage et al. 2005).

Hence, despite citing a communitarian commitment to the local as a contributory factor in choosing their children's schooling, apart from sending their children to local comprehensives, their most significant social networks, comprising family and friends, were mainly independent of the local area. We can glimpse this rhetorical allegiance undercut by what is in effect a disengagement from the locality, in what Trevor Wells, a London parent, says:

We believe in schools being a community project...If my politics is anything to do with it at all it's the politics of the community. *Interviewer: but are you a member of anything locally?* I don't think so, Jackie will know. No, no, I don't think so.

When parents were able to articulate a sense of belonging, an embeddedness in a tangible as opposed to an imagined community, the communities they described were white middle-class ones. So Sheila Moss asserted that:

> We have settled here mainly because of the benefits of the community and it really is a strong community and most of that is based around the primary school for people like us.
>
> (Sheila Moss, Norton)

In Riverton too we see the coalescing of a kind of middle-class bubble centred around a popular school. Bakers Lane in Bakersville was portrayed as a tight-knit middle-class community. Similarly, City Wall School was located in a gentrified area that appeared to be developing in a similar way:

> The school changed in the time that we were there in the same way that Broadway changed. There's been a huge influx of young middle class [professional] couples, who then grow like us really, get families, move from the small houses to the bigger houses and it's become a lot more go getting and popular. The school is much more middle class now.
>
> (Ann Epsom Riverton)

The families were either detached from their localities with families suspended in a global world that rarely made contact with the predominantly working-class residents of their city (Nayak 2003), or else their communities of reality rather than desire, were, as Watt (2009) also found, located in a small number of adjacent streets. These were almost exclusively populated, as Sheila, above, pointed out, by 'people like us' and frequently focused on the predominantly white, middle-class primary schools their children had attended. Despite strongly expressed desires, particularly in London, to be part of wider multicultural communities, the majority of the families were most at home in small almost exclusively white middle-class enclaves. So Lindsey Malone, living in East London, felt like 'a local almost as soon as I got here'. However, as she indicates, her locality is very narrowly bounded both geographically and culturally:

> This street is a cul-de-sac which helps I think. In the summer there are games of street cricket, things like that and people go in and out

of each other's houses so I know people on first name terms, certainly in this half of the street. I do feel very much part of the community.

Similarly Karen Sollazzi in Riverton asserted, 'I am very into community. We have street parties here which I was quite big in setting up' but she went on to describe her street as 'a very homogeneous street, I must say, very white homogeneous, safe though, a very nice place to bring kids up'. There are similarities here with Butler with Robson's (2003) white London middle-classes grouped together in small tightly bounded communities which provide the security they need in order to venture further afield culturally (May 1996).

Amongst the parents therefore we have those occupying bounded enclaves, with others acting as pioneers, largely in London, confident in their sense of self in shaping the social space that they have occupied as outsiders. According to Massey (1994) 'a place is formed out of the particular set of social relations which interact at a particular location.' Hence the ability of a particular group sufficiently dominant to 'produce new social effects' (p. 168).

Yes, it [City Wall Primary] is more diverse ethnically, but still it's vast majority white. Given it's mainly middle class majority now, it's still got quite a high percentage of... like for example, free school meals. [It's] just below the cut off for being very high free school meals. It's a nice mixture, it lends itself for a very global feel actually of being community... Even without the ethnicity, yes. Well, with and without it [ethnic mix], it's a nice place to teach, a nice place to hang out because you get to meet on an equal level, all sorts of people and working in a class there, you get the impression that some children are dragged up by other children. It's a nice [place]...

(Ann Epsom, Riverton)

Conclusion

The parents' relationship to their geographic locality is aligned to their relationship with their child's school, not in the sense that they moved house in order to access a desirable school but in the sense that they made their 'space' work for them in a similar way to which they also made the school work for them (Crozier et al. 2007). Given that over half of the families lived in high-income areas, this was arguably not challenging or risky. However, in London where 42 per cent of our families lived in these areas, a 'high-income street' can run parallel with a low-income, disadvantaged street or estate.

May (1996) argues against the polarised position of bounded space and the notion of a progressive sense of place. He is also questioning of the motivation of those he refers to as the new cultural class residents who draw on multiple place identities (p. 210). The engagement with difference or extracting the global from the local, as we have shown, is, it would appear, about accruing cultural capital and generating metropolitan habituses: both to enable operating in a twenty-first-century complex and diverse world. The impact of the middle-class families on their locales is often quite significant, but the effect is to further advantage themselves such as in leading to house price rises and also raising the status of local schools which then become oversubscribed.

In terms of school choice, within each of the areas, location provides different contexts for school choice which in turn has an impact. Parents' commitment to the local comprehensive school plays out differently given the distinctiveness in the local school economy. Compared to the other areas, for most of the Norton parents the choice was relatively straightforward, since they lived near to an acceptable urban comprehensive and one that was on an upward trajectory in terms of the GCSE measure. In Riverton and London, choice of state schooling was generally problematic and this minimised the options for the parents.

In all of the areas critical mass and the need for assurance that there were other children at the school 'like us' was regarded as an important issue. In Norton given the size of the middle-class as a small percentage of the population, there were fewer 'like them' to compete with for an urban comprehensive school; therefore they were in an advantaged position secure in the knowledge that they/their children would be desired by schools. By contrast, in Riverton the competition for acceptable school places was intense. In London, however, the opportunities and availability of useful resources and networks were more extensive and these mediated the risks and difficulties, to a greater extent than in Riverton.

The three regions therefore provide different opportunities and challenges for this class fraction of white middle-class parents in their choice of secondary school.

4
Against-the-Grain School Choice in Neoliberal Times

Introduction

An appreciation of the practices and consequences of 'against the grain' secondary school choices needs to be set within some understanding of the wider policy framing of choice, and indeed the nature of 'mainstream' choosing, in relation to schooling. Accordingly, this chapter looks briefly at the emergence and recent development of choice in educational policy in the context of neoliberal thinking. It then focuses on practices of school choice, arguing that a finer distinction (that between commitments and preferences) is necessary for understanding the gulf between the rhetoric of choice and the much more nuanced sets of practices and effects revealed in the research. We then discuss the nature of general orientations amongst our sample of parents, highlighting in particular the low incidence of communitarian commitments and the prevalence of instrumental orientations. Finally, the chapter looks at the related issues of 'hot knowledge' and parental intervention.

Choice in neoliberal times

It is worth giving some consideration to the nature of 'choice' and the context for the emergence of its contemporary significance in schooling. There are now several attempts to compare the rise of parental choice between different countries and to weigh up its effects. For example, Plank and Sykes (2003) present an edited collection accounting for marked increases in parental choice in Chile, New Zealand, England and Wales, Sweden, Australia, South Africa, China, Czech Republic and Hungary. Whilst choice takes many different forms across these examples, Plank and Sykes argue that there are two essential features that run through all of them in some form. The first is a 'demand side' shift, in that policies give parents more choice about the schools to which their children will go. The nature of this shift depends on the starting point on a continuum, at one end of which is the state-centred system in which children are simply assigned to schools using a set of criteria typically including geographical residence and ability. The second is a 'supply side' shift, whereby there is more 'explicit or implicit competition among schools for students and revenues...With the advent of school choice policies...schools no longer "own" their students' (Plank and Sykes 2003 p. ix). Yet whilst these two features can be said to appear in all their cases, the authors acknowledge that there is also considerable variability:

> ...under some policies parents may be *required* to choose a school, while under others they retain an entitlement to a place in the local public school. Some policies restrict the competition among schools to schools in the public sector, whilst others expand the market to include private and religious schools as well. Countries also vary in the extent to which governments provide ancillary services to support parents' choices, including such things as student transportation and the production and distribution of information about schools. The extent to which these services are publicly subsidized has a powerful effect on how the emerging market for schooling operates.
>
> (p. ix)

As well as highlighting this variability, Plank and Sykes also address the question of why these shifts are occurring. They write that it is not so much due to the power of arguments *for* greater school choice, but rather due to 'the collapse of a plausible argument in favor of standardized, state-centred educational provision' (p. x). They identify four points of view on this issue. The first is the argument that the bureaucratisation and standardisation of schooling has undermined the construction of community – both within and around schools. Secondly, there is support for extending school choice on equality grounds, such as the argument that state systems have trapped some people into unsuccessful provision. Thirdly, there are arguments based on dissatisfaction with the nature of government, with levels of inefficiency or corruption, and a related thrust towards decentralisation and the use of private agencies to achieve state goals in the name of greater efficiency. Plank and Sykes couple this line of argument together with the desire to increase global competitiveness and the pressure this makes governments bring to bear on education systems. Fourthly, they group a set of arguments under the heading of 'neoliberalism and free markets', in which:

> The enthusiasm of economists and others for the 'magic of the market' has produced recommendations for privatizing virtually all the activities of the public sector, from pensions to prisons. In education, these arguments have been deployed in support of vouchers and increased private-sector participation in educational provision. Arguments that urge governments to 'unleash' market forces in the education system have been powerfully influential in a number of countries, including Chile, the Czech Republic, the United Kingdom, and the United States.
>
> (p. xii)

Plank and Sykes also point to the role of trans-national agencies like the World Bank and the OECD in influencing governments, though they do not offer an integration of these observations with their suggestions about neoliberal ideology. This theme is however taken up by Forsey and colleagues in their book *The Globalisation of School Choice?* (Forsey et al. 2008). They describe how 'in the past three decades or so we have witnessed and experienced a dramatic increase in the influence of economic theory on social action and political practice' (p. 11). This does not refer to all kinds of economic theory, but to a particular form originally exemplified in Milton Friedman's work and characterised by a strong model of individual self-interest and its maximisation through rational choices. Many have criticised this model and pointed to its inadequacies. As early as 1977 the economist Sen described 'purely economic man' as a 'social moron' [*sic*] and complained that economic theory paid too much attention to this 'rational fool decked in the glory of his one all-purpose preference ordering' (Sen 1977 pp. 335–336). Nevertheless, there is no denying the pervasiveness of this way of thinking at the level of the political, and how its application in the Thatcher and Regan governments set in train a direction of travel that is still apparent and which has 'long since washed up onto many a shore around the globe' (Forsey et al. 2008 p. 12). This is not to imply a uniform effect: like other global trends, policies for school choice take specific local forms depending on historical and other aspects of context. Nevertheless, Forsey et al. point to two important general ramifications. Firstly, that

choice frameworks can incorporate the interests of even those
actors who otherwise have little affinity with market thinking in
education...Beyond its neoliberal advocates, religious, ethnic and
linguistic minorities in many countries are adapting the phrasing of
'choice' to suit their assorted interests.

(p. 22)

And secondly, that

choice is often not the most appropriate term to use when describing
what has happened in recent reformation of school systems. While
the movement towards private educational options can in theory
open up educational opportunities in state sectors that always operate in a limited financial environment, in practice it often results
in further diminution of state-run schools...the options available to
people have all too often become more limited in the new choice
environments produced across the globe.

(pp. 22–23)

Forsey et al. argue that 'current forms of neoliberalism are closely associated with the push for a globally unified economy' (p. 13) in which the
state's role becomes one of providing the conditions in which such an
economy can flourish. Similar points can be found across the now considerable volume of writing about neoliberalism and its consequences.
For Olssen, the last 25 years or so have seen a trans-national pressure
to release economic activity from state regulation, presenting a major
obstacle to democracy and leading to '...a huge escalation of inequality
in the distribution of incomes and wealth', both between countries and
within them (Olssen 2004 pp. 231–232; see also Blanden and Machin
2007; Rutherford 2008). Tabb has argued that the aim of neoliberalism
is '...to put into question all collective structures capable of obstruct-
ing the logic of the pure market' (Tabb 2002 p. 7). But it is perhaps
Harvey's account of the origins and spread of neoliberalism that does
most to explain the political forces accompanying the economic shifts:
'The assumption that individual freedoms are guaranteed by freedom
of the market and of trade is a cardinal feature of neoliberal thinking'
(Harvey 2005 p. 7). He adds:

to presume that markets and market signals can best determine all
allocative decisions is to presume that everything can in principle

be treated as a commodity... The market is presumed to work as an appropriate guide – an ethic – for all human action.

(Harvey 2005 p. 165)

So the notion of greater choice seems inherently attractive, and not just because it goes with ideology that makes 'the market' appear to be the natural order of things: choice is also easily conflated with ideas like freedom and respect for individual rights. In part, and as Plank and Sykes (2003) suggest, the rhetoric of choice appeals because it promises a break with structures of state-managed provision in which nation-states used bureaucracies to attempt to deliver services and social welfare in an equitable fashion, but with quite variable success. For present purposes, the central point is that neoliberal policies around school choice have re-shaped earlier discourses of equity, inclusion and social welfare, changing the meaning of the terms themselves. Although the rhetoric of choice appears politically neutral, its introduction discursively shifts the responsibility for social inequality to individual citizens.

Practices of school choice

The research evidence on whether choice policies 'work' is at best equivocal. One study by the Organisation for Economic Development and Cooperation showed that the introduction of choice policies had increased social class segregation in schools in seven different countries (OECD 1994). In the UK context, the rise of such policies from around 1988 'benefited all sections of the middle classes' (Tomlinson 2005b p. 174). Several studies in the United Kingdom explored the mechanics of middle-class advantage in the period when choice policy took real hold (e.g. Gerwirtz et al. 1995; Ball et al. 1996; and see Ball 2003). For Tomlinson, governments adopting such policies have continued to make it possible for the middle-classes to avoid both 'the poor' and those types of educational provision associated with lower status:

The middle classes who could not afford private escape have usually had at their disposal strategies to avoid their children being educated with the poor, to ensure that their children attended well-resourced schools, and avoided stigmatised forms of education.

(p. 177)

There has also been some research on parental views of choice. An earlier small-scale study of secondary school choice in England reported that '... three-quarters of parents said there were particular schools to which they did not want their child to go', and 'the predominant reason given was its "bad reputation"' (West and Varlaam 1991 p. 22). In their research on British parents, Boulton and Coldron (1996) suggested that even those who had not been particularly concerned about choosing schools for their own children nevertheless placed high value on the *availability* of choice. Yet in contrast to this, Tomlinson cites studies that suggested that apart from those parents seeking to 'go private' or who aimed for particular selective secondary education,

> ... what most parents wanted was a good local comprehensive school, wellresourced and staffed and offering equality of treatment for all children.
>
> (Tomlinson 2005b p. 54)

Many observers have pointed to the rather limited meanings of the terms 'choice' and 'diversity' in respect of actual parental interactions with school systems. Without a doubt, our sample of parents had more choice than their working-class counterparts, but most of them nevertheless *felt* that they had very little. It is likely that despite continuing government pronouncements about the power of parental involvement and parental choice, parents as a whole continue to have minimal choice of secondary school unless they are part of the political and cultural elites (see also Butler and Hamnett 2010). Perceptions of limited choice were commonplace across all three locations. For a few parents, there seemed to be an absence of choice. Choice was often described as mythical or illusory. Oliver Dorling (London) expressed this view whilst also recognising the link with the housing market and his personal desire to put a stop to the middle-class practice of moving house for school proximity:

Interviewer: How would you describe the choices you've made about your children's education? Would you say they were moral choices, political choices, pragmatic choices, or a mixture?

A mixture.

Interviewer: In what way?

Well, pragmatic in the sense that you've only got a local school or you've got to pay for them to go to another school. This idea of choice – I mean I don't like the idea of choice, either, because it's a total fallacy. You don't have a choice. It's either you've got the local school, or if you put another school down as a second choice, you won't get into that one. And what people need is a good local school and a good local hospital. You don't want to have to send, drive halfway across London. So it's meaningless having a league table. It's easier for the middle classes because they can buy their way into a catchment area. Which is another bee in my bonnet. If I could work it out, if I could think of a way that that could be clamped down on, I would agree to it or vote for it. I'm not clever enough to work it out yet.

(Oliver Dorling, London)

Oliver Dorling was unusual in our sample for his voiced opposition to this practice, and as we noted earlier, some 69 per cent of parents were 'incomers' to the areas in which they now lived. Whilst some (such as Julie Hextell – see Chapter 3) described as 'lucky' the proximity of a particular school, others gave indirect acknowledgement of the relationship between choices of location and the reputation of a school. In some families, choices were effectively made many years ahead of any actual transition from primary to secondary school, through a decision about where to buy a house. Lynne Heslop (Norton), for example, having described how happy they were with the local comprehensive school, spoke about the semi-conscious figuring of school quality as part of choosing a 'nice area' to live:

I suppose in some ways, because we lived near, we'd chosen a very, very good school we'd selected by living here...I don't know if I'd have felt the same, if I'd stuck to my principles, in (another area of town) or somewhere, I might have found that hard. And I think we might have reconsidered something then.

Interviewer: This is very hypothetical but what would your choices have been if you were living in (that other area)?

I would have had a problem

Interviewer: Would you have considered private school or would you consider moving house, for example?

I think probably...I would have done, I don't think my husband would...he's a very true sort of, state education for everything, end of story, and wherever you are. But I think we actually were selective in where we actually bought a house, if we're honest. I mean, we lived in a very nice area.

Interviewer: Do you think that was just fortunate that you happened to be living here or do you think somehow, when you were even making the choices in the first place about living here, you sort of assimilated that this was a nice, safe area?

Yes, probably, probably. I mean we were guided by the people that were already here. So we looked here, here and here at housing and we didn't know anything about Norton at that time, but obviously they did, so we were guided to here. We have friends in (that other area) who were in a very difficult position, he finally sent his children to the church school. I mean that would have possibly been another option, that we might have wanted a church education rather than a state education. That would have been another possibility.

(Lynne Heslop, Norton)

Mongon and Chapman (2009 p. 114) note that '...Diversity across the offer from publicly funded schools is largely marginal.' However, they also point out that there is always 'a local pecking order that can be influenced by style as well as substance and in which Choice is played out for staff as well as parents'. 'Playing out' is a useful term for this particular process, because the process has both real and imaginary elements at one and the same time. Even those parents who are dubious about there being any real choice cannot avoid the way that the process positions them as completely responsible: They could make 'bad' choices and would only have themselves to blame. At the same time, the powerful idea that successful secondary schooling is the result of parents making 'good' choices at the point of transition is itself something that conceals the maintenance of inequalities:

national policies to promote choice and diversity are working within and compounding existing patterns of inequity and social division. What diversity there is in school provision owes more to historical factors... The ways in which parents exercise choices (or not) reinforce inequities and local authorities are largely powerless.

(Ainscow et al. 2007 p. 7)

As we saw in the previous chapter, the operation of the housing market means that many middle-class families will find themselves near schools that already have a high proportion of middle-class students.

The historically high correlation between social class and educational attainment will usually make these schools look 'good' in conventional terms. Where they do not, or where even 'better' schooling is desired, some parents will fight hard for places in specific, high-performing schools. This may involve buying a new house and moving, renting a new or an extra address, paying fees for private schooling, renewing religious affiliations, or if all else fails, assembling a strong case in an appeals process. Some parents are prepared to engage in fraudulent or deceptive practices, such as using a false address so that they appear to live closer to a desired school (BBC 2008; Harvey 2008).

A further problem here is that the positive halo around the concept of 'choice' can make it harder to understand the social processes at work. In what Hargreaves calls the political period of the 'second way', characterised by standardisation and market competition, '...many Anglo-Saxon governments...imposed prescriptive and sometimes punitive reforms in the shape of increased competition between schools fuelled by public rankings of high-stakes test and exam results' (Hargreaves 2009 p. 18). Hargreaves also notes that in England, '...increased parental choice between schools and reduction of local authority control' were particularly evident (2009 p. 18). Many such elements have persisted, despite the claims that 'second way' policies gave way to 'third way' policies that emphasise other routes to 'improvement', including cooperation rather than competition between schools.

Choice, preference and commitment

In regard to public services such as education, there is still a widely held view that greater choice, together with more or better information which the public might use in making choices, is of itself a desirable goal. As suggested earlier, one reason for this is probably that greater choice appears on the surface to be a self-evident proxy for freedom. However, there is an inherent tension in all this, which parts of our study reveal. Firstly, standardisation and marketisation are only plausible if we can conceptualise the key parties as potential producers and consumers. Secondly, these potential producers and consumers have to be assumed to be striving for the same goals. To put this another way, there must be a shared definition of ends, of what amounts to 'a good education'. Our study shows up the inadequacy of this 'consumerist' perspective for grasping the subtleties of practices that involve choices of secondary school. Many of the white middle-class parents we interviewed were dismissive of league tables of examination results and were critical of the idea that these might tell one anything useful at all about the qualities of an education or a school. Thus, whilst all of them valued academic success *per se*, many also rejected the dominant discourse and therefore much of the market information that was made available to them. To understand this, it is helpful to differentiate between different kinds of 'driver' or 'motivation' for choice. Sayer's (2005) work on 'investments' is particularly helpful in this task.

In his constructive critique and development of Bourdieu's concept of *habitus*, Sayer suggests that tensions between some of the philosophical streams underlying Bourdieu's work led to an underplaying of a range of ethical and emotional dimensions of habitus and social practice which are nevertheless present in Bourdieu's own writing. For example, Sayer (drawing also on the work of Margaret Archer) discusses the nature of investments and argues that a distinction between *preferences* and *commitments* is especially useful in appreciating different kinds of investment that people have in the social world. Preferences are what we have when we choose between two items on the grounds that one is liked a little more than the other. Choices during the purchase of goods and services are often about preferences. Commitments are qualitatively different, going deeper than preferences and having a stronger bearing on practice. They are the *felt* as well as the *thought* aspects of social life, to do with habitus and the psychic dimension of social class (cf. Reay 2005). They arise from values and have an emotional element, forming part of an identity. As Sayer puts it, 'I am committed to certain people, ideas and causes and I can't be bought off, for they are ends in themselves, not merely means to other ends' (Sayer 2005 p. 41).

Drawing upon Sayer's distinction, the argument we wish to make here is that policies based on standardisation and marketisation operate as if all school choices were in the realm of preference. Investments that in fact entail *a range of commitments and preferences* are assumed to be much simpler than they are. This homogenisation of *ends* in the name of raising standards and educational achievements also pretends that for all their differences, schools are *really* on a single continuum and the key measures of position (principally league tables and Ofsted inspections) can be taken to sum up all that really matters in school processes and quality. In our interviews it became clear very early on that many more factors were involved in the choices being made, and these factors were often deeply rooted, derived from particular sets of experiences, from family history (see Chapter 2), from values, and from various forms of 'hot' and insider knowledge. What we have termed 'parental managerialism' (James and Beedell 2009) sees parents putting great efforts into constructing a broad educational project in which actual school choice is just one element, albeit the most important single feature. Such parents have a *commitment* to particular notions of society and to particular kinds of socialisation: Their choices make sense in relation to their commitments.

In Chapter 5 we discuss the significance, for many families, of the proximity of 'the ethnic other', derived from commitments to a multicultural society. However, commitments were sometimes more generic: Families like the Smiths (Riverton) valued academic success, but they were also committed to a particular vision of 'good socialisation' which was in some conflict with dominant assumptions about how educational success was to be secured. Indeed, as we saw in Chapter 2, one of them worked in a University in which they met students who were highly successful in conventional academic terms, but whom they found to be 'clueless' about the real world. The Smiths had commitments that were of sufficient strength that they (a) put time and energy into broadening their daughter Sadie's group of friends during primary school, (b) overruled Sadie's desperate wish to go to a nearby private school along with her three closest friends from primary school and (c) held fast to their choice in the face of a protracted episode of bullying during the first year of secondary school.

The distinction between preferences and commitments is also helpful with regard to another feature of our data that were a little unexpected. It appeared to us that most of the parents we interviewed were trying to act ethically, or in accordance with certain beliefs and values that had clear reference points in the political and moral landscape. However, several mentioned a distinction between, on the one hand, 'politics' or 'principles', and on the other hand, 'what's right for your own children'. We should add here that in terms of political orientation, the parents we interviewed shared broadly 'Centre-Left' and 'Green' positions, and that direct involvement in party-political or pressure group activity (such as the miners strike, Greenham Common, Rock Against Racism, the Womens Movement and campaigns for gay rights) was a frequent feature of background. However, and somewhat surprisingly given the antecedents, there was also an uneasy ambivalence with contemporary Party politics, in many cases exacerbated or brought to a head by the UK role in the Iraq war.

The contrast between 'political principles' and 'what's right for your own children' is both interesting and important. It is interesting because it is a line of reasoning that one would expect to find with *conventional* white middle-class school choices, and not so much with our 'against the grain' choosers; it is important because it re-positions 'politics' or 'principles' (usually taken to mean deep *commitments*) as dispensable surface phenomena, as belonging to the realm of *preferences*. At the same time, 'what's right for your own children' is seen as a more thorough and authentic expression of interests or concerns. There is a notable irony here too, in that several of the parents in our sample reported that they had been accused by other parents of being selfish and of sacrificing their children's education in the name of a political principle. We give more specific consideration to civic engagement and the links with political positions in Chapter 8.

Orientations, pragmatism and provisionality

Almost universally, the parents in our sample were supporters of the welfare state, so as we began to analyse the data we were surprised at how few of them seemed to explain school choices with reference to a political commitment to comprehensive education. In just one or two cases there appeared to be an orientation to secondary school choice that was thoroughly centred on community, locality and a sense of solidarity, and might be summed up by the phrase 'this is where we live, the local school is good enough, if it needs to be better we can help it to improve – and if everyone did the same, all schools would be good'. Laura Franklin (Riverton) described both the primary and secondary schools attended by her children in these terms. We had been asking her how much she knew about particular schools when they had moved into the area:

> For us the school was just a school, we didn't actually know if it was technically good or not, it was just there. And I do remember about a year before my oldest was due to start there, walking past the playground and hearing one kid call the black kid in the playground 'coon' and I thought 'oh shit'. And had a slight wobble and wondered if St Margaret's would have a better racial mix, but then thought 'If this is what we've got, that's the school they're going to'.

Further into the interview, Laura described the 'principle' that underpinned decisions on school choice in the family:

> We explained the principle to the girls and they completely understood it, to the extent that towards the end of Year 5, my younger

daughter was under the impression that Hammerton School (an out-of-city State school that many children of professionals go to) was a private school

Interviewer: Explain that principle to me.

That comprehensive education only works if everybody sends their child to their local catchment school... of course comprehensive education truly only works if you close down private education and everybody sends their child to the local catchment school. And that is totally fundamental to what we think

Interviewer: So for you, there was no question of dithering?

No. Some people thought it was very hard. When the kids were about 5 and everyone thought that Redwood School (the local comprehensive) was all bullying and low achieving, a lot of people said 'You'll change your minds, you'll suddenly move to Mountstevens School...'. I thought 'Redwood does look a bit hard'. But I thought, they'll be older by then. So we never went to another open day... the kids wanted to go to Redwood

Interviewer: Is that where most of the kids from (the primary school) went?

I think possibly in Claire's year, the majority of her year possibly did. Certainly half of her year went, I'd say, but amongst her friendship group, a lot of them went somewhere else. It seems a long time ago now. But she was quite happy, she felt that was the school for her, it was her local school. We had discussed the whole principle with her and she agreed with it and was quite happy with Redwood School, a bit scared obviously, but she would have been just as scared if she was going to Hammerton or independent (laughter).

Interviewer: And how was that process for you? How did you feel about it? What were you aware of in that process? Did you notice any fracturing of people into working class, middle class?

Well... one middle-class person after another informed you that their child was just too clever to go to Redwood, or that they were too arty to go there... [they would say] 'I admire what you're doing'. Admire? – what is admirable about your child going to the local school? I talk as if we were saying 'This is our principle.' It was far more organic than that... It's just the way it was, that's what was happening. But I did despise people who gave me all the reasons why their particular child couldn't do it... [saying for example] 'I'm sure Redwood's very nice, but my child's too clever'.

We have quoted Laura Franklin at length precisely because to our surprise, the position she articulated, whilst it was shared by her partner Alan, was so unusual across the sample. There were more instances of a 'softer' communitarian orientation, where for example 'walkability', convenience on environmental grounds, a desire to be 'local', or more general notions of staying within the community, were important:

> I think (for us) there was a strong feeling... about the significance of 'local'. You know, so in the same way that I would choose to go to small local businesses rather than out to North Park [a large out-of-town shopping mall], I would rather support local schools.
>
> (Martin Brandt, Riverton)

We return to this 'softer' communitarian idea in Chapter 8, where we make reference to the idea of a 'vocabulary of association' (Jordan et al. 1994). On the whole, however, the parents we interviewed were not strongly committed to comprehensive education as a general concept, and only a few were explicitly wedded to 'the local'. There was instead a combination of pragmatism and instrumental orientation woven through most explanations of the choice of an ordinary state secondary school and the outcomes it had yielded or was expected to yield. Indeed, much of this book could be said to be about teasing out the main themes amongst these instrumental orientations and their ramifications.

Whilst the choice itself was often described as pragmatic, the consequences of against-the-grain school choice were often described in terms of benefits or gains of one sort or another. The most prominent of these were to do with social mix. However as we go on to discuss in Chapters 5 and 7, a mix of ethnicities was far more likely to be sought out and celebrated than a mix of social classes. There was also much talk of how the ordinary school provided the right context for the young people to stand out or show their 'specialness' or 'extraness'. Furthermore, some parents acknowledged that they and their children were amongst a few especially valued clients of the school, and felt more or less guilty about their privileged access to resources, to staff or to influence.

A consciousness that a secondary school choice could be undone, that it was in a sense provisional and conditional, was a frequent theme in parent interviews, especially in Norton and Riverton. Janine Barker

(Riverton), a parent whose child was going to Meadowood school, told us at length about how the parents of *all* of her child's close friends were either 'going private' or moving house a year or more in advance of the primary–secondary transition, so that their children would be able to go to Mountstevens school and could avoid Meadowood. They had considered these options in the family, but Janine's own view was that moving house or buying or renting a flat just ahead of the qualifying period was a kind of antisocial behaviour. She had both personal and professional insight here, having worked in a Local Authority in Housing, and said that sadly, the strategy was rife amongst the better-off families in Riverton. Janine's views on the benefits of exposure to ethnic diversity were similar to many other parents in the study. However, later on she acknowledged that there were particular risks associated with the choice of school, and that the family was in a position to reverse the decision they had made if that became necessary:

> You know, I think we've got more options than a lot of people around us have ... and that if we really had to, we could do something about it.
>
> (Janine, Riverton)

Here, 'doing something about it' means getting their child into a different school, and the 'options' include paying fees for private education. The awareness of and reference to this 'safety net' underlines the extent to which the transition is being managed, and monitored – in a sense, the fundamental choice is provisional and can be undone should the need arise. This suggests that for against-the-grain secondary school choice, the analogy of a risky financial investment has some utility: in such investments, profits are higher than average, but the arrangement is also more volatile than a conventional one, and a high level of vigilance is therefore required, plus a willingness to 'change tack'. It is to vigilance, and the importance of insider knowledge to support it, than we turn next.

Hot knowledge and parental intervention

We were surprised by the high proportion of families in which at least one parent was or had been a school governor, and we discuss the significance of this in Chapter 8. Being a school governor appeared rooted in a desire to make a civic contribution, and there were elements of the community-minded building of social capital in the sense described by

Putnam (2000). There were also many other connections with the world of education: For example, 13 per cent of the parents in our sample were university academics, and in Riverton alone, some 40 per cent of families had at least one parent with a teaching qualification and/or working as a teacher. Proximity to the school offered by such roles and similar connections were valued for providing opportunities to gain insider information.

Ball (2003) and Ball and Vincent (1998) discuss the role of information in a marketised service such as education. Against a background of different networks and contacts, information is a vital matter:

> Information is a key dynamic in the workings of all markets and has been a particular focus and a powerful mechanism in the reform of education systems. That is the generation of judgemental and comparative performance information which is intended to allow consumers to make better choices between providers.
>
> (Ball 2003 p. 100)

Ball and Vincent (1998) distinguish between the formal information ('cold knowledge') that is produced by or about providers (and which is freely available to all), and informal information that people share and which circulates in social networks, namely 'hot knowledge'. Ball's later study suggests that hot knowledge was privileged by parents choosing schools, and that various 'weak ties' in social networks are used heavily in decision-making. Like Ball's study, ours shows high levels of anxiety and uncertainty amongst the choosers, and the extensive use of 'hot knowledge'. But importantly, this goes well beyond the periods in which the main choices about transition were made. We suggest that 'hot knowledge' continues to be important to many white middle-class parents once the young people are established in the school, and it contributes to high levels of continued intervention with elements of 'mangerialism'. Most parents of school-aged children are likely to have some level of engagement and intervention, but many of those we have studied went much further than this. The term 'managerialism' usually refers to beliefs and practices in workplaces and organisations. It is '...underpinned by an ideology which assumes that all aspects of organisational life can and should be controlled. In other words, that ambiguity can and should be radically reduced or eliminated' (Wallace and Hoyle 2005 p. 9). Like its workplace counterpart, parental managerialism rests on the idea that all the important variables are controllable and within reach. It is a reflexive project of the self of the

child which necessitates a certain confidence in relation to organisations like schools, and then a great deal of intervention. There were
many examples in our data. Tricia Simpson (London) described at length
how the deliberate and concerted efforts of a few middle-class parents,
including Tricia herself, had made a local primary school 'the most
improved school in England' and that this had a lot to do with 'increasing the percentage of kids from high achieving backgrounds'. Linda
Stubbs (Norton) described how she and another parent had decided to
do something about a weakness in the area of performing arts at The
Park School:

> Well actually myself and another parent we're on a bit of a mis-
> sion to try and improve performing arts at the minute. I don't know
> what will come of it, but we um, my kids are very musical and my
> daughter's really, really interested in dance as well. We found out
> that (a dance organisation) had offered The Park free dance work-
> shops as part of their education outreach, and they refused them,
> which slightly took our breath away. And they've had a lot of prob-
> lems with performing arts and with staffing, and they took drama
> off the curriculum last year... although they offer it as a GCSE, you
> don't get it in years 7, 8, 9. The performing arts is abysmal, it's com-
> pletely and utterly abysmal, to the point where if my kids wanted to
> do GCSE in music I would tell them not to do it there because it's so
> awful... which I think is immoral. So we met with the head, we wrote
> a couple of times and got the standard letter back saying it's all fine,
> we wrote back and said no it's not fine and then we got a meeting
> with the head, that was about three weeks ago, and this afternoon
> she's actually meeting with the head of performing arts, whose view
> is that apparently everything's fine.
>
> (Linda Stubbs, Norton)

Linda and her fellow parent refused to accept the first responses provided by the school, and also a second set of responses which offered
the explanation that there had been 'behaviour management problems'.
(Her view of this was that the school had not appointed the right staff
and needed to take this area of the curriculum more seriously.) Similarly,
in London one of our young interviewees told us about the nature and
level of her mother's engagement with the school:

> My mum is like a big complainer if anything doesn't go right at
> school she is like first there talking to the head teacher. She's good

friends with him now. In Year 7 she managed to get an English teacher sort of sacked, she is a bit like that, she is a bit of a tyrant. She'll like, if I come back and they haven't marked my book for a while, then she will be 'ok I am going to go and tell the school' because she wants me to have the best education I can and whereas I would rather just think oh let's wait for someone else to do it she is the one to do it. She is really involved with the school she is standing for governor. Yeah she really like feels strongly about trying to get me to do the best... and also she really wants to try and get more middle class people to go to Capeland School. And she has drawn up like made a little committee and this year when people were being shown around the school as a middle class parent she tried to like get other middle class parents to send their kids to Capeland.

(Ella Harding, London)

There are parallels in all this with the social class tendencies in chil-drearing noted by Walkerdine and Lucey (1989); Crozier's (2000) study of parents and secondary school relationships; Reay's work on parental engagements with school and how the success or productivity of these encounters differed for mothers with different resources of cultural cap-ital (e.g. Reay 1998b); Lareau's (2003) study of processes of 'concerted cultivation' amongst middle-class parents in the United States; and strong resonances too with a UK study of parental voice which showed that whilst there were similarities across all parents, one group who were highly involved with schools had a particular habitus in relation to education which included a '... responsibility to monitor children's achievement *and the school provision*' (Vincent and Martin 2002 p. 125. Emphasis added).

The significance of insider hot knowledge is further illustrated in the following extract from our interview with Jocelyn and Bob Humphries (Riverton). Both were teachers. We asked them if they thought there were any particular risks being taken in sending their children to a poorly performing (by conventional measures) local comprehensive:

Jocelyn: No.
Bob: No.
Jocelyn: Not for our own children
Bob: Particularly not at the time. I suppose there might have been a slightly different question had the school gone into special mea-sures at around about the time that Johnny was going and if we

didn't, at that time, have the knowledge that we subsequently had. So that might have been a question.

Jocelyn: I don't agree because – and this comes from being in education – the best time to send anybody to a school is when they're in special measures, because they've got tons of money, lots of extra teachers and you're quids in. As far as I'm concerned, that's the time to send your child to the school.

Bob: Well we did send them there, although if you like, there was a perception in the neighbourhood, that it wasn't a good school. We weren't concerned about it, we felt it was a good school, not necessarily a popular school, but it was a good school. By the time Zoe went there... I think when Zoe went there it was in special measures.

Jocelyn: Yes, I think so too, because Mr Mears (Head teacher) was still there.

Bob: Yes he was... we weren't concerned because actually we felt that the school wasn't, I felt anyway, the school wasn't as bad as the special measures label on it.

It would be difficult to imagine a conception of quality any further removed from the mainstream preference-ordering on which choice policy depends.

Conclusion

In the broadest sense, school choice has been re-shaped by neoliberal thinking that has changed the meaning and significance of ideas like equity, inclusion and social welfare, and which has positioned the individual as more responsible for the outcomes of whatever choices they make. Some of the research suggests that policies that drive families and schools in this direction have contributed to increased social inequality. Looking at such issues through the lens of data about 'against the grain' choosers shows that much more is going on than a market model can possibly admit. Our analysis suggests that the economistic concept of choice conceals more than it reveals. Firstly, even at the level of individual decisions, it conceals an important distinction between preferences and commitments. It does this via the insistence that the quality of schooling can be summed in one way that everyone agrees on. Secondly, it conceals the significance of social positioning (such as choosing to live in a 'nice' area that does not contain the 'worst' of state schools, even many years ahead of the birth of a child or ahead of a primary/secondary transition). Thirdly, it conceals the *continuing* operation of social practices such as the parental monitoring and intervention, and the associated ongoing and provisional nature of choices that we have outlined in this chapter. Our study shows that the actual choice of secondary school at a particular time is only one small part of the overall story of 'against the grain' middle-class practices.

The commitments of our sample of parents were actually more diverse and much less 'political' than we had expected at the outset. The distinction between 'principles' and 'doing what's right for your child' is a reminder of Zizek's assertion that politics has not only become 'a dirty word', and increasingly so in the contemporary context, but also that the language of political intervention no longer appears to make sense of, and in, the contemporary climate (Zizek 2006). Even this left-leaning, pro-welfare segment of the white middle-classes rarely couched their choices in political terms. Their rejection of dominant assumptions and (to some extent) practices is a rejection of a contemporary political re-shaping of public services, but it is not one that is anchored in a shared alternative political vision: One could say that against-the-grain school choices seem to reveal more of what people do *not* believe in than what they *do* believe in.

Although superficially these families might appear to be 'acting against self interest', they are in fact doing nothing of the sort. Most were seeking, or claimed to have acquired, specific social, cultural and ideological returns from the school as a microcosm of a politically, socially and ethnically diverse society. Hence, we would argue that the neoliberal approach to education provides opportunities for these 'mutating' and evolving middle-class families, already predisposed to social and ethical flexibility, to adapt to the system and construct new forms of advantage as their existing capital interacts with the resources of 'ordinary' urban schools.

Over 50 years ago at the inception of the comprehensive schooling system in the UK Anthony Crosland, then Minister of Education, wrote:

The system will increasingly, if the Labour Party does its job, be built around the comprehensive school ... All schools will more and more be socially mixed; all will provide routes to the Universities and to every type of occupation, from the highest to the lowest ... Then, very slowly, Britain may cease to be the most class-ridden country in the world.

(Crosland 1956 p. 207)

Comprehensive schools have of course been constrained in realising Crosland's vision, either by the continuing existence of selection alongside them in some areas or by the proliferation of other types of school, and also by the immense rate of change at the level of policy. But our research suggests that far from providing even a slow or partial remedy for the 'most class-ridden country in the world', comprehensive schools are themselves caught up in processes that reproduce social class relations. We would argue that though it appeals in common-sense terms, it is sociologically naïve to expect social mix to produce social mixing, rather as exposure to steel bands and samosas do not add up to anti-racist action. Nancy Fraser writes of a conflation of a politics of recognition and a politics of redistribution, identifying a 'problem of displacement' (Fraser 2000 p. 108), where redistributive struggles look as if they are served by cultural processes of recognition whilst actually being displaced by them. We have described elsewhere the mutuality of interest between league-table-conscious schools and white middle-class parents (e.g. James and Beedell 2009): Elsewhere in this book we address the extent to which this might produce gains to white middle-class families whilst being potentially disadvantageous to others.

5
A Darker Shade of Pale: Whiteness as Integral to Middle-Class Identity

Introduction

Drawing on the growing literature on whiteness in the United States and more recently in the United Kingdom, this chapter interrogates whiteness as integral to white middle-class identity. The first part of the chapter describes the high value attributed to multicultural schooling by the parents, mapping out positive aspects of their self-interested altruism. It then discusses more problematic aspects in which the differential values attributed to classed and raced others is often strongly related to the extent these others share the same or similar values. While for many parents and children, there are very positive gains from attending socially diverse schooling, and ethnic diversity is often valued for its educative potential, there remain many difficult and uncomfortable issues around whiteness in multi-ethnic contexts. Even those parents who actively choose ethnically diverse schooling appear to remain entrapped in white privilege despite their political and moral sentiments.

The chapter focuses on the complicated question of value; of having value, finding value in, getting value from and adding value. While knowledge and understanding of different cultures was emphasised by both parents and children, encapsulating an openness to difference and multiculturalism, even these white middle-classes committed to multi-ethnic schooling face the perils of middle-class acquisitiveness, extracting value from, as they find value in, their multi-ethnic 'other'. The chapter examines these processes of generating use and exchange value in which the 'multi-ethnic other' becomes a source of multicultural capital.

The importance of habitus as a sense of place again permeates the data. Although all the families expressed sentiments of tolerance and openness to difference, for the most part, the Norton parents were not dealing with the lived experience of multiculturalism and all their children attended schools where minority ethnic groups constituted a small minority. Both Norton and Riverton were among the 13 local areas that a recent Institute of Community Cohesion Report (Mansell and Curtis 2009 p. 13) described as 'increasingly segregated, deserted by white parents if they find their children becoming outnumbered by pupils from ethnic minorities'. The percentage of ethnic minorities in the schools the Norton families were sending their children to ranged from 18 to 3 per cent. In Riverton the range was 54–4 per cent with less than a quarter of families sending their children to schools where more than half the pupils were from ethnic minorities. Rather, it is primarily the London parents who are living 'the multicultural dream', with 95 per cent of the schools attended by their children having at least half the pupils from ethnic minorities (Reay et al. 2007).

However, regardless of the level of immediate proximity to ethnic others all the parents were investing symbolically in processes which position the ethnic minorities as a symbolic buffer between themselves and a pathologised white working-class. In particular, a majority of both the white working-classes and the black working-classes, those who are perceived not to share white middle-class values, come to be residualised and positioned as excessive in white middle-class imaginaries across all three locations. The chapter concludes that the white middle-class interest in difference and otherness can thus be understood not only as recognition and valuing of 'the ethnic other' but also as a project of cultural capital acquisition. This was particularly the case for the London and Riverton families who sought to display their liberal credentials and secure their class position by equipping their children with the capacities to cope or thrive in a multicultural society.

Adding multicultural value

There is a growing body of literature across the global north that reveals the advantages and unacknowledged normativity of whiteness (Frankenberg 1997; Nakayama and Martin 1997; Hage 1998; Lipsitz 1998; Giroux 1999; Back 2002; Hill 2004; Byrne 2006). bell hooks (1992) argues that privilege habitually passes itself off as embodied in the normative as opposed to the superior. Privilege works in a peculiarly seductive way in relation to whiteness, which is seen to be rooted in a whole range of things other than ethnic difference and skin colour. However, theorisations of whiteness as a privileged identity have been complicated by notions of whiteness as generating intense ambivalences and anxieties, as well as denial and defensiveness (Brodken 2001; Perry 2002). It is this multi-faceted understanding of whiteness that we are attempting to elicit through a focus on white middle-class identities.

Value lies at the heart of white middle-class identity (Skeggs 2004). In a class-ridden, racist society, to embody both whiteness and middle-classness is to be a person of value. It is also to be a person who makes value judgements that carry symbolic power; a valuer of others. And despite the rhetorical flourishes around difference and diversity, it is sameness that routinely gets valued. A majority of white middle-class parents in the United Kingdom seek out schools where there are children like their own (Reay 1998a; Ball 2003).

Culture has become a central site for the exchange of value. As Skeggs (2005 p. 47) asserts, culture can be converted into a highly mobile commodity and is regularly used in transnational advertising to generate multicultural appeal. However, cultural differences have rarely been analysed in terms of their appeal to members of the majority white culture within educational fields. Yet, many of the families did feel passionate about the need to produce well-rounded, tolerant individuals and they saw multi-ethnic comprehensive schooling as an important component in this process. They spoke of children who were 'socially fluent and adaptable'; children who became 'more resilient' and this resilience is sometimes counterpoised to the 'softness' of children who attend selective and private schools. In particular, multiculturalism is seen as an important value reflecting inclusivity in a diverse, global world. This positive value in comprehensive schooling emerges strongly in what Avril Smart, one of the London parents and a journalist, said:

> This is a speculation but I think there is definitely something about not being arrogant or not appearing arrogant. There is some kind of modesty that some people might see as them not being confident. You are not being educated to be a woman of the world, to be in charge; you are being educated to take your part, a place alongside everyone else.
>
> (Avril Smart, London)

We glimpse, throughout what Avril Smart says, a sense of attending comprehensive schools as almost a humbling experience for the white, middle-class child; one that makes children both better people and better equipped to understand and respond to ethnic diversity. Avril's sentiments were widely held. They are reflected in the words of Karen Charles, a Norton mother. Speaking of her two teenage children she asserted:

> They just have a great experience of people. I mean they share classes with completely different types of people with different backgrounds, with various different problems, and I think that's hugely beneficial. I think they've learnt tolerance, they've just learnt so much about other people's lives, how fortunate they are, I think it's been a really positive experience.

In both the women's words, and those of the vast majority of the other parents we interviewed, we are presented with a progressive inclusive image of twenty-first-century citizenry in which comprehensive schooling is seen to play a key role in promoting cultural openness and understanding. Edith Jennings, another London parent argued that this was a case of putting rhetoric into practice, of living as well as espousing democratic, civic values. Our parents were emphasising a social and cultural fluency in which an active engagement with difference is signalled as a highly valued attribute:

> I think we would automatically spout all the stuff about the importance of cultural and social differences but I don't think it would mean much to our children if we sent them to either private or selective state schooling. Sending Jack to the local comprehensive means that we mean it.
>
> (Edith Jennings, London)

It became clear that many of the parents saw ethnic diversity itself as an important and highly positive educative feature, equipping their children for a globalised, multicultural future. Examples across all three localities revealed the strong emotional engagement of many parents as they described the 'marvellous advantage' of ethnic diversity. One parent described her son's

> ... incredibly ethnic range of friends and it is a marvellous advantage, I mean it is not something that most people of my generation would have I think. At his 15th birthday party last year 19 friends came and they were from 9 different ethnic origins from all round the world

and I found it rather moving actually. They were just lovely, they were just lovely, they were all over the house they were doing whatever they were doing.

(Deirdre Johansson, London)

Another described how he valued a social mix:

I think it is really important for them to be exposed to a social mix, which I think must be a big part of what I hope they get in going to a state comprehensive school.

(David Gordon, Norton)

Whilst another celebrated ethnic mix together with exposure to challenging circumstances:

I think that aspect of Meadowood School was just an amazing education for my kids and it was just there, it was just how school life was. There were dealers outside the gates at lunchtime – well they had to learn to cope with that, they've got streetwise and they've not been protected from the seamier side of life. And the political refugee children – they (my children) had so much education.

(Carinna Chandler, Riverton)

There is a strong expectation here that the social and ethnic diversity of a school will produce a 'better', 'nicer' person – one who is capable not only of recognising, knowing and respecting qualities of 'the other' but also by doing so, having an enhanced capacity to negotiate their own way through life:

Marcus has been so happy there, he doesn't do any work but he's turning in to such a nice person, that's partly [how] he is anyway and I think we're quite a loving family. But I think that Marcus will do well academically wherever he is because he's able and he's socially very happy there which I think at fourteen is more important than anything. He feels very well looked after, he was telling me the other day saying that it was quite challenging to start with when he was confronted with all this sea of different coloured faces, he said he'd never been in that sort of environment before and didn't know how to deal with it, but he's just got used to it. He said he found it quite shocking to start with because it was so new. He's just turning in to a really nice person.

(Karen Sollazzi, Riverton)

While for Stuart Spedding, another Riverton parent, the working-class and ethnic minority students that white middle-class children meet when going to urban comprehensives

> are actually quite an important part of education, and learning to deal with people who are a bit difficult or have different views or different backgrounds is actually what it is all about.

For many of the parents, social and ethnic diversity was a form of capital to be weighed against the more conventional concern with the GCSE results that their children might achieve.

Andrew Sayer (2005) argues that while it is analytically possible to separate in abstract the moral from the instrumental and the conscious from the habitual, in practice the two are complexly interrelated. Multiculturalism may be valued in itself, as may be an understanding of other cultures so as to be able to better relate to other people. There is however an important difference in principle between the moral and conscious articulation of such 'valuings' and, on the other hand, holding them *in the knowledge*, (or even *because*) they gain an advantage vis-à-vis others. So inner city multi-ethnic schooling is seen to be a good in itself but also important for acquiring an understanding of, and proficiency in, multiculturalist capacity. Amongst the high principles, moral integrity and openness to cultural diversity is a powerful strand of calculation regarding the gains to be made from multicultural urban schooling. Our data reveal how both civic commitment and a self-interested altruism can be woven together in a complex amalgam, as in this example from a London-based barrister speaking about his daughter:

> Sophie will be, already is, totally different to us, all our friends are white and middle class, hers are from all sorts of class and ethnic backgrounds. And to be honest I'm quite uncomfortable with people from different backgrounds. I never had the experience either at school or university, and we didn't want that for Sophie. We wanted her to be a fully paid up citizen of the twenty first century and

I think she is and that is all down to the school. She has a real social confidence and can get on with anybody.

(Richard Harding, London)

There are shades here of Van Zanten's (2003) public sector urban professionals with their cosmopolitan view of contemporary society and an instrumentalised view of local multicultural state schools as 'major agents of preparation for this heterogeneous type of modernity, typical of metropolitan areas' (p. 119). Tolerance, understanding and proximity are all valorised as positive, and clearly there is much to be commended in white middle-class practices of sending your child to multi-ethnic urban comprehensives, but such practices are also motivated by self-interest as well as more selfless civic motives. As Gibbons (2002) argues, the ethic of multiculturalism reflects the realities of professional life and increasingly needs to be espoused in order to secure professional success. The global economy requires individuals who can deal with people of other races and nationalities openly and respectfully. So within the professional social fields these parents inhabit as workers multiculturalism is increasingly a source of cultural and social capital. In fact we would argue that these white middle-class families are *consciously* – or at least partially consciously – setting out to acquire valuable multicultural capital in order to better equip their children for an increasingly diverse global world.

In common with many of the other families, Richard Harding's reflections on his daughter are also redolent of 'omnivorousness'. North American research (Erickson 1996; Peterson and Kern 1996), and more recently work in the United Kingdom (Warde et al. 2000; Bennett et al. 2009), maps out a particular kind of middle-class self-formation, the cultural omnivore, who can access, know, take part in and feel confident about using a wide variety of cultural mileux, from high to low. Sophie is a classic middle-class omnivore. She is an accomplished pianist, loves classical music and the theatre but also enjoys Black music and clubbing and has friends from a wide range of ethnic backgrounds (although all of them are middle-class). She had also been predicted four A grades at A level and intended to study English at Oxford. Sophie like many of the other white middle-class young people in the study is 'a real multi-cultural kid' (Marcus Smedley, London) but also one who, through her cultural activities, remains firmly embedded in white middle-class social networks. This ability to fit readily and easily into very different social milieux is characteristic of many of the young people in the sample. London teacher Dan Adkins' comments about his daughter also exemplify this omnivorousness, though it was also clearly evident across all three locales:

Emily for example goes to a school where predominantly it's a kind of working class environment, a lot of children come from difficult yes difficult, disadvantaged domestic situations. And it's roughly 50% non white. And so she's got this kind of middle class background and goes on middle class holidays with a middle class family, and has got reasonably wealthy grandparents who have left an inheritance for her kind of thing. And she goes and spends several hours a day with people who come from very different backgrounds, so she's exposed to both and is totally comfortable with both.

(Dan Adkins, London)

Yet, despite the importance of social mixing with the classed and racialised other expressed by parents across the sample, the vast majority (over 90 per cent) of the white middle-class young people remain firmly and primarily anchored in white middle-class networks (Reay 1998b). Parents expressed varying degrees of concern about this, ranging from Isabel Webb's (Norton) surprised tone:

Andrew has stuck with exactly the same friends as he had at primary school. I think it's extraordinary, I've tried to say invite people back . . . but they're all from families like us, they're always from white middle class families.

To Audrey Caisey's (Norton) ironic humour:

I can't remember the figures but it's something like 20 percent of the children [at the school] do not have English as a first language. There is actually a huge ethnic mix but having said that my children never seem to have found them.

The white middle-class interest in difference and otherness can thus also be understood as describing a project of cultural capital acquisition through which these white middle-class families seek to display their liberal credentials and secure their class position (Bourdieu 1984; May 1996). Ghassen Hage (1998) argues that in the context of multiculturalism migrant cultures exist in the service of the dominant white culture. He writes about 'ethnic surplus value' (p. 128) in which the white middle-classes further enrich themselves through the consumption of ethnic diversity. The ability to move in and out of spaces marked as 'other', whilst part of these white middle-classes' performance of tolerance and acceptance, is simultaneously a process through which they come to know themselves as both privileged and dominant (Razack 2002).

The classed and racialised 'others' of white middle-class multicultural identity

Lying beneath omnivorousness and inclusive multicultural attitudes and practices are more instrumentalised, and at times fearful, impulses and attitudes. The instrumentalisation, the extracting of value from others, is never far from the surface as a number of parents reflect on the 'value-added' gained in terms of confidence and self-esteem that comes through attending schools where many of the children are far less privileged:

> The funny thing is, something I didn't realise is, I think it is very good for their self esteem, I mean we are free loading in a way, partly because they have got all these opportunities and a lot of them are cheap and/or free, but also they are top of the tree academically at a school like that and if they went to another school they would be average... But I think they think they are great and so that is very good for their self esteem.
>
> (Sally Rouse, London)

And:

> Bryony has come out very confident because she was top of the pile as well in that school and she overcame all her fears and worries at the beginning and has come out extremely well adjusted socially and emotionally, very confident and knows where she wants to go.
>
> (Julian Drew, London)

More buried are the fears and we discuss these in depth in Chapter 6. We glimpse white middle-class fears of potential danger from the negative influence of white and black working-class peers on their own children's attitudes and behaviour. But more common are fears of a negative impact on children's educational attainment as a result of being in pupil peer group cultures where educational achievement is seen to be insufficiently valued. This is most clearly articulated by Vickie, a London charity worker: 'there's fear, a fear that you're sending your child into a lesser environment, somewhere where they're not going to be able to do as well.' Such fears are simultaneously rational and irrational, and perfectly understandable, and result in the high levels of parental intervention discussed in Chapter 4. Our parents constitute a segment of the white middle-classes who are actually facing up to fears prevalent among the white middle-classes more generally. However, both sets of fears also reveal something more troubling, namely the ways in which black and ethnic minority children are often used symbolically to put even greater distance between the white middle-classes and their other 'other', the white working-classes. Jenny Etches, a Riverton mother, expressed clearly the underlying white middle-class value hierarchy that positions the ethnic minorities as a more acceptable working-class when she comments:

> Parents I've spoken to are more concerned about their children mixing with the white rather than the black working classes. I can see a fear here.

But many of the white middle-class parents make more explicit value distinctions between 'the valueless' white working-classes and those ethnic minorities who are seen to hold more value. So in a significant number of the transcripts a segment of the ethnic minority children are separated out from the excess of blackness and come to represent the acceptable face of working-classness, and of ethnic/'racial' difference: they are the children who 'are exceptionally bright and very nice', 'are doing their best', those who are a paler shade of dark, and come from families 'where the parents really care about education' 'have high aspirations' and 'are really ambitious for their children' – the 'model minority' (Leonardo 2004 p. 129). This status is not however attributed to all ethnic groups. As Paul Western differentiates:

> Whereas you go to beyond where the secondary school is there's a council estate and its very much a white school but it is in terms of class very working class and its very much not aspiring middle classes, whereas the school that Hal went to which has lots of ethnic minorities a lot of the parents aspire very strongly for their kids.
>
> (Paul Western, London)

Within dominant symbolic systems the aspiring ethnic minorities are ascribed with moral value despite – or we would argue, because – of their ethnicity. This is perhaps unsurprising, especially as research has consistently documented (Chen 2004; Tomlinson 2005a) that economic migrants adopt middle-class values towards education often regardless of class position. They also stand out from the working-class majority (both Black and White) because of shared values. They are perceived to be committed to the same values as these white middle-class parents. They, too, have an aspirational habitus (Baker and Brown 2008) which, despite their difference, makes them not too different, unlike the white, working-class who are seen to be 'beyond the pale'. So, for many of our parents, the aspirational ethnic minorities come to be defined as good and having worth in a middle-class process of drawing boundaries and attributing value. And despite the deep-rooted institutional racism within the labour market, such ambitions and aspirations are slowly being realised, as a higher than expected number of upwardly mobile young people are from ethnic minority backgrounds. A recent study (Ridge 2005) found that 56 per cent of people from Indian working-class families take up professional and managerial jobs in adulthood, while more generally new generations of not just Indian, but also Chinese, Caribbean and African families are moving ahead in the employment market (Platt 2005).

However, more troubling, as some of the earlier quotes indicate, are the ways in which the working-class is represented in the accounts of a number of our white middle-classes. Whilst there is much valuing and validation of the multi-ethnic other what is also interesting here is what is being displaced and to whom it is being displaced. This is made explicit in James Mount's account of 'the white trash factor'. The interview had been covering the features of a good school:

> Plus, the other factor that goes into making the school actually good is, I don't know if it's particularly politically correct, but actually it is very low on the white trash factor you see. What you've actually got, is you've got people from all over the world basically and particularly you have got the Muslims, about half or a third of the intake or whatever. It has got much more of a tradition of education and like real fascist parents really (laughs) and so actually you don't get the same kind of disciplinary problems. You know they might be poor and they might be refugees but they have still got a very, erm, positive [attitude] towards the benefit of education as opposed to like the white trash families basically who are the third generation of Thatcher's dross or whatever. Actually if you get too many of those in

the school then that is actually much worse than people of different colour and races frankly.

(James Mount, London)

In this parent's words we can see a privileging of the white 'multicultural' self through the pathologising of 'the other'. As Bourdieu argues in *Acts of Resistance* (1998), moral stigma is frequently attached to those who are worst off in class terms while moral superiority is attached to higher classes, in a process of what he terms 'class racism'. And this is what is at work here. In the process of gaining multicultural capital the white working-classes are residualised. They come to simultaneously represent excess and nothing, in the sense of having and being of no value. Very similar processes are at play here to the ones Haylett (2001) describes in which the white working-classes are marked as the abject constitutive limit by which middle-class multiculturalism is known and valorised. They are Warren and Twine's (1997) 'very white...naked, pasty, underdone: white white', embodying a whiteness that is some- how excessive, excrescent and incommensurably 'other' (Haylett 2001 p. 360). But the association of excess with Blackness never entirely goes away and there is still the fear/paranoia about 'big Black boys' or in Steve Davies, A London parent's words 'racism pure and simple'. Both 'White working-class trash' and 'big Black boys' are positioned here as 'abject', the embodiment of that which is valueless (Skeggs 2004 p. 23).

Hierarchies of value and valuing

In all of this values are paramount, both in the sense of having the right moral and educational values (the shared values discussed earlier) and in *being of* value. In fact there appears to be a powerful causal rela- tionship between the two in so far as the multi-ethnic other needs to share in normative white middle-class values in order to be of value, while those unruly white and black working-classes who refuse norma- tive white middle-class values come to simultaneously represent excess and abjection (Reay et al. 2007). They are of no value. Yet, this is not quite as depressing a scenario as the one that emerges in *Class, Self, Cul- ture* (Skeggs 2004). As we have illustrated in the earlier section on 'adding multicultural value' nearly all white middle-class families in our sample find value in as well as get value from multi-ethnic, inner city school- ing. However, it is only a section of the working-classes whose affect and dispositions are desired: those minority ethnic 'working classes' who are working-class primarily in the traditional sense of having few economic resources. They are Byrne's (2006) excitingly different yet acceptably the same 'cultural other'. To a large extent they share the same aspirations, hopes and desires for their children as the white middle-classes. Unlike their white working-class counterparts, they offer acceptable aspects of working-class culture 'that can be put to use for the enhancement of the middle-class' (Skeggs 2004 p. 12).

Furthermore, the white middle-classes do not simply want their children to gain from contact with their ethnic other, they want them to be friends, although, as we have said, this happens less often than they desire (see also Chapter 7). The multi-ethnic other then is not only a source of multicultural capital, but it also becomes a symbolic buffer between the pathologised white working-classes on the one side and the traditional white middle-classes, criticised for their separatism and racism, on the other. Yet, to view the minority ethnic students *only* as a way for the white middle-classes to gain multicultural capital would miss out on the gains that work in the other direction, however secondary they may be. We glimpse these gains in what Martha Sage says about the learning benefits an Asian twin has acquired through being placed in a class with a critical mass of white middle-class students:

> It's quite interesting because this friend who is Asian and lives on one of the estates is part of Charlotte's little group as it so happens she is a twin and they are in separate classes. The one who's in Sophie's class is doing a lot better than her twin sister. They're not identical twins and there could be all sorts of differences but even Charlotte points to that and I think it is because they have very different friendship groups.
>
> (Martha Sage, London)

These gains were expressed more crudely by Ann Epsom, a Riverton mother, who commented that in classes with all sorts of different children 'some children are dragged up by other children'. As both mothers identify, learning gains come through social mixing. Sociology of Education has been concerned about the benefits of social mix for a long time (Coleman et al. 1966; Thrupp 1999) but traditionally the benefits are all seen to flow in one direction from the middle to the working-classes, from white to minority ethnic children. Furthermore, the gains from social mix are only seen to work if there is a majority of white and/or middle-class students. What we have here challenges such orthodoxies. A critical mass of middle-class children may 'drag up' some working-class children academically, but simultaneously the white middle-classes are heavily reliant on their ethnic minorities and working-class 'others' to provide the real-life experiences that these parents value and feel that they are not able to offer themselves.

So for much of the time having value, finding value in, getting value from and adding value to are inextricably entangled in the data. As Lorraine Reeves (London) states, multi-ethnic schooling is 'good for white, middle-class children. It keeps them real', and her sentiments are echoed across the interviews with parents. Nearly all the parents referred to their children's improved skills in dealing with what was termed 'the real world' or 'dealing with real life': 'it's important for being able to deal with life' (Jane Marsden, London); 'She's got a stronger sense of reality, learning how to deal with all types of people' (Jacqueline Fenton-Lawley, London); 'It gives them a taste of the real world ... She has really understood what life is really like so she is much more worldly wise' (Liz Welland, London). As these quotes make clear, many of the parents welcome the resilience and worldliness that comes with attending inner city comprehensives. So threaded through the discourse of valuing the diversity represented in urban comprehensives is a powerful theme of the value gained from diversity that we have discussed earlier. This opens up a tension across the data between two qualities – 'of value' and 'of use'. As Baumann (2001 p. 164) points out, they are 'notorious for being confounded and confused: is not a thing valuable because it is useful'? But as he goes on to argue that value is the quality of a thing while usefulness is an attribute of the thing's users:

> It is the incompleteness of the user, the dearth which makes the user suffer, the user's urge to fill the gap, which makes a thing useful. To 'use' means to improve the condition of the user, to repair a short-coming; 'using' means to be concerned with the welfare of the user.
>
> (Baumann 2001 p. 165)

A different way of approaching what is desired would be to value the other for its otherness, to nurture that otherness and make it flourish and grow. This for Baumann is akin to love and he asserts that 'use means a gain for the self; value augers its self-denial. To use is to take, to value is to give' (p. 166). We want to argue that there is a deep, irresolvable ambivalence among our white middle-class sample in relation to 'use' and 'value'; between what we have earlier distinguished as 'value in' and 'value from'; a tension between the acquisitive individualised self and commitments to civic responsibility and the common good.

As Thompson (2003 p. 7) argues, 'progressive whites must interrogate the very ways of being good for the moral framing that gives whites credit for being anti-racist is parasitic on the racism that it is meant to challenge.'

Challenging privilege? Doing whiteness differently

Sayer (2005) asserts that behaviour is often shaped by mixed motives and influences. While individuals often decide on a course of action because they hope it will have beneficial consequences for them, they are also acting out of a moral sense of the right thing to do. In many of the parents' narratives the effort to do the right thing is difficult to separate out from 'getting the best for my child'. On one level this is because 'getting the best for my child' is itself positioned as ethical behaviour (and as we saw in the previous chapter, it can trump 'political' perspectives). Problems arise when it is at the expense of others. Yet despite the mixed motives of white middle-class parents, many of the young white middle-class individuals who attended socially mixed comprehensive schooling, at least from the perspective of their parents, were seen to be developing key citizenship skills of tolerance and understanding difference that are increasingly vital in a society with growing class and ethnic intolerance. As Sarah Davies, a deputy head teacher of an inner city comprehensive, put it:

> Going to an inner city comprehensive has made both boys socially able to mix with anybody, having a real understanding and tolerance of other people. Being the kind of people I think their sort of moral attitudes are very, very strong. I think they are both very much full of concern for others and they are not competitive in any way. They don't look at life that you know I have got to get to the top I have got to be better than other people. They are both very understanding and definitely don't think they are better than other people.
>
> (Sarah Davies, London)

Roediger argues that whiteness is all about absence. 'It is the empty and therefore terrifying attempt to build an identity on what one isn't and on whom one can hold back' (Roediger 1994 p. 13). Such empty identities are ripe for filling in and one of the ways in which white dominance in the context of urban multi-ethnic comprehensives is 'rationalised, legitimated and made ostensibly normal and natural' (Frankenberg 1997 p. 3) is through processes of 'shading in', adding 'colour' to the white middle-class self. There is a blurring and shading in of whiteness that serves to mask its privilege. These omnivorous practices produce alternative white middle-class identities – streetwise, globally knowledgeable, tolerant, inclusive young white middle-class individuals, who, in a number of parents' words, are better prepared for a global economy (James et al. 2010). Sometimes, however, this can become problematic particularly when acculturation goes too far and white, middle-class children are deemed to be over-enthusiastically playing with other identities. As Lesley Mitchell comments:

> I mean Andy can do a wonderful imitation of a South London Black kid and that dismays me sometimes I say 'why do you want to talk like that'. But you know I don't think he's going to do it forever because the whole environment is very important and he doesn't come from a home where he is not expected to do well.
>
> (Lesley Mitchell, London)

Implicit in Lesley's words is the white middle-class propensity to move in and out of different more 'colourful' identities. White middle-class omnivores can both dip in and out of black culture unlike their black working-class counterparts.

Caught within multicultural capitalism

It is important for critical social science, on the one hand, to identify hidden instrumental strategies and power relations behind apparently innocent and disinterested action and, on the other hand, to uncover genuinely unintended advantages deriving from ethical behaviour (Sayer 2005). Initially our project was a naïve one in that we expected to find, in the white middle-classes sending their children to urban comprehensives, a fraction of the middle-classes characterised by altruism and a sense of civic responsibility. We did indeed find those qualities in our sample, and we can see clearly in what parents say about their children some of the intended and unintended gains from ethical behaviour. However, this altruism and sense of civic responsibility was tempered by a degree of instrumentalism we had not anticipated. Writing of her American white middle-class neighbours, bell hooks (2000 p. 3) argues that:

> They may believe in recognising multiculturalism and celebrating diversity...but when it comes to money and class they want to

protect what they have, to perpetuate and reproduce it – they want more. The fact that they have so much while others have so little does not cause moral anguish, for they see their good fortune as a sign they are chosen, special, deserving.

Only a minority of the white middle-class parents in our study made explicit claims about their children's 'extraness', their specialness. However, at the same time the vast majority did not question their privilege, even though it was particularly apparent in the multi-ethnic, working-class schools they chose to send their children to. In fact most of the parents, while distancing themselves from the more exclusivist white middle-class majority, continued to deploy their greater economic, social and cultural capital to get more educationally for their own children. While sometimes such practices were accompanied by a commitment and even practices to improve educational resources for other less-privileged children, on the whole actively seeking to enhance the common good was not normative for this group of white middle-class parents either. Like Butler with Robson's (2003) London middle-classes these parents constitute 'a class in and for itself'. Theirs was a multicultural, but only rarely a socialist, egalitarianism. While they were anxious not to refuse or misrecognise cultural others, they do not see themselves as implicated in the injuries of class (Sennett and Cobb 1973), especially the injustices suffered by those termed 'Chavs' or 'white trash'.

So is there an innocent white middle-class? One that is not either putting cultural and material distance between itself and its ethnic and classed others by rushing into elite geographical and educationally separate enclaves, or else 'making use' of a conveniently accessible and acceptably valuable ethnic other in order to gain valued global multicultural capital? Certainly, our research indicates that the future-projected, strategising, capital-accruing self that epitomises middle-class subjectivity can never be completely held in abeyance. Attending multi-ethnic urban comprehensives becomes yet another, if slightly risky, way of resourcing the middle-class self. There are glimpses of future-projected strategising in most of the interviews but it is most clearly articulated by Martha Sage:

We looked at our own educational experience and we had both done reasonably well at school and got into prestigious universities and we felt, you know, we were successes of the education system from that point of view. We thought, what in life has ever stood in our way and has it been to do with exam grades and we thought no, actually it's been things that we would rather be better at; it's other stuff, not passing exams. It's to do with social fluency, social skills, time management, self-confidence, knowledge of other cultures and the real world, whatever it might be. We thought that those things if anything are more likely to come from going to a school like Capeland.

Martha Sage and her partner, Jeremy, have already mapped out the skills that their children will need for professional success in a multicultural global economy and have calculated that attending an urban compre-hensive is a better context for acquiring them than a more traditional grammar or selective school. This is where we come back to the discom-fort of our own positioning as researchers in relation to the research and whether there is a way to rescue the white middle-classes from their relentless acquisitiveness. Those of us, now precariously perched on the moral high ground, who critique materialism and consumerism, frown on elite choices and social snobberies perhaps neglect the gains we enjoy on the back of our consumption of all the 'right on' capitals including multiculturalism.

Conclusion

Despite their espousal of a cosmopolitan identity, there was little sense amongst our white middle-class families of cosmopolitanism as 'an imagination of a globally shared collective future' (Beck 1992 p. 27). While the practices of Savage et al.'s (2005 p. 206) Mancunians work to efface 'the other', the London families, together with many of those in Norton and Riverton, seemed to be directed towards 'consuming the desired other' in an act of appropriation. Cultural validation is entwined with acquisitive valuing. And this is mostly a partial and narcissistic valuing; one that is primarily about recognising a more colourful self in the ethnic other in a process that residualises both a hyper-whitened white working-class and an excessively black working-class who come to share the same symbolic register in the white middle-class imagi-nary (Sibley 1995; Haylett 2001). We can see the paradoxical way in which the embracing of an acceptable ethnic 'other' is, in effect, an excluding inclusivity. 'The "unities" that identities proclaim are, in fact, constructed within the play of power and exclusion' (Hall 1996), and this process of partial inclusion produces the too black working-classes and the too white working-classes as unacceptable 'others'.

Yet it is important to remind ourselves that these parents are negotiating an impossible situation that individually they can do little to improve. They are left with the quandary of trying to behave ethically in a situation which is structurally unethical (in terms of entrenched inequalities), and radically pluralistic (in terms of different moralities and value systems). The wider social context of structural injustices is bound to throw up impossible moral dilemmas and lead to all sorts of morally inconsistent behaviour. Marx argued that ethical behaviour is only partially achievable in a society which is structurally unethical in the way it distributes resources and opportunities and with them, possibilities for equal recognition (see Avineri 1968). And contemporary society has changed little in this respect. When the white middle-classes make choices that are directed towards the common good, greater benefits and value still accrue to them rather than their class and ethnic others. This is a case of entrapment in privilege and constitutes powerful evidence that we need effective policies that work towards the dismantling of economic and social privilege.

We are left with two powerful challenges: first, to develop critiques which, whilst recognising how people negotiate inequitable situations, also constantly keep in play the structural injustices within which they are situated. The problems of capitalist multicultural society do not derive largely from the moral failures of individuals but from society at large; second, to recognise the complexities of whiteness, and the need for more empirical studies of how whiteness is lived and experienced by different fractions of both working and middle-classes, and across different contexts. The research indicates that, whilst the white group in society share the same skin colour, they are not 'equally white' (Bonnett 1998). Paradoxically, while the white working-classes are perceived to be excessively pale, and are too white to possess dominant cultural capital, the white middle-classes in our study accrue valued (multi)cultural capital by presenting themselves as 'a darker shade of pale'.

6
The Psycho-Social: Ambivalences and Anxieties of Privilege

Introduction

The main focus of this chapter is the frequently overlooked anxieties, conflicts, desires, defences, ambivalences and tensions within middle-class identities, what we have termed the psycho-social. Although they are rarely made explicit, either by Bourdieu himself or the many scholars drawing on his theory, there are strong links between the psycho-social and Bourdieu's concept of habitus (also see Bourdieu 2007; Steinmetz 2006). As Bourdieu himself asserts, habitus as the interiorisation of social history is fundamentally about the degree of integration across the disparate experiences that make up a biography (Bourdieu 1990). However, although he writes powerfully about his own ambivalence at being in an unfamiliar field (Bourdieu 2007) and the defences of the working-classes whose 'habitus of necessity operates as a defence mechanism against necessity' (Bourdieu 2000 pp. 232–233), he does not engage with the psycho-social manifestations of middle-class habitus. It is these we are attempting to uncover in this chapter.

As we mentioned in Chapter 4, the dominance of neoliberalism and the increased emphasis on educational credentialism has intensified parental anxieties about the consequences of *not* making educational choices for their children which might be seen as indicative of being a 'bad parent' (Butler and Hamnett 2010). White middle-class families making counter-intuitive choices have to deal with the psychic costs and tensions of having different notions of 'the best' for their child to those normative within white middle-class culture. As one London mother succinctly pointed out, 'Not everyone can have what is best because the best is an exclusive thing.' Yet, as we have seen, our sample was far from homogeneous. The 125 families were differentiated by different positions on a number of cross-cutting spectrums. They ranged from the established upper middle-class where even grandparents attended elite universities to tenuously positioned new arrivals in the middle-classes; the UK equivalent of Bourdieu's (1986) 'inheritors' and 'newcomers'. There were also varying degrees of commitment and ambivalence to socially diverse urban schooling, which we will be exploring further in the next chapter, as well as the range of levels of detachment and embeddedness in localities that we explored in Chapter 3.

However, the focus in this chapter is the psycho-social-affective spectrum with on the one extreme a tiny number of confident, relaxed parents who know their child will do well wherever they go to school; and on the other, the highly anxious parents, often mothers, who feel compelled to micro-manage their child's school experience. The chapter presents data to illustrate that while this psycho-social spectrum does not map readily on to social class fractions, it does nevertheless have a strong connection with the levels of risk involved for parents in making non-normative white middle-class educational choices. In turn levels of risk are connected both to degrees of security and establishment as middle-class and to the level of educational attainment and market positioning of the school attended. While higher degrees of anxiety are apparent in the narratives of the 'first generation', the more recent arrivals and less secure members of the white middle-classes, there were also regular glimpses of anxiety and fear in our interviews with the securely established middle-classes.

Narratives of white middle-class choice reveal both powerful defences and the power of the affective, and these are explored through a number of in-depth case studies that highlight complex moral and ethical dimensions of white middle-class identity and, in particular, the psycho-social basis of 'principled choices'. Central to the analysis are white middle-class relationships to a classed and ethnic 'other'. We are attempting to understand the psycho-social impact of relationships and representations in the formation of white middle-class identities in predominantly working-class, multicultural contexts.

Before focusing on the case studies it is helpful to rehearse aspects of the wider political and economic context that both feed into and intensify white middle-class ambivalences and anxieties. The past 40 years have witnessed a growing and alarming disparity between rich and poor (Lansley 2009). While state surveillance and regulation have grown apace, over the same period the welfare state has shrunk in a number of senses. Governments have reneged on the earlier ambitious and optimistic remit of universal provision, and there has been a largely hidden yet remorseless process of privatisation. The egalitarian, social justice underpinnings of the welfare state have been consistently undermined by dominant ideologies of free markets and choice. In place of wider structural state provision we now have the expectation that we can all become self-entrepreneurial individuals capable of optimising from the wide range of choices that markets provide. At the same time, as Lynne Layton points out:

> Government has increasingly retreated from providing any functions that might contain anxiety and trauma; on the contrary, government, in concert with the media and corporate policies, has done its best to keep people frightened. Fear has led to splitting and projective identification, and large segments of the population, traumatized in different ways depending on social location, have taken up polarized positions of 'us' vs 'them'.
>
> (Layton 2008 p. 69)

However, as Layton goes on to argue, instead of challenging these developments and the policies that sustain them, most people have sought refuge in the narcissism of minor differences and/or an intensified individualism. Rather, when government and public institutions abandon their responsibilities to their citizens, as Layton asserts (p. 3), 'there is a pressure to create ever more individualistic identities that repudiate the vulnerable and needy parts of the self.' Against this backdrop we attempt to explore the psychic tensions the white middle-class families in our sample were grappling with. On the one hand, the many expressions of anxiety and ambivalence indicate a white middle-class still in touch with its own vulnerabilities, yet on the other hand, there remained a defence of distinction which entailed a repudiation of moral accountability. We see this most clearly in the powerful discourses around 'brightness' exemplified in the case study of Clarissa, discussed later in the chapter.

Personalising social class

Class is still an objective formation about 'who gets what and who ends up on what pathway', but it is also '... about subjectivity – how one understands and positions self and other, rationally and emotionally, and one's sense of potency and possibility' (McLeod and Yates 2008 p. 359). Lois McNay argues that constructionist approaches, in general, lack attention to 'the more troubling and destabilizing effects that irrational and unconscious motivations may have upon an individual's behaviour' (2000 p. 122). The preoccupation of constructionist approaches with the meanings people give to their behaviour and the discourses which interpolate them tend to mean a corresponding lack of attention to what Paul Hoggett (2000) terms the power of what is unthought, unspoken, unthinkable and unspeakable. We would argue that shifts in conceptions of the citizen and wider social processes of individualisation and consumerism, together with the ways in which these influence processes of educational choice for families, coalesce to generate a set of dynamics that are both social and psychic. Consequently, it is important to focus on the inner conflicts as well as the outer rationalisations. Wendy Hollway (2004 p. 7) contends 'we are psychosocial because the real events in the external, social world are desirously and defensively, as well as discursively appropriated', and it is this combination of 'the desirous and the defensive' that we are trying to elicit. Ironically, although both clients and professionals in 'the psy industries' are predominantly middle-class (Rose 1989), when there has been a focus on the psycho-social within academic writing the emphasis has largely been on the working-classes – their defences, projections and paranoia – usually in relation to their ethnic other. However, social inequalities take shape psychically for all individuals through binaries such as middle- and working-class, rich and poor, white and ethnic minority, straight and gay. And as Layton (2004 p. 46) argues:

> They do so by defining what affects, behaviours, thoughts, and modes of attachment and agency are 'proper' to each falsely split half of the pair. Within each pair in the hierarchy, a negative cultural valence is assigned to the attributes of the degraded identity, a positive valence to the dominant one. Thus these identities are often lived as painful, conflictual, binary (either/or) structures.

The process then of internalising such invidious social norms, even for those positively positioned by them, is complicated, conflictual and often painful. Habitus is striated with ambivalences. The unfamiliar educational fields the white middle-classes find themselves in generate conflicts and tensions, as well as the difficult and uncomfortable feelings that accompany them.

As we have already stressed nearly all the families were dealing with the psychic costs and tensions of having different notions of 'the best' for their child to those normative within white middle-class culture. However, as we have discussed in Chapter 4, rationales for choice of urban comprehensives were couched as much in pragmatic terms as moral and political ones. While across the sample parents expressed a sense of regret at social inequality and many felt that by supporting their local school they were making a commitment to the local community, parents who spoke passionately about the ethical reasons for choice were in a minority. Rather, for a majority of the parents it was the psycho-social consequences of choice that dominated their narratives.

The ambivalence at the heart of white middle-class counter-intuitive choice

As we have seen in the previous chapter, parents expressed a complex mixture of pity, sympathy, disgust and fear, towards the working-class 'other' but had more positive responses to their ethnic other. There were strong spatial aspects to parents' perspectives (Reay et al. 2008). In London the 'other' was frequently a minority ethnic other, who was recognised and represented as having similar attitudes and aspirations to the white middle-classes and thus seen to be of value. There was a degree of mutuality, respect and the identification of common interests. In Norton, with a far lower percentage of minority ethnic pupils in the secondary schools, and to a lesser extent in Riverton, there was primarily a focus on the working-class other who was, for the most part, denigrated by parents and labelled as 'locals', 'Chavs' or 'Charvers'. In particular, for our Norton middle-class parents living in a city where the middle-classes constituted only 8 per cent of the city population the figure of the Chav was represented in disproportionate and emotive ways that revealed underlying anxieties and fears.

Although the majority of parents expressed an anxiety about the white working-class, many minority ethnic children were seen in terms of the 'model minority' (Leonardo 2004) with similar values to themselves. A number of the minority ethnic children were middle-class, particularly in the Norton context, but a substantial number of those who were not were represented as coming from middle-class backgrounds in their countries of origin (see for example Yvonne's quote later in this chapter). This conscription of the other as a source of learning was undoubtedly a genuine empathy for some, but could also become superficial and detached as many maintained their distance. Sympathy was tempered by high vigilance against damage to their children's prospects. A surprising finding was how often parents viewed the others' disadvantaged circumstances, particularly those of the white working-classes, as a cultural rather than a structural issue. Dominant discourses of individualisation, meritocracy and self-responsibilisation seem to have had a powerful influence even on this left leaning, pro-welfare fraction of the middle-classes.

These then are families who have chosen against the middle-class grain, sometimes out of strong moral and ethical inclinations. However, ambivalence lies at the very heart of inclination (Adkins 2003) and what the data show are the psychic costs of ethical choice and often a more than fleeting ambivalence in relation to their children's schools and particularly the other children that attend them. They were managing deeply felt and unresolved tensions in relation to their children's schooling.

There were strong signs of Bourdieu's 'divided habitus' (Bourdieu 1999 p. 511). The white middle-class subject produced through 'acting against the normative middle-class grain' is split, divided between the acquisitive self-interested self and a more altruistic, public spirited self and has to live with the tensions generated through the contradictory interplay of cooperation and competition, consumerism and welfarism (Miller 1993).

These are the white middle-classes who do not have the fortress mentality of the majority white middle-classes. While exclusion remains a crucial strategy for 'fearful' middle-classes (Vincent and Ball 2006) in ensuring the social and educational reproduction of their children, the middle-classes in our study are not putting up the barricades but boldly, or in few cases rather hesitantly, going where most white middle-classes fear to tread. Anxiety and fear about a potentially contaminating other affected all fractions of the white middle-classes. For example, Catherine, a London mother, whose parents and grandparents attended university, talked about 'the danger' of sending children to schools where 'there are too many working classes'. She perceived such schools as characterised by indiscipline but more crucially as places where children like her own would no longer be seen as 'the norm'.

Yet, despite fears like these, it could be argued that the white middle-classes have colonised normativity across society. Middle-classness in the contemporary is about what is normal, good, appropriate and proper (Skeggs 2004), while whiteness is also about a normalcy that historically has meant a displacement of race onto racialised others (Byrne 2006). And while the growing literature on whiteness is endeavouring to make whiteness visible as a racialised identity (Frankenberg 1997; Perry 2002; Ware and Back 2002), we still seem to be a considerable way from seeing a discursive shift that opens up whiteness as a range of racialised subject positions. For many, the white middle-classes continue symbolically to represent the ideal towards which others should aspire; paradoxically the social grouping with all the culture but none of the ethnicity. Both middle-classness and whiteness then are positioned as the universal and, as Lucey et al. (2003) argue, 'the universal marks the particular as the particular in order to attain its hegemony and with that evades the universal's own particularity.'

Beyond rationality: Passion and politics in white middle-class choice

Middle-classness traditionally has also been about containment and restraint; in fact these qualities are part of the reason the middle-classes have come to represent the social ideal. As we have alluded to earlier, it is the working-classes who have always been portrayed as repositories for excess (Stallybrass and White 1986; Carey 1992). However, we would argue that emotions and affect seep beyond the edifice of 'the rational subject', and this seepage was powerfully articulated in Yvonne Scott's narrative. Yvonne, a London parent, was a coal miner's daughter before becoming a dancer and marrying a middle-class man. When her oldest daughter went to Copethorpe comprehensive it was bottom of the LEA league table with 17 per cent A* – C at GCSE. At the time of Yvonne's interview the local newspaper had an article on Copethorpe entitled 'Worst in London: Secondary school exam results hit rock bottom' on the front page. The newspaper was lying on Yvonne's kitchen table while she was being interviewed. Throughout her interview Yvonne reiterated her deep commitment to comprehensive schooling, but this strong commitment was in constant tension with Yvonne's fear of the consequences of acting on her belief:

> I was totally freaked out by the whole prospect of secondary school and all Tanya's friends went to Drayton Park and I thought I was like minded with these mothers, but it wasn't until the secondary school thing I thought no, they are not and I was panicking about it and Tanya wanted to go to Drayton Park, she said her friends were picking their school and why couldn't she pick hers. I said Tanya they are not picking their school, their mum is picking their school and if you go to Drayton Park, their mum will have picked your school. I said I don't believe in segregation of any kind, whether it is single sex, faith schools, fee paying, whatever people do to divide us, and I wholeheartedly mean that and so you have to go to a mixed school

with no special faith where there is a mixture of kids and this is our local mixed school.

(Yvonne Scott, London)

The calm reasoned explanation Yvonne provides to Tanya belied her anxious feelings about school choice. In many ways Yvonne is one of the least ambivalent of the parents (but see Laura Franklin, a Riverton parent, in Chapter 4). She is passionately committed to comprehensive schooling and told us that 'there is no way I'd move my kids. I think it is the responsibility of parents like us to make sure these schools improve.' Yet despite her resolve Yvonne found the transition process, in her own word 'excruciating':

> When her primary class went to visit Tanya was terrified because it was chaos. Not just that, the kids were pretty crazy, they weren't in the classrooms, the ones in the classrooms weren't getting on with their work and the teachers didn't seem to have much control, it was just chaos. I rang up the head and said I came today and do you know, we want to send our daughter to this school, we really want to support this school because everything we believe about putting into your community and not taking from it, this encompasses everything we believe, we want to come, and we will help. And I said look today was a complete disaster and my daughter already asked not to go to the school and had to listen to her friends saying oh why are your parents sending you to that crap school, my mum would never let me go. And we are getting flak from them and then we are getting her here and it was a disaster. So it was just excruciating.

For Yvonne her investment in doing what was best for society rather than just her own children was producing considerable anxiety not only in relation to her daughter's fraught experience of their local comprehensive but also in terms of her own self-perception as a mother who in sending her child to what is perceived to be 'a bad school' may herself be seen to be 'a bad mother'. We can see very clearly the conflict and tension between being a good citizen and a good parent (Oria et al. 2007):

> She went on the first day and literally I was not sleeping at night and everything I was really worried. And I am not a worrier, I am really not, but the first day she went, I took her there and me and John both took her and she went up the stairs to the door to the

assembly hall and she didn't know anybody and she walked off and her face, I will never forget her face and she went bye mum and then I went and worried all day, all day I was looking at my watch and worrying.

Such conflicted feelings are further aggravated by a nagging sense of anxiety that such choices may result in children 'under-achieving' educationally. While such powerful affective responses were most common in the London context there were similar concerns in both Norton and Riverton, as the following quotes from Isabel Webb show:

Um, we had a very unfortunate first term ... he was horrendously bullied. Um and that was all just, just about everything that I feared was all coming true ... it was just terrible, it was horrible, it was horrible hearing what he'd gone through and bless him he'd kept it all bottled up and it was awful. The first we'd heard about it, it was sitting, was at a parents' evening and it was this time of the year, it was about, it was around about his birthday. We went over there and sat down with the form teacher and, um, and the teacher said, she handed me this piece of paper which was Luke's assessment of how he was getting on in different lessons, you know and he went through it and bless him he'd sat there and filled it in so honestly and it was things like I'd like, I like geography but in geography I get a lot of um, a lot of teasing, do this and do that. German, I'd like to learn some German but it's, you can't learn any German because of all the disruptive behaviour in it. PE, I get, you know, I get bullied in, they take my clothes away from me in the changing rooms and make them wet under the taps so that my clothes are wet. You know, and just things like that and I just sat there and I'd never, I said this is just shameful, absolutely shameful.

Isabel added

... we were so upset, we were so upset, John was just so upset about it, that whether they would have that response had we not been that upset, had we not been that articulate, which we can be if we have to, you know, standing up for your child. Um we made it quite clear to them that we weren't accepting it and, you know, we were expecting this, the boys were not used to that, we're not used to that kind of ... And you know, they went to a really good primary school, that school's fantastic, and I don't think, you know, by the time they

left Birchwood I don't think I could have paid and got better education to that. Um, so then going to that over there, it was, it was just
awful.

(Isabel Webb, Norton)

Across our data we noticed how these white middle-class parents
retained a strong sense of entitlement in relation to the education
of their children. But that entitlement was often infused with and
under-cut by high levels of anxiety. In the quote below Karen Sollazzi,
a Riverton mother, describes the widespread hyper-anxiety among
Riverton parents in relation to a new secondary school located in a
multi-ethnic working-class locality:

> It's fear of not achieving and fear of the unknown, it's like almost, it's
> stereotyping at ethnic minority kids, it's sort of almost . . . buying in
> to this notion that just because these kids are from different races or
> different ethnic or different economic backgrounds they are automat-
> ically going to be difficult children or they're going to be disruptive
> children, which is a load of rubbish as we all know. But it's almost
> feeling that your child is going to be sucked in to this place and is
> never going to achieve their potential. It's just a faceless fear.

Class out of place: The discomforts of 'lesser places'

Stephen Ball argues (2003 p. 162) that for the middle-classes, concerns
and anxieties about getting it right and doing the right thing are engendered and reinforced with social networks. If white middle-class parents,
in part, become moral subjects by learning and acquiring behaviours
and attitudes from others in their class setting, then when those others opt for the private and selective state sector parents like those in
our sample are often left with a sense of abandonment and righteous
indignation, but also anxiety and guilt. There is no reassurance of community. Instead we have a language of panic in which the psychic
costs of principled choices becomes evident. Unsurprising then that
anxiety, guilt and contradictory responses permeated our interviewees'
responses including some of those who were well established within the
middle-classes. Cathy Beattie, a London mother, went to private school
as did her husband. She sent her two oldest children to private school
before deciding to send Ben her youngest to the local comprehensive.
In the quote below, we can see the powerful conscious and unconscious
conflicts permeating Cathy's narrative, and gain a strong sense of the

middle-class fear of contagion through contact with the working-classes (Layton 2008):

> They are very seductive the private schools, they sort of, you know, into thinking they're the best and I think it's, yeah you could say it's racism it's classism at the start, but it's fear, it's fear that you're sending your child into a lesser environment, somewhere where they're not going to be able to do as well.
>
> (Cathy Beattie, London).

Here Cathy articulates a prevalent middle-class fear that state comprehensives are in some way inferior. Her emphasis on state schools as 'lesser' places is telling. Skeggs (1997 p. 90) argues that class is internalised for the working-classes as 'an intimate form of subjectivity experienced as knowledge of always not being "right"'. Concomitantly, the internal fears and defences of white middle-class parents like Cathy are supported in the wider social world through discourses which themselves contain enduring phantasies about the inferior intellectual capacities of the working-classes (Carey 1992). Although she is clearly struggling against these perceptions, Cathy's 'lesser places' reveal 'the middle-class use of class as a defence, to create the illusion of superiority and false confidence, warding off fears of failure and inadequacy' (Ryan 2006 p. 60). Here habitus is operating as a defence mechanism against privilege. We can see clearly a defence of distinction and the ways in which the white middle-classes, most apparently unproblematically but in the case of these parents more conflictually, defensively use their own investments in class to distinguish themselves as superior to others. What is also evident in the quote below, and the later example of Ross, is that the white middle-classes do not view the majority working-class white and ethnic minority students in their schools as people they easily fit in with.

> You know also he was the only...he was alone, he didn't have a single mate, he didn't know anybody, he was by himself, whereas virtually everybody else came up with a peer group, so he was sitting by himself and you know he is very white and he's very middle-class. So looking round, all the groups are mixed, there isn't a sort of 'white middle-class group' he could go and slot himself into...So I think he found it really difficult. I know he did, it was horrible, we used to walk to school and it was a nightmare. The first term I just felt sick, the whole time. I would like it to be the norm for people to go to their local school and not to be scared in the way that I was scared.

> I would like people like me to send their children to Broomwood and
> not be scared. I think a lot of my fear was irrational. I'm sure it was.
> I didn't even go and look at the school, so how rational can this be?
>
> (Cathy Beattie, London)

Like many of the parents, Cathy is ambiguously positioned and
expresses a great deal of ambivalence. At different points in the interview she spoke about 'the terrible, terrible reputation of local state
schools' and her sense of panic when considering them as possibilities
for her own son. On the one hand, she projects her discomforts onto
lesser people in lesser places, those through whom she can maintain her
privileged status (Hughes 2007). But on the other hand, she adopts a
strong moral stance in relation to 'the good society' and asserts that if
she wants society to be more equitable then she needs to act in certain
ways despite her fears. This tension between doing the best for one's
own child and doing the best for wider society was there, to a greater or
lesser extent, for all the parents. Yet again we glimpse 'a habitus divided
against itself, in constant negotiation with itself and its ambivalences'
(Bourdieu 1999 p. 511). These parents were managing the psycho-social
strains of trying to behave ethically in a situation which is structurally
unethical, in terms of entrenched inequalities, and radically pluralistic,
in terms of different moralities and value systems (Sayer 2005).

Objectifying the classed other

Within private and selective schools the middle-classes are one of a
social group or collective of individuals that offers 'the two-fold bless-
ing of being someone and not having to be alone in doing it' (Berking
1996 p. 199). For these families, and particularly those choosing the
lowest performing schools, that is not the case. We can see this very
clearly in Cathy's description of her son Cameron's isolation. It is also
apparent in Ross' account. Ross, who achieved four Grade A passes at
GCSE Advanced level and a place at Cambridge, was at a school at the
bottom of the Local Authority league table. While we cannot determine from Cathy's words whether Cameron's isolation is chosen or
imposed, isolation for Ross has a distinctly ambivalent character; it is
both imposed and deliberately chosen. In the quote below, he articulates clearly a boundary drawing process that separates him off from his
ethnic minority working-class peer group:

> I did my own thing but with lots of support and like yeah, I was never
> held back and I was always really pushed by my teachers. In class

things I always felt a bit uncomfortable because I would always be kind of straining myself from sounding like a twat (laughs). But in general I was, allowed to write like a twat in my books and I just got on with it. I am not saying I found things easy it was just that I compelled myself to do more than anyone else did. Like I just worked longer, it's kind of like a neurosis.

(Ross, London)

He hints at some of the costs in this process but his father, himself from a working-class background, makes them more evident when he explains why Ross dropped out of a Gifted and Talented leadership programme:

Anyway they wanted three kids for this gifted and talented leadership scheme, and he was chosen for one of them. And I remember him coming home and saying 'oh great'. And the next day he was just crying for no reason at all and so they took him to the office and it happened again. And so they took him to the doctor and they arranged a visit, it was amazing, within a week, with the educational psychologist. And then we got 6 sessions with him and me almost straightaway and it turns out that I had been putting too much pressure on him and that was the last straw.

(Steve Davies, London)

The family may have a powerful commitment to socialist egalitarianism but as we can see from both son's and father's quotes, these principles must be managed in tension with the pursuit of academic excellence, a conflicting desire to be 'the best'. This constitutes a difficult painful enterprise in working-class educational contexts that requires constant vigilance and pressure in and over the child. These processes of stretching the child and ensuring that his talents and abilities are fully realised against the institutional odds are both exhausting and isolating. As Ross says he 'compelled himself to do more than anyone else'. But this is not simply a self-inflicted disciplinary practice, his father admits that he too 'had been putting too much pressure' on Ross. This joint pursuit of academic excellence results at one point in psychic collapse.

Ross' relationship with his classed other illustrates the ways in which despite valuing the other there is still enormous ambivalence about children connecting or becoming allied with the working-class majority in the comprehensive schools they attend (Reay et al. 2007). One consequence is the semi-detachedness evident in what he had to say about working-class students at the predominantly working-class comprehensive he attended:

> At Sixth Form College they had got no idea about how most people live. They'd had no experience, unlike me. I'd seen it at first hand. I knew what life was like for kids who lived on the estates. Not that I agreed with how they behaved a lot of the time. Mostly, I kept my distance.
>
> (Ross, London)

Here knowing is not the same as empathising. Rather, Ross is demonstrating the dispositions of the white middle-class cosmopolitans that Bev Skeggs writes about. She argues (2004 p. 158) that 'to be cosmopolitan one has to be able to appropriate, distinguish and claim to know the other in order to generate authority and disposition from this knowing.' And Ross has this appropriating knowledge that becomes a resource for the self rather than an empathetic connection with the other. But at the same time this is no easy knowing rather it is undercut by the discomfort of being in culturally different and difficult spaces. This was especially the case for those families whose children like Ross attend schools with a sizeable majority of working-class children (some 60 per cent of the schools attended by the London children had over 25 per cent of their pupils eligible for free school meals). Tricia Simpson, a London mother whose daughter attended a comprehensive with 52 per cent minority ethnic and 40 per cent free school meal pupils, had a reflexive class analysis. Yet, while she expressed sympathy with the white working-classes, she still positioned them as a problem to be faced up to. Talking about the white working community adjacent to her daughter's secondary school, she commented:

> They are really an indigenous community and have long histories of being servants to the military and now that military has gone, everything has crumbled around them. They don't have so many jobs. The army has just kind of left them and that's actually an erosion of hundreds of years of history. You may not like the attitudes, you may not like the lack, you know, the quite aggressive culture, the racism in that culture, you may not like it, but to pretend that it never existed and that it is unimportant is only to create problems for yourself. And the problems that you deal with: schools are the only places, I think,

the only places, where you actually confront those issues, because particularly state schools are pulling in everybody.

(Tricia Simpson, London)

Bourdieu's theory of identity formation focuses on habitus as the internalisation of hierarchical social relations, an internalisation that produces dispositions that reflect the individual's position in the social hierarchy. And Tricia's microscopic analysis, her privileged view from above, displays the classic middle-class habitus. We can also see in Tricia's words Layton's (2008) 'failure of empathy'. Tricia epitomises the attitudes and affective responses of many of the parents and children to the working-classes, and particularly the white working-class other. On one level they are to be pitied, and, in common with Ross, she stresses the importance of knowing and understanding their situation intellectually. But there is also the emotional impossibility of putting yourself in the position of those who are defined in the middle-class imaginary through 'their lack', 'their aggression' and above all 'their racism' (Haylett 2001). Rather than developing any empathetic understanding the challenge is to learn about and understand the working-classes as a problem to be dealt with. Sheila Moss, a Norton parent, expressed a similar condescension laced with distaste, disdain and a slight sense of mockery:

I go into school frequently as a governor and I see horrendous children, children that you think what is going to happen to them? Where are they going to go? And my poor children who are really nice have to be in amongst them.

The key distinction here is between 'nice' middle-class children and 'horrendous' working-class ones. Despite over a hundred years of universal state education the working-classes continue to be discursively constituted within the educational field as an unknowing, unreflexive, tasteless mass against which the middle-classes draw their distinction (Tawney 1931; Carey 1992). Despite their left-leaning, communitarian impulses these families have complex and difficult feelings towards their classed other, ranging from Joan's ironic distaste to Ross' ambivalent but still defended response. Dealing with the discomforts of privilege in disadvantaged contexts all too often results in varying degrees of repression, sublimation and dis-identification (Skeggs 1997). These parents and their children are attempting to do class distinction work under conditions of anxious proximity (Raisborough and Adams 2008).

Claiming the intellectual high ground: Brightness as the white middle-class defence of distinction

Of all the young people we interviewed, Camilla, a Londoner, was the most transparent about the difficult feelings that class differences can arouse. In her mid-twenties by the time of the interview, she reflected on how when she was at secondary school 'there was an element of being embarrassed about being middle-class'. She explained that this was especially so as secondary school was the first time in her life that she was confronted with people she describes as 'having a lot less than anyone I had ever met'. Her recollections of her secondary school experiences illuminate difficult tensions between empathy and desires to distance herself. Once again the divided habitus that results from the ambivalences and tensions that characterise many of these middle-class individuals is evident. On the one hand, she was:

> ...quite upset to see it though and I remember feeling really sorry for them because although I knew it happened and I knew it was an issue, you know, until you actually see if for yourself you don't actually think about it. And then knowing that we had so much more and knowing that when I came back after my first day my mum was going to ask me how it went. And there were so many kids there whose parents obviously probably didn't have hardly anything and you know weren't going to ask or didn't care sort of thing and that was quite sad.
>
> (Camilla, London)

However, on the other hand, permeating Camilla's sense of empathy and embarrassment at her own privilege was a countervailing sense of superiority in relation to her working-class peers at school. Her words also poignantly reveal her need to defend against a sense of inferiority in relation to her parents who are both senior academics:

> I think the other kids at school looked up to me to a certain extent and I didn't sort of consciously think it but I subconsciously felt slightly superior to them in that I had everything that they didn't have. You know everything that my mum and dad had given me and I was more intelligent than they were and there was more going for

me than there was for them. And I think also because my mum and dad had achieved so much I think I probably felt quite second rate to them and being friends with these people made me feel like the one you know who was achieving you know and was superior to them.

We have drawn on Camilla's uncomfortably honest account of her comprehensive school experiences because, in many ways, she seemed the least defended of the white middle-class individuals we interviewed, and her openness allowed us a better understanding of what was at play in the claiming of intellectual superiority by the vast majority of our participants. We would argue that the norm among the sample was to take refuge in what Freud terms 'splitting'. Freud (1940) argued that when faced with a traumatic situation that calls into question one's integrity, the ego often deals with what appears to be an irreconcilable dilemma through processes of disavowal that leads to a splitting of the ego. What is seen to be shameful, in this case any responsibility for very visible inequalities, is split off and projected onto subordinate groups. But as Layton (2009 p. 116) asserts, 'the split polarities that result from the shaming instantiation of oppressive social structures such as sexism or racism [and we would add, classism] proliferate in the dark.'

Skeggs (2004) provides a very powerful account of how excess, vulgarity and stasis are projected on to the working-classes, in order that the middle-classes can preserve their hold on respectability, reflexivity and responsibility. Through such processes of 'making classed selves' (Skeggs 2004 p. 119), the working-classes come to be seen as lacking in value as value is attributed to 'distinctive' middle-class ways of being and doing. In our research it was primarily through discourses of middle-class 'brightness' that middle-class distinction was asserted and defended. Across 251 interview transcripts there were a staggering 256 references to brightness, made by the parents, and to a lesser extent their children, without prompting by the interviewers. We would argue that such discourses, which position middle-class brightness as both normative and a justification for middle-class privilege, are one of the main means through which the middle-classes defensively use their own investments in class hierarchies to distinguish themselves as superior to others. Splitting, and the othering of the working-classes it generates, enables the middle-classes to hold on to brightness and intelligence as key aspects of their identities whilst generally denying these characteristics to the working-class other (Holt and Griffin 2005). Brightness then becomes a rationalisation for holding on to more: educationally, socially and economically. Furthermore, investment in brightness defends against the fear of failure. For the white middle-classes educational failure is often intolerable and needs to be projected elsewhere.

The desirous white middle-classes: Positive identifications with classed and racialised 'others'

At the beginning of the chapter we described both the defended and the desirous white middle-classes. However, the majority of the data reveal a defended white middle-class subject with varying degrees of ambivalence and anxiety. We gain a whiff of white middle-class fear of softness; a fleeting anxiety, but one present in many of the interviews, that privilege puts children at risk of becoming flaccid, in some ways weak and unable to deal with the real world. This is expressed in particularly vivid terms by Caroline, a journalist based in London:

> I also feel very strongly that private schooling doesn't prepare you in any way at all for real life once you leave. I mean our best friends down in this road, their daughters are exactly the same age as ours and they go through the private system. And I just look at their daughters and I think at some point you're going to have leave school and you're going to have to be out there with some rough dysfunctional people and you won't know what's hit you. Whereas my daughter is in classrooms with some very, very difficult behaviour of children, and she's having to learn to concentrate and get on with what she's doing. And I think that is tough for her but she is learning that in order to do well at school she's got to be an independent learner.
>
> (Caroline Friar, London)

Evident in Caroline's words is the conviction that attending inner city comprehensive schooling is the best preparation for dealing with the real world. This is comprehensive schooling as a provider of 'character' or 'backbone', ironically in one sense, and in this sense only, a twenty-first-century successor to a prime function of the old public schools.

Most of the white middle-class desire for the other was complicated by differing degrees of dis-identification with what was seen to be conventional middle-classness and in two or three cases whiteness, although this latter small group of mothers either had ethnic minority partners or had mixed race children. Brenda, a London mother, who has a black partner and a white daughter from an earlier relationship, makes a strong statement about the desire not to be privileged in terms of either class or race:

> Brenda: She had a group of black friends and so she was she was not seen as like, posh like the white middle-class kids.
>
> *Interviewer: But she was*
>
> Brenda: She was but she wasn't, she was and she wasn't because you know it depends on how you look at it doesn't it. I mean yes she is white but I don't think she's, I don't think we are particularly posh and certainly her experience growing up has been very, very diverse. You know who our friends are and who we mix with is definitely not mostly middle-class.
>
> (Brenda Gresham-Worthing, London)

First it is important to recognise that Brenda's daughter is not typical of our sample. Most of them did mix mostly with other white middle-classes. But also if we look at the psychic processes at play we can see a strong dis-identification with white middle-classness as a defence against the anxiety of being part of, and benefiting from, a prejudicial class system (Reay 2005). She continues repeatedly to dis-identify her daughter from white middle-classness and convince herself of the success of this dis-identification with 'I don't think...' '...certainly she is not...' '...she is definitely not...', suggesting powerful processes of dis-avowal. Like a majority of our sample Brenda has unresolved anxieties around privilege (Ryan 2006), and we glimpse the ways in which habitus can be susceptible 'to a kind of duplication, to a double perception of the self, to successive allegiances and multiple identities' (Bourdieu 1999 p. 511).

But denial of privilege and powerful psychic investments in dis-identifications from one's subject position are not quite the same as desiring the other, and certainly not, as was the case for Skeggs'(1997) working-class young women, in part a desire to be 'the other'. According to Elliott (2004) one of the defining characteristics of contemporary culture has been a longing for cultural difference, for a sufficient sense of otherness, particularly a desire for multicultural communities. So where were the desiring white middle-classes in the sample; those embracing otherness? Christopher Bollas (1995 p. 22) writes about 'the ultimately self-enhancing projective identifications by which we invest the world of external objects with aspects of ourselves'. And we do glimpse self-enhancing projective identifications, and even at times more socially desirable empathetic understanding. Below Avril, a London mother, who might be best described as upper middle-class as one of her parents was a member of the aristocracy, talks of both openness and understanding. While clearly recognising that other white middle-classes might misread such openness negatively as lack of confidence, she is very definite that such qualities are positive, that to learn with other cultures rather than of them is an asset:

> One of the most important things is an openness . . . and also I think it is an understanding of others you can only have if you are sort of with them all the time. It is something to learn of other cultures, but to actually learn with other cultures, of other cultures, it is a completely different thing.
>
> (Avril Smart, London)

In Avril's words we can see the desire for inclusion and openness; an attempt to reconcile unity with difference (Hoggett 2000). Similarly, Maria Lowenthal, a London mother, who comes from a solidarist working-class background, talks of an openness and desire to understand rather than to know of one's 'ethnic other':

> I know some people didn't send their children to Capeland because they'd heard about it focusing too much on black kids and racism in the school. And I just thought I wouldn't want my kids to go to a school where they didn't do that. I thought it was very positive, that's what a good school should be doing and Max had a number of black friends and very positive for them and for Max to see it and to hear about it was good for him. They were able to talk about these things and when he did his sociology research project he looked at the differences between black young people and white young people at Capeland and he wouldn't have done that if he hadn't have been in a school where it was actually seen to be important to do and where they didn't see it as threatening.
>
> (Maria Lowenthal, London)

A significant minority of our white middle-class parents expressed similar sentiments. A particularly vivid example is Yvonne, who, despite the enormous anxieties we have seen in her earlier quotes, articulates a powerful recognition of the self in the ethnic other:

> I said to my kids 'who do you think refugees are'? If they were bombing this country what do you think we would do? Do you think if

I thought there was a chance you might have your leg blown off every time you went to school I would get you out of here. Of course I would, we would go, there are some other people who are maybe not quite as intelligent as us, who would stay here to have less idea about how to motivate themselves to get out, that is who these people are, they are the people like us, from these other countries. When they get here they are like, there is an opportunity for you. And you grab it by both hands.

(Yvonne Scott, London)

But even here, the identification with, and valorisation of, the ethnic other is accompanied by the denigration and residualisation of the white working-classes, those others who are not 'intelligent' or 'motivated' enough to move either geographically or educationally.

Conclusion

Paul Hoggett (2000) argues that in relation to citizenship and the welfare state the key issue is that of difference, the idea of the individual or group who won't fit in. In particular, school choice policies and the construction of quasi-markets reveal powerful kinds of defensive formations. The provocation of anxiety at both individual and collective levels can result in a splitting between 'good' and 'bad', 'us' and 'them' at the levels of schools, students and communities. The defended habitus that Bourdieu writes about in relation to the working-classes (Bourdieu 2000) is just as prevalent among the middle-classes. All the families are struggling with the wider psycho-social context, the macro level, in which collective imaginaries are increasingly about divisions and what divides rather than unity and openness to difference. However, at the micro-level, the 'otherness' white middle-class families confront in these urban comprehensives undermines the traditional middle-class confidence about being able to control the educational process and its values, further reinforcing defensiveness and generating anxiety for a majority of the parents. But more hopefully for a significant minority, like Avril and Maria, anomalies and questions of otherness are construed 'against the grain', 'as novelty, enrichment, and as a focus for the extension of the self's possibilities, as the source of "wonderment"' (Young 1997). We glimpse a yearning after and for difference.

Judith Butler (1997 p. 86) points out:

... the psyche, which includes the unconscious, is very different from the subject: the psyche is precisely what exceeds the imprisoning effects of the discursive demand to inhabit a coherent identity, to become a coherent subject.

Normatively speaking, the middle-classes do not 'do' excess and incoherence: both are supposed to be the province of the upper and lower classes. But those of us who are middle-class know that excess and incoherence can be part of middle-class identity. Rather, we would like to suggest that normatively, excess and incoherence are not owned and integrated. They are the unacceptable parts of middle-class identity, defended against and projected elsewhere, usually on to those white and black working-classes who are normally kept at a comfortable distance. However, the white middle-class families we have studied have chosen what is at times an uncomfortable proximity to their class and ethnic other. This generates both defensive anxieties and fears, but also sometimes, and more hopefully, a desirous openness.

A crucial social issue then is how to cultivate and grow dispositions of desirous openness because even amongst this group of left leaning cosmopolitans they are uncommon and increasingly under threat (Page 2007). Within the public arenas of the social, and more specifically the educational, world, there is a growing emphasis on competition, instrumentalism, and 'being the best' (Rodger 2003), while the demonisation of the working-classes and, in particular, the white working-classes within official, media and public discourses has increased over the last 50 years (Skeggs 1997, 2004; Lawler 2005; Reay 2006). All these developments have impacted powerfully on the inner dynamics of the boundary constructions necessary to collective identity. Stallybrass and White (1986 p. 202) describe the middle-classes as:

a class which, whilst indeed progressive in its best political aspirations, had encoded in its manners, morals and imaginative writings, in its body, bearing and taste, a subliminal elitism which was constitutive of its historical being. Whatever the radical nature of its 'universal' democratic demand, it had engraved in its subjective identity all the marks by which it felt itself to be a different, distinctive and superior class.

The white middle-classes sending their children to urban comprehensives are struggling, with varying degrees of success, to resolve the tensions between desirous openness and sublimated elitism. We would argue that this is not just a challenge that they alone should face, especially when a majority of the middle-classes continue instrumentally, and from a distance, to use their Others 'in order to play out the disorders of its own identity' (Stallybrass and White 1986 p. 200). Rather, the challenge for the white middle-classes, and for social justice more widely, is how to resolve the tensions between desirous openness and sublimated elitism to the benefit of all classes. In the next chapter, we move on to look at the experiences of the children and how their white, middle-class identities are reproduced or reconfigured in the context of multicultural state schooling.

7
Young People and the Urban Comprehensive: Remaking Cosmopolitan Citizens or Reproducing Hegemonic White Middle-Class Values?

Introduction

Middle-class parents, ambitious for their children, tend to have a sense of 'futurity' (Prout 2000) or what Butler with Robson (2003) term 'horizon', that is middle-class parents are confident in how they envisage their children's future trajectories and how to ensure these (p. 141). Underpinning these objectives lies a strong, implicit desire to socially reproduce the family. However, our middle-class parents have not been as strategic in such intent (through their choice of school) as for example those studied by Ball (2003) or Butler with Robson (2003). They do not engage to the same degree in the competition for reproducing their class advantage. As we have seen, one of their intentions in choosing the urban comprehensive school was to provide a more expansive and diverse experience for their children which would provide them with opportunities to prepare them as global twenty-first-century and even cosmopolitan citizens (Beck 2006). The question for us is whether they have merely found new strategies to ensure their social and cultural reproduction or whether their actions reflect an attempt to re-orientate or reconstruct their and their children's middle-class identities based on a more equitable cosmopolitanism. Through the preceding chapters we have seen the tensions and struggles that surround these endeavours and have also shown that the parents are beset with contradictions and moral ambiguity (Sayer 2005; Crozier et al. 2008), although in Chapter 4 we demonstrated the assurance with which parents made potentially 'risky' decisions. In this chapter we turn to the views of the young people themselves and explore from their perspectives and through their voices the impact of the urban comprehensive experience on their identities.

We look at the young people's experience of the urban school in terms of their achievements and their attitudes to their peers; their own sense of fitting in, their identifications or dis-identifications and their coping strategies. And we discuss how their views and attitudes echo or diverge from those of their parents, examining the complex dynamic between reproducing parents' views and asserting independence and difference. This issue is also important in relation to the extent to which the parents impose and reproduce their own attitudes and values on or in their children. Given the desire for their children to develop cosmopolitan experiences and identities through their diverse schools we discuss the extent to which this took place and consider the difference between social mix and social mixing.

As we have explained earlier, the schools the children attended were regarded as average or below average according to league-table position. The most ethnically mixed schools were in London (of the 40 schools in London only four had less that 50 per cent ethnic minority intake, and 14 schools had more than 70 per cent). In Norton[1] the school that most of our respondents attended had a significant minority of mainly South Asian pupils which apparently had one of the largest percentages of Black and Minority Ethnic (BME) pupils in the city. In Riverton three schools had between 27 per cent and 54 per cent of BME children; two schools had 19 per cent and 15 per cent, six schools had 10 per cent or less and two had no BME children at all. The average number of BME children in Riverton comprehensive schools was, in 2005, 8.2 per cent. There were 270 children/young people in our 125 participating families, of whom five children were mixed 'race'. We interviewed 68 white children (that is, 25.2 per cent of the 270). These ranged in age from 12 to 22, plus one 27-year old. There were 39 girls/young women and 29 boys/young men.

Young people and choice

Whatever the intentions of the parents, the children were not entirely passive or pliable beings but exercised agency to a greater or lesser extent. At the point of choice there were clear examples of the children exerting their own preferences but there was also a whole spectrum of coercion and subtle orchestration exerted by the parents, behaviour in keeping with others' findings that middle-class parents tend to assert their own views in the school choice process (Ball et al. 1995; Reay and Ball 1998; Butler and Hamnett 2007). Generally speaking, the levels of stress and anxiety engendered by these processes were lower for the children than for parents, although at the point of transition, predictably, many children were a little intimidated by the size and differences presented by the secondary school and some also were disappointed or upset not to be accompanying their friends.

A few of these choices, mostly in London, were against the wishes of children who wanted to remain with a group of primary school friends for the transition to secondary school. However, on the whole, the children interviewed were happy to be at the school their parents had chosen for them and despite occasional episodes of social and/or academic difficulties, most young people ended up making positive assessments of their experiences of school. Not one child in Norton expressed a desire to be at a different school. In London, only two children, both boys, had an overall negative experience and two girls wished, in hindsight, they had gone elsewhere, and in Riverton only two children expressed some unhappiness.

In general, children echoed their parents' well-rehearsed arguments about the choice of secondary school and about the issues surrounding it, such as the pros and cons of private education and the quality of education in the chosen school. There are also examples of children across the three locations reiterating, often quite passionately, the moral and political arguments against private education and for a more egalitarian school system:

> Well it's hard to think what I thought then cos I've obviously got a view now, but um I think I thought that it was maybe fairer, er, having state schools and yeah, I'm not sure whether I had a very sort of socialist view of it or anything, but I think I maybe understood that I was going to a state school because, not because we couldn't afford to go to a private school, but because it was sort of better in a way.
>
> (Natasha Hann, 17 years, Norton)

> I think that you shouldn't have to pay to go to a school because at the end of the day you shouldn't have to pay to get an education. It's like everyone is entitled to one and it shouldn't be you can't get that education because you can't afford to pay for it, or 'oh no, you can't get that education because you are not clever enough' [...] if you go to a private school, I don't know, it just feels like it is unfair...
>
> (Angela Baker, 12 years, London)

Children also echoed their parents' desire that they should have and learn from 'real life experiences'; as Zach (14 years, London) somewhat pointedly said, 'I ain't going to meet a range of people, if I go to [a private school].' These shared narratives of distinction between types of school and school experience or values different schools can provide, indicate that schooling is a shared project in the home: the *family* has a relationship to the school rather than just the child or the parent. Here we saw something of the passing-on (reproduction) of values and ideas with the child learning to think like the parent.

As we have seen, the choice of school was often influenced by a range of principles and pragmatic factors. For instance a number of families (particularly in London) made different secondary school choices for their different children and this was especially noticeable where one or more children had Special Educational Needs. Not surprisingly then the young people themselves expressed the view that the choice of school depended on the individual child and on the sort of person you were:

> There are people that wouldn't fit into an in inner city comprehensive school environment and people that wouldn't fit into a private school environment. There is nothing worse or better about them, (they are) just different experiences. That has been my outlook on life. That is another thing my Dad has given me. There is no better or worse, just different. [...] I would want the experience that suited them [his children, if he had any]. I can't say what would suit them because I don't have any. I would pick the school that suited them the best.
>
> (Ed Jennings 16 years, London)

At times, however, this viewpoint is expressed in less egalitarian terms. Like their parents the young people constructed a binary between themselves and the Other, and in this way set themselves apart. Fourteen-year-old Noah, for instance, feels going to the socially mixed school is of benefit because you get to learn about the real world and have contact with, and knowledge about, 'the not nice people out there' which in turn prepares you to deal with them:

> I feel that non private schools are always better because you learn more and it's more diverse and it kind of toughens you up. Not exactly, but you are not exposed to much if you go to a private school, like, there aren't that many fights and you don't really know how to deal with stuff. It is not really the real world because there are a lot of not nice people out there and for people who can afford to go to a

private school they don't see much of that. And so I definitely think public school or non private school is better, but it is still not good.

(Noah Malone, 14 years, London)

Maintaining advantage and dispelling urban myths?

Academic achievement is crucial in terms of social reproduction. According to Bourdieu and Boltanski (2000) '... the reproduction of class structure operates through translation of the distribution of academic qualifications held by each class...' (pp. 220–221). As we have discussed earlier, parents' choice of school gave rise to anxiety and dilemmas about their children's well-being and fundamentally about their academic fulfilment. With regard to the latter such concerns seemed in most cases unwarranted. Across all three locales the young people were generally doing well at school. Most were performing well compared to their age equivalent peers, with some performing significantly above average. The choice of school their parents made did not seem to have had any negative impact on academic development and in fact the children seemed to have benefited from being in inner city comprehensives. In terms of measurable academic success, of the 117 young people who had reached at least 16, all except three boys and one girl did well in GCSEs; two of whom because of personal family circumstances and the third was found a highly paid job eventually by his father in the film industry. Of the 71 who were over 18, eight went on to Oxbridge after A levels (six from London) and the others went to a range of pre- and post-1992 universities, with only one girl leaving education at 18 years and two boys going to specialised further education (one sports and one arts foundation). As we have argued, in the context of a performative target-driven school culture, teachers/the schools appear to value highly (white) middle-class children who they see as helping them meet their targets. Whilst they might be irritated by middle-class parental interference (see for example Crozier 2000) this is a small price to pay for children who display consonance with the values of the school and have the requisite capitals to ensure success. In a minority of cases parents did acknowledge the pressure that the school's expectations placed on the children particularly where middle-class children were in a small minority:

I believe they have high expectations for some children, for the children they can see who are putting in the effort, for the children they can see who are going to succeed, whether that be A-level, university, whatever, then yes I do think [they] have very, very high expectations. An example of that is my niece, one of my nieces, um very bright child, stayed on to sixth form and originally said she was going to go to university, then she changed her mind. Still does her A-levels but she's going to get a job. The teachers hounded her, absolutely hounded her because she said she wasn't going to university. And you know, I was saying to her look it's your choice, if that's what you want to do that's your choice, at least if you've got the A-levels you can pick it up later in life if that's your choice. But she was really, really sick of the teachers hounding her and obviously because to them it was a waste of talent, might have something to do with their achievements, you know, their reports and it's one less picture on the wall in the sixth form block, you know, um a child in a cap and gown. Cos I've noticed in the sixth form block that every child that's gone to university, once they've graduated that's it, there's a photograph up there.

(Sharon Cole, Norton)

Sharon Cole insightfully identifies the importance of the middle-class child to urban averagely performing schools. Although in this instance the pressure is unwelcome, its presence indicates how the school can share the parental view we explore below, that the middle-class child is 'special', 'extra'.

High educational achievement is synonymous with being middle-class. As we have seen the parents themselves are educationally very well endowed and correspondingly they want the same for their children. Moreover, as Brantlinger (2003) has argued, middle-class parents' self-definitions are strongly related to their children's own successes: 'high tracks, good grades... marked children and mothers as smart' (p. 48). Although the parents did not leave academic success to chance (Crozier et al. 2007) they are confident their children are 'intelligent', 'bright' and able to achieve; there is no doubt in their minds. This is apparent very early on in their children's schooling:

She had some problems initially with reading they told me she was struggling with reading which I wasn't particularly bothered about to be honest. They gave her some extra help with her reading but I just knew that she'd learn to read because you can't not really if you are in a literate household with parents who like reading and you know where books are around all the time. I just knew she would get there in her own time and of course she did.

(Brenda Gresham-Worthing, London)

This confidence extends to a universal assumption that their children will go onto university or some form of higher education; the pursuit of a 'normal biography' (Du Bois-Raymond 1998):

> The thing is it was always ever, since she was little, assumed that she would go to university and I don't know if we laid that on her really but its just she came from a family where her parents had two degrees each you know and the house has always been full of books.
>
> (Beth Cannon, London)

This is such a natural assumption for their middle-class identity that it leaves one Riverton mother slightly bemused (and amused) when her son, along with some other top set pupils at his poorly performing comprehensive, was given a university mentor to encourage him to think about going to university:

> Now, I'm not quite sure why they chose him. There's a few of them that have been chosen, but they obviously think that he's, y'know, suitable. The thing is, my expectation is that he's going to go on anyway, to university [smiles, laughs].
>
> (Gill Harrison, Riverton)

In almost all cases, the young people were in top sets (ability setting, in the core subjects at least, was prevalent in all of the schools attended by the young people) and most were selected to benefit from the Gifted and Talented scheme. This had the effect of creating a two-tier system in the schools and as one Norton mother said her children's school was like two schools in one. This separation added to a sense of 'specialness'. In London, for example, where the child was often the only white middle-class child in their class or year group, this sense of educational superiority seemed to be exacerbated, sometimes supporting a perception that their children were uniquely 'gifted' or 'special':

> Mary and I went to see the head about it who was very defensive and thought we were complaining and we weren't we were just saying he needs help. I mean he was very bright and he wasn't getting enough stimulation and he was feeling 'extra' all the time if you know what I mean because he always knew the answers and the other kids didn't and so you know he felt excluded. And the school was fantastic he got extra lessons they celebrated his 'extraness' if you like within the

class and got the other kids to celebrate it as well and so you know they cheered him on rather feeling he was different from them.

(David Goldblum, London)

She has got on really well academically she got lower fives in the SATs [Key Stage 2] and she has just continued to progress. She got very good results in the Key Stage 3 SATs. When I went to see her teachers before the school broke up, they are looking for her to get quite a lot of As and A* at GCSE, and the science teacher was so thrilled that she was crying because [Susannah] is the only person who has ever got 20 out of 20 in the tests [laughs]. I think that they don't usually get the chance to teach bright kids and so when they do they are really excited and go for it really. Instead of just trying to manage them, they'll actually try to recognise it.

(Diane Prichard, London)

We see again here the affinity in Diane Pritchard's identification of the link between middle-class parents' desires for their children and the school's desire for middle-class children in the context of league tables. Added to this many of these young people had been selected for the schools' 'Gifted and Talented' schemes. The Gifted and Talented Scheme educationally privileges the white middle-class children, placing them at the pinnacle of the comprehensive school. Whilst many parents were ambivalent towards the scheme and didn't see it as offering their children anything they didn't already get, either at home or in the out of school activities they themselves provided, there is a contradictory sense that parents liked the fact that their children had been identified as 'Gifted and Talented' as it affirmed their educational superiority:

She's a bright girl, you gather she's got on the gifted and talented but, we weren't looking for that, but she was approached. And I'm sure she is at that level of ability and em, I'll be interested to see how that translates into GCSEs in terms of the blessed As and A*s and goodness knows what, but it feels ok.

(David Gordon, Norton)

I am very pleased that she is doing that [i.e. participating in the Gifted and Talented scheme] and I have parental pride that she is doing that. I wouldn't deny that.

(Patricia Forrester, London)

This would explain why despite some parents' apparent ambivalence, they questioned the school if their children were not included in Gifted and Talented activities and even went so far as to lobby for their child's inclusion.

Even when the children did falter slightly within the comprehensive system, there was a strong belief from parents that it was the system that was at fault and had let their children down. There was no doubting of their children's ability and in fact their sense of intellectual superiority was often reinforced by the fact that their children overcame the pitfalls of the comprehensive system and did manage to achieve, though not as highly as they might have done within a more academically conducive environment:

> Yes, I mean, if I look at [Peter's] GCSE result, he got eight As and he got three Bs and the rest were Cs and most of that was because he didn't do his course work and I just know that at any of those other schools there was no way that they could have got away without doing course work. I mean, it's very difficult. I mean, how involved do you get? When they get to 16 or so they have to do it without you encouraging. I could see he was more interested in other things but we kind of encouraged him along and chivvied him along a bit but I doubt those other schools, even if the teachers write it for them, it's there and it's done. [With Peter's] ... design technology, the teacher said to us at parent's night, 'well, do you know he's hardly done a thing and it's 60 per cent course work and 40 per cent on the exam, he's going to have to get 95 per cent in the exam to get a pass'. And what did he get, he got a C so he went into that exam and got 95 per cent!
>
> (Liz Allum, London)

Although the choice of comprehensive education did not come without anxiety, parents were able to draw on their vast reserves of social and cultural capital and to ensure educational success. The importance of maintaining family status gives rise to parents' school interventions and pressure or influence on their children. The parents were intent on the children securing the best possible resources and outcomes from their schooling. Whilst their choice of school may have been influenced by egalitarian principles subsequent actions and their relationship to the school do indicate more individualistic intentions, such as the parents' endorsement of the institutionalised stratification through setting and as already mentioned, through the Gifted and Talented scheme in the school. There was some disquiet felt by the children, about the fairness of such singling out for academic privilege within a notionally egalitarian, comprehensive system:

I think it is good if you are in a higher set like you know you are in Set One because you are at the top of the pile and I guess like the classes were a little bit more [well] behaved. But I don't think it is good, like people who were in Set Five just thought what is the point... I know all the Set Five people were unbehaved and sort of loud and everything they just thought we are all in Set Five and we are not going to get up to Set One and so there is not really much point. And I think it really like dampened your spirits if you got put in a lower set and you think you can't move up.

(Davina Wansell, 18 years, London)

The language of 'top of the pile', or as another student described it 'the smart class', is interesting and clearly indicates the sense of superiority such structures simultaneously build upon and maintain. However, the benefits of separation were welcomed by others. A key motivator for being in the top set was to ensure academic success, but this was also linked for both the parents and young people to the desire to be separated off from the putative 'disruptive elements in the school' – the undesirable Other. So whilst one argument for going to the urban comprehensive was to experience a diverse social and ethnic mix, the reality was often quite different (see also Lipsitz 1998).

As James Gordon (12 years, Norton) explained when talking about his views on his school:

I thought it was good. Yeah, it was just getting used to the fact that there were some Charvs as we call them, and they're quite annoying, and that was just quite tough in the first year, but then now I'm in the second year it's fine, cos I've moved up into the higher sets and they've moved down, so I'm sort of away from them, I don't have to deal with them as much as last year, so it's not... whereas last year it tended to be in most lessons, they'd be disrupted by that, but we weren't set in the first year.

In relation to the structures of schooling and academic progress, many children and young people echoed their parents' views of streaming/ setting and the Gifted and Talented programme, recognising the benefits for the individual but also a desire to be kept apart from those not perceived as 'good enough'. Overall there was limited recognition amongst the young people of their own relative advantage or the impact of an inequitable system on the life chances for the majority. Rather, many of them seemed to espouse a meritocratic view of society and educational success – that it is 'all down to the individual' to make their own success in life and also take the responsibility if they failed. Talking about her working-class peers Louise says:

> A few of them towards the end of their secondary school really thought 'I'm going to get through this, I'm not going to be one of these people that fail...because they wanted to break the vicious circle almost really because you know it can be a hard cycle. I mean a lot of them were very young mothers who got pregnant when they were teenagers and a lot of them sort of said you know, I'm going to learn from this, I'm not going to sort of go through that because when you're in those circumstances it really is hard you get trapped in a cycle and its just constantly repeating itself, so I was really sort of proud of a lot of them for you know just really wanting to break through so and I'd say in terms of statistics and like Austin Friars not having like a high pass rate or whatever, its because of that social cycle rather than it being a bad school or the teaching being bad. And I think at the end of the day its really down to the individual to just decide whether they're going to break through that or whether they're going to succumb to it and so I know a lot of my friends you know, did really well and went onto go to college I suppose. That's quite pleasing for me.
>
> (Louise Cannon, 18 years, London)

In his work on the middle-classes and class advantage, Ball (2003) discusses the need for the middle-classes to achieve social closure (Parkin 1979) and the need of the middle-classes not just to maintain their class advantage but as Moore put it (2004) 'to advance their own particular "virtue" and its associated status, culture and the situation of its members' (p. 82). In a world where there is an expansion of education and for all of its flaws, an orientation towards increasing educational achievement for all, the middle-classes cannot remain complacent:

> ... Once higher levels of education become recognised as an objective mark of elite status, and a moderate level of education as a mark of respectable middle-level status, increases in the supply of educated persons at given levels result in yet higher levels becoming recognised as superior, and previously superior levels become only average.
>
> (Collins 1977 p. 131 cited in Moore 2004)

As we have seen here, school choices that might have been construed as a handicap for the middle-class families in this endeavour have not been. However, social and cultural reproduction is not merely about mastering school knowledge but perhaps more specifically the role that school plays in the development of habitus and the cultivation and accumulation of cultural capital (Moore 2004 p. 82). An indication of the 'right' conditions for the cultivation of white middle-class habitus is arguably evidence of the expressive order in terms of discipline, behaviour, attitudes, demeanour and so on (Bernstein 1996). Given that, according to parents' accounts, the urban schools portrayed the antithesis of the type of behaviour that they wanted their children to adopt, this goes some way to explain their endorsement of the system of setting which in effect created a separate existence in school for their children from the unacceptable Other.

Classed and gendered: White middle-class boys and girls fitting in to the urban comprehensive

The extent to which the white middle-class children felt 'out of place' in the context of their school was contingent on the different social class and ethnic composition of the schools and the ethos of the school, but also the agency of the child, with several families having differences between siblings. Interestingly there appeared to be a gendered dimension to this with more parental anxiety about their child 'fitting in' in the case of boys (see also Williams et al. 2008).

Although bullying was not a dominant theme in the data, there was a strongly held view among the parents that the transition to secondary school was not a smooth one for some of the boys in particular. More boys seemed to experience difficulties 'fitting in' than girls. The conception of ourselves is shaped by the social worlds we move in and 'the way in which individual identity relates to social, cultural and spatial contexts' (Sibley, 1995 p. 4) and secondary schooling is for many of the young people the first time that they experience being in a minority (in numerical rather than status terms). The sense that white middle-class boys struggle socially when they are in the minority is articulated by Stephen who did not mix well at school;

I always didn't feel I fitted in very well...I always felt a bit different to be honest. And it just got worse when I went to secondary school. [This was]largely because I didn't play sport very well and I was (pause) quite a bit, I don't know if you would say brighter...but I was kind of a bright kid and found it difficult to kind of stay at a level that we were being taught at, at primary school.

He added:

> I was a very scared kid and secondary school and like Pittsville feels
> like a rough place to be when you are 11 and a little bit soft! The kids
> at Pittsville are anything but soft!
>
> (Stephen Goldblum, 22 years London)

It could be argued that there are no classed and gendered patterns in
relation to who gets bullied at school and who does the bullying, as
it is down to power relations which can be based on strength, 'street
cred', personalities and characteristics (see for example Duncan 1999).
As Stephen pointed out: he was 'shy,' and 'nervous; and this made him
'weak' and vulnerable to bullying in an inner city comprehensive, or in
any situation in fact. However, we argue that this masks the structural
nature of his position within the school. His sense of isolation and being
'out of place' at Pittsville is both classed and gendered, as his father was
well aware: Stephen did not fit in because he was privileged. Privilege
operates to create a sense of division between Stephen and 'the kids at
Pittsville'. The alternative masculinity he brings to the school provides
him with a marginal space at school, one that is valued by staff and
adults which may aid his social reproduction but keeps him at a distance
from his peers.

Parents encouraged their sons into particular kinds of (especially
creative) activities and many boys struggled to maintain the balance
between the alternative masculinities fostered at home with the normative masculinity they encountered at school. But this balancing act
can come under strain as Sarah Davies makes clear; for her son Ross the
stress of managing both becomes too much to bear especially as his plu-
ral masculinities cause resentment amongst his peers and he eventually
has to reject football in favour of pursuing English and poetry:

> I suppose Ross had some conflicts when he got to round about Year 9
> because he was very much an all rounder he was very good at football
> as well as being good at music as well as being very, very good at
> English and everything else. And some of the people in the football
> team resented him being there because their attitude was well you
> are academic and so why aren't you doing that why are you here.
> And so he had to make that choice was he going to go along and
> think it was important to do football and put up with a bit of hassle
> from them or was he just going to cut his losses and think I have
> got enough to do I will keep with the music, I will keep with the

English and the poetry and the writing and all that. And he made that decision he decided he would opt out of the football. He had enough to do.

(Sarah Davies, London)

This creates a difficult balancing act for a number of the young men who find the range of masculinities that they can perform in school limited by teacher and peer expectations and that this, coupled with their parents' expectations, often leads them not to 'fit in'.

In general, whether they had sons or daughters or both, parents believed that it was harder for boys than girls at the comprehensive school.

... from my own professional experience [as a clinical psychologist] um, it's mainly um, a number of boys that get referred to us who are very unhappy, anxious about schools and it tends to be the brighter boys who aren't into the sports and other things like that and who want to get on with their work.

(Beverley Hann, Norton)

Boys were often constructed (by their parents) as delicate and fragile in contrast to the characterisation of their sisters as 'easy going' but 'robust'. The notion that boys need to be protected but that girls are more able to 'take things in their stride' was a widespread view amongst the parents.

In addition parents saw the presence of girls as mediating the over-whelming threat of classed and raced masculinity:

Because more often than not parents who don't or won't send their own children there are talking about badly behaved black boys and it takes a critical mass of little blonde girls to begin to change their minds.

(Avril Smart, London)

The sense that girls neutralise problematic masculinities is strongly embedded in these parents' discourses as is the construction of girls as socially able copers:

When Olivia was in Year 6 she got on really well – and always has done – with the awkward boys, particularly the awkward Caribbean boys she really likes them and they really like her. I remember her saying that she was working with one in the English class and he turned round to her and said, 'You're well posh, aren't you, Olivia?' But she feels comfortable around these people.

(Pat Levy, London)

Pat's use of the term 'these people' emphasises the distance between her family and the forms of masculinity that the 'awkward boys' represent. It seems that their awkwardness is their inability to fit in with white middle-class masculinity or indeed their distance from her daughter's restorative femininity. Parents are more tolerant about 'awkward people' at schools their daughters attend:

> You know I am aware that there are, sort of, there are people who find either the behaviour or the slight wildness about some of the kids there, erm, difficult but Charlie doesn't seem ... she seems to take it all in her stride and ... Bob and I try to take it in our stride too (laughs).
>
> (Diana Pilkington, London)

Positioning girls as copers, and indeed the focus on boys (in a family) can silence the problems that girls face (Mahony 1998; Francis and Skelton 2005) and serves to make invisible the problems that are reported by them (Hey et al. 1998). In contrast to parental perspectives on their daughters as 'robust' and 'easy going', many of the girls themselves talked about difficulties in managing friendships and about problems such as sexual harassment which they didn't discuss with parents:

> I remember when I was in year 7 actually, it was really horrid I'm just walking along and this boy likes gropes me in the back and it was horrid and I hated it and I have never admitted it to anyone, I mean I have to my friends but I was really shocked and I was in year 7 and it was horrid – and he was in year 11 and it was horrid, I hated it.
>
> (Olivia Levy, London)

Social mix or social mixing? Young people's friendships and social groups

While there is a social mix in the urban schools these white middle-class parents send their children to, there is little social mixing particularly between social classes. This seemingly stands in contradiction to the often declared desire for mixing by parents, a number of whom as we have seen lament their children's lack of minority ethnic friends. However, embedded within the desire for 'mixture' is also a fear of 'over-exposure' to difference. Even where there is a degree of social mixing with the classed and racialised Other, the data reveal that nearly all the white middle-class young people remain firmly and primarily anchored in white middle-class networks. This is underscored by the primary schools these children attended and the after-school, extra-curricular activities the children and young people engaged in such as dance, drama, instrumental classes and woodcraft folk which are pre-dominantly accessed by other white middle-class young people. Over half of our middle-class parents sent their children to primary schools that came in the top third of the primary school league tables for their local education authorities. As a consequence most of the children in our sample arrived at multi-ethnic, class diverse secondary schooling from predominantly white middle-class primary schools. It was a minor-ity of families in the sample – and largely those from first generation middle-class backgrounds or those recently returned from living over-seas (mainly in London and Riverton) – whose children had been to primary schools as diverse as their secondary schools. Also the majority, from the data on young people over 16, seemed to be moving on to sixth form provision that was similarly predominantly white and middle-class. This was especially so in London where there was a trend towards children/young people moving into 'whiter', more middle-class spaces for FE and HE. This meant many did not retain beyond secondary school any mixed friendships they may have had. Frankie Cadogan (aged 18) admits to having a completely new set of friends now he is at a highly performing sixth form college in a gentrified London borough, and Fiona Richards (London), reflecting back on her educational trajectory which took her to Oxford, remembers sixth form as 'much whiter'.

Attending inner city comprehensives was on the whole seen to be a positive experience for the children/young people. As we saw in Chapter 5, a key element underpinning parents' anxieties stemming from having placed their children in an urban comprehensive is the anxiety of the undesirable, troublesome black and white working-class Other. The parents are intent upon distinguishing their children from these others and indeed their children are constructed in contrast to what they are not. The white working-class is often denigrated, and there tends to be a reluctance on the part of both parents and children to see anything of importance or of intrinsic value in white working-class culture. There is a strong sense of fear of contamination and also of what

Stephen Ball (2003 p. 114) calls a sense of 'other' families as not 'normal', as unintelligible in terms of 'our values, attitudes and behaviour'.

As well as the structural division in the organisation of the school which is strongly linked to class and 'racial'/ethnic stratification, parents and children pointed to overt differences marked out by cultural differences. In Norton and Riverton several parents described how their children's school was divided internally, between 'Chavs' or 'Charvs' and the groups that their own children belonged to. For example, white middle-class children at The Park School got called the 'Poshies' or the 'Hippies', with clear social class connotations (the term 'poshies' clearly denoting middle- or upper-classness, and 'hippies' having their roots in middle-class radicalism (Parkin 1968) or at least alternativism. Gemma Foster (age 13) explained how in her school in Riverton 'generally you stick to your own groups'. In a process of boundary making (Southerton 2002) children in Norton and Riverton were very keen to define themselves in opposition to the Charvers or Chavs, as one mother (Anne Downie, Norton) explained about her daughter, 'she's part of an interesting little [laughs] friendship group, who define themselves as non-Charvers.' As Holt and Griffin (2005) argue,

> Othering enables the middle classes to focus on aspects of their identities which they wish to hold up as defining their groups' characteristics (for example Middle class taste, intelligence, refinement), while denying these characteristics to the working class Other.
>
> (p. 248)

The othering of the 'Charvers' defined by their violence, bad behaviour, crass taste in clothing and lack of interest and ability in education served to set the white middle-class children apart as well behaved, with the 'right taste' and 'natural' educational ability.

Social class distinctions are important in most of the children's accounts of school experience and friendships, and were usually expressed, as Nayak (2006) has shown, via visible markers like style, accent, attitude and appearance.

> [...] while social class may rarely be discussed directly by young people it continues to be threaded through the daily fabric of their lives: it is stitched into codes of respect, accent, dress, music, bodily adornment and comportment. In short, the affective politics of class is a felt practice, tacitly understood and deeply internalised.
>
> (Nayak 2006 p. 828)

Terms like 'Chav', 'Charver' and 'Hippy' were common. However, many of the young people did wish to convey they knew that these sorts of generalisations were partial and inadequate for summing up the characteristics of others and in talking about this also displayed a certain discomfort:

Interviewer: So are Charvers working class would you say?

Not all of them, that's the thing. It's ... just as superficial as any other sort of classification like a hippy or a, you know like you can be, it doesn't matter what like class you're from, like anybody can be, I would say like the majority of people, the majority of Charvs probably are like sort of working class, but I wouldn't, I don't really like to say that cos it sounds stupid.

(Oliver Todd, 19 years, Norton)

Children in Riverton talked about Goths, and Chavs or Townies but most often they situated *themselves* outside any of these groupings. William Smart (aged 15 Riverton) elaborated how there are Chavs, but there were also:

... Jitters, Skaters, people who dress like Skaters but can't actually skate. And there was Indies and a few Emo's and a few Goths, but, yeah, it's changed a lot, there are a lot more Emo's. And a lot of the boys are Emo's.

There was some awareness of themselves as marginalised in all three locales but for these children whilst this may have been discomfiting it had no significant impact on their school experience. To deal with this they most often when necessary developed different personas for in and out of school, including the use of different accents in different settings:

Um well I still say I sound posh in comparison to some people, but we're not labelled as that any more, cos we've kind of blended with other groups from our form.

(Lucy Gordon, 14 years, Norton)

Or else they created their own distinctive groups:

Well me and my friends would often refer to other people as Chavs in their groups and they would call us something like Jitters I guess although we didn't particularly think of ourselves as that, we didn't really know where we fitted in so I guess my group of people were the people that we weren't, we didn't fit in, in any of the other groups so we were kind of like the odd ones and most of us were from the same backgrounds, we were just quite different I guess. So we didn't fit in and we made our own group I guess.

(Laila Bailey, 15 years, Riverton)

In some cases they sought to transcend such classifications and asserted their individual or even unique identities compared to the majority. Todd Western (aged 19, London), at a coeducational school which had 90 per cent Asian pupils, told us:

Well I got into heavy metal and stuff but no one else at the school listened to it, that I knew of, and *so I always felt a bit out of place there*. I mean it wasn't like they all excluded me or anything to be honest; I wasn't like forced out of any groups or anything, everyone still talked to me. I was quite happy to go off on my own really. In terms of having friends there- most of my friends that I ended up with were outside the school.

(Emphasis added)

When asked more explicitly about class and ethnicity, he replied:

Well ethnicity doesn't bother me at all but most of my people who are into what I'm into are white.

Another boy, Frankie Cadogan (aged 18) who had moved school to a sixth Form college across the other side of London, also talked about his own difference from the other(s). He talked about the school being predominantly working-class, with a large Bengali population and he reflected:

I think everyone was just sort of different [to me] everyone was from [the immediate local area] and was just sort of into different stuff and I was going up to Camden and there were some people who hadn't really left [the immediate local area] in their life.

The percentage of BME children in schools which differed dramatically within and across the three cities appears to have a strong effect on children's sense of themselves in the world. In schools with a small proportion of BME children it is as if ethnicity is invisible. We find little of Fortier's (2007) 'intimacy of multiculturalism' and young people giving up aspects of originary habitus in order to identify with classed and raced Others. More often distance is maintained:

> It is really difficult because I think in some ways it is quite idealistic to say that every like school should have a perfect mixture of different classes and different races. I think it does cause problems. I don't think by sticking lots of different people together in one place it doesn't get rid of the difference it just intensifies the conflict. I think it just makes, I think people from like unfortunate backgrounds, I don't think they appreciate having other people that have come from more privileged backgrounds. I don't think they think 'oh that's really good of them to come and mix with us' I think it is almost as if it is rubbed in their faces.
>
> (Jemma Johnson, 20 years, London)

Jemma Johnson's experience and viewpoint represents a direct challenge to the strong parental expectations placed upon social mix in the secondary school, illustrated by so much of our data and discussed earlier in the book. Rather than the benign positive influence of social mix we glimpse here an antagonism engendered by close proximity.

Conclusion

The white middle-class parents are strong advocates for their children which in turn transmits a strong sense of entitlement, 'specialness' and with that a sense of superiority. At the same time there is evidence of the young people developing or trying to develop egalitarian perspectives and socially just frameworks for praxis. However, within the limits of the research, it is not possible to weigh up the degree of success that they had in this regard.

A dominant theme in our data is around disparagement of the working-class Other and the strong desire and strategic intent to separate themselves off from this group. The structure and organisation of the school in a number of cases (if not most) facilitates this to some extent and as the children get older that separation is increased. However, there is some evidence of children trying at least in terms of accent and or dialect to 'blend in' but this does not seem to be a major concern. The issue around boys' masculinity may be a concern for the boys but it would seem to be a greater concern for the parents. If they (the boys) (think they) have something to hide such as an interest in dance, then they hide it, but overall the white middle-class children set themselves apart and so it becomes less of an issue. The young people tend to have a very strong sense of themselves and part of that is a sense of superiority – superiority in terms of: academic achievement; family support; cultural attributes and tastes; and in terms of material wealth. Whilst they do get called names because they have the affective and cultural resources to counter the effect, these are not apparently significant events for them.

Whilst there were similarities in terms of classed experiences of school across the three locales, this was less the case with respect to their different ethnicised experiences. Here critical mass seemed to influence the young people's 'racial' awareness and reflectivity with more awareness being displayed in the London context. Positioning as a minority white middle-class child in a majority black or Asian school played out in particular ways in the school context; a number of young people variously described their experience as 'shocking though not necessarily in a bad way' to 'exciting' and 'revealing' as indicated in the experiences recounted earlier. However, it was rare for the young people to describe these relationships as friendships.

In terms of the overarching question of social reproduction the young people are clearly working through the kinds of developmental experiences that young people need to do and given the dissonant contexts within which they have to engage in that process they have an added challenge to cope with. Nevertheless there is evidence to suggest that in many cases the young people have interpellated (in the Althusserian sense) their parents' values and views on the urban comprehensive and their raced and classed peers. Perhaps this is an explanation for the seemingly limited evidence of teenage rebelliousness and ensured focused academic success which was intended for them.

8
Reinvigorating Democracy: Middle-Class Moralities in NeoLiberal Times

Introduction

This chapter examines the democratic possibilities that emanate from middle-class identities which are grounded in sociality and openness to difference. In what ways might these identities work against, and disrupt, normative views of what it means to be 'middle-class' at the beginning of the twenty-first century? In the US context Kahlenberg (2001 p. 62) argues that middle-class parents constitute powerful resources within state schools, intensely involved in their children's schooling, driving up standards and drawing in additional resources. For Kahlenberg middle-class parental involvement not only has a positive influence on their own children's educational experiences and achievements, it enhances the experience of all children in the school (p. 63). We interrogate Kahlenberg's assertion in the light of our own UK-based data. There is also an examination of the role of social mix in parents' understandings of, and levels of commitment to, notions of 'a common good', and the extent to which the idea of the school being an extension of the local community is valued but more importantly put into practice in their actions. While the focus is on processes of 'thinking and acting otherwise' in order to uncover some of the commitments and investments that might make for a renewed and reinvigorated democratic citizenry, what also emerges strongly are the difficulties of turning these commitments and investments into more equitable ways of interacting with class and ethnic others. The chapter explores some of the possible reasons why the translation of sentiments into practices is a real challenge for this left leaning, pro-welfare segment of the middle-classes, concurring with Cucchiara and Horvat (2009) that the benefits of middle-class parental involvement in disadvantaged inner city schooling are more limited than its proponents have argued. The wider political culture and discourses of neoliberalism that valorise competition, individualism and the market are seen to make it increasingly difficult to convert inclinations into actions, even for these white middle-classes who express a strong commitment to community and social mixing.

Civic engagement and moral ambivalence

White middle-class parents make up the vast majority of parent representatives on school governing bodies, and the parents we interviewed were heavily involved in school governance. In 58 per cent of the London families (36 out of 62 families) at least one parent was currently serving or had served as a school governor. There were 11 chairs of governors (these were all secondary apart from a mother who was chair at a primary school). Of the 20 primary school governors 75 per cent were mothers. Of the 23 secondary governors 61 per cent (14) were mothers. The figures in Norton and Riverton were lower, as was the proportion of mothers, though still unexpectedly high. In Norton 22 per cent of families had a parent who was a school governor, and of these nine parents, four were mothers and five were fathers. In Riverton 43 per cent (13 out of 30 families) had a parent who was a school governor, of whom seven were mothers and six fathers. For a majority of these families becoming a school governor was rooted in a desire to make a civic contribution, and it demonstrated a commitment to the wider community. However, it also very clearly constituted an additional way of managing the risks in sending children to inner city state schooling. Other than being a governor there was little civic engagement across the sample, despite nearly all the parents describing themselves as politically left of centre. London had the most politically active parents (22 per cent), including three Labour party activists, a chair of the local neighbourhood society and a couple who were campaigning against a local Academy. But for the most part civic engagement and activism lay in the parents' past histories, and many talked about their disillusionment with politics, and in particular, New Labour, although almost all talked about their commitment to the welfare state. We would argue that this pervasive sense of activism as 'a thing of the past' is an indication of the ways in which neoliberalism has worked to 'incorporate, co-opt, constrain and deplete activism' (Bondi and Laurie 2005 p. 2).

Across all three locales the parents held broadly 'Centre-Left' and 'Green' positions. In the face of the primacy ascribed to the market by New Labour, the fervour with which communitarian ideals were once pursued by the parents had mostly given way to pragmatism and pessimism about the possibilities of political action. There was little evidence of the high levels of social responsibility that Etzioni (1993) argues are essential for communitarianism to thrive. However, this is not to posit some kind of loss of moral bearings. Most of the parents worked as public sector professionals, and they sometimes cited beliefs about their work in a general support for public sector institutions. But rather than expressing recognisably political positions in relation to public sector provision, support for state education tended to be voiced in terms of individual morality and what was ethically desirable, and in terms of what sorts of people their children would become (see Crozier et al. 2008 p. 265). We saw a good example of this was the quote from Audrey (Norton) in Chapter 2.

While there was a wide spectrum of civic engagement across the sample there was a significant minority of white middle-class families, predominantly in London, who demonstrated a strong 'vocabulary of association' (Jordan et al. 1994 p. 43). Jordan and colleagues describe those who, despite the ascendancy of individualism and imperatives to make something of oneself, still give a high priority to the public life of participation, membership, community and democracy. These families had a commitment to a local community that was broader than 'people like them' and they expressed strong views that it should be the focus of civic responsibility with local schooling as a key community project. For this group comprehensive schooling was strongly valued as an opportunity to put democratic, civic values into practice as well as for the related identity-work it can perform. They saw schools as central to community-building, viewing them, as Etzioni advocates, as places where children should learn responsibilities to the common good. Avril Smart, a journalist in the London sample, put it like this:

> There is definitely something about producing a different kind of middle-class child. Comprehensives are all about producing a different kind of middle-class child...We didn't want our girls to think they were superior to other children who didn't have their advantages...There was no way we would have sent them anywhere else.

However, for the majority of the parents there was more provisionality than this, and the happiness of their children was deemed paramount. Their commitment to local comprehensive schooling was conditional on the individual educational success and emotional well-being of their children: As Isabel Webb in Norton said:

> We've wrung our hands and still do about whether we should send them private... We'd have buried all our, all our socialist principles [laughs]. If you, you know, if um you ask John that's the one thing that he would ban, private schools.

Similarly for Elaine Booth in Riverton:

> Everyone has a right to be a hypocrite for their children, 'cos whatever your politics you just... when it comes to your children, you just have to do what's right for them, and that's what I did.

The ambivalence and provisionality expressed by Isabel and Elaine was much more common than the unconditional commitment of Avril. In the rest of the chapter we look at the sample in terms of this division between the 'brave few' who express few qualms about their commitment to comprehensive schooling and the 'more fearful majority' who are still on some levels 'hedging their bets'. But first we explore the wider political landscape in general, and the neoliberal discourses in particular, that have led to the withering away of democracy and politics, and a diminishing of the public sector.

Neoliberal subjects?

We can find some of the reasons for the fearful retreat of the white middle-classes from the public sector in the wider social and economic context. The contemporary cultures of individualisation and privatisation have eroded commitments and investments in the public sphere. The last three decades have seen the evaporation of a strong public sector ethos under sustained political attack, first by Thatcherism and, more recently, under New Labour (Hutton 2010). Furthermore, the reduction of graduate jobs at the same time as the rapid expansion of higher education has resulted in middle-class anxiety and a loss of certainty. In addition, the growing gap between the rich and the poor has exacerbated class divisions and increased mistrust and fear of the classed and racialised 'other'. Local democracy and civic engagement, particularly in our inner cities, is becoming increasingly elusive as state centralisation continues apace and local power becomes vested more and more in the hands of a small privileged minority. Teresa Caldeira

(2005 p. 335) argues that 'among the conditions for democracy is that people acknowledge those from different social groups as co-citizens, that is, as people with similar rights'. But that recognition is probably less characteristic of the white middle-class majority in the 2010s than it was 50, even 100 years ago (Szreter 2006), and appears to have diminished over the last 40 years as egalitarian and more inclusive perspectives on social differences, and especially class differences, have faded in the onslaught of neoliberalism (Bourdieu 1998).

In Chapter 4 we explored the impact of neoliberalism on notions of choice. It is also important to trace the consequences of neoliberalism for public sector education. As Nick Stevenson (2008) emphasises, neoliberalism is a profoundly educative project that seeks to produce flexible, consuming, enterprising individuals. It is concerned not simply with structural features of society but with the making and remaking of cultural practices and understandings in ways which centre the individual and sideline society. A growing culture of marketised self-improvement has marginalised wider concerns with the needs of others or more civic responsibilities. The neoliberal culture of hyper-individualism has resulted in a prioritising of the self at the expense of care for others (Elliott and Lemert 2006). But more important for the families in our study it is increasingly the dominant lens through which their actions are viewed; one in which the responsible committed solidarity of parents like Avril is viewed either as reactionary passivity or the wilful selfish prioritising of individual principles over children's best interests. In contrast, the more calculated provisional preferences of parents like Isabel are valorised as part of active entrepreneurship in which 'individuals are encouraged to strive to optimise their own quality of life and that of their families' (Miller and Rose 2008 p. 79).

Although the families in our sample are amongst those middle-classes most resistant to dominant discourses of neoliberalism, even the bravest amongst them never entirely escape the reach of these discourses. As noted above, neoliberalism is a profoundly educative project concerned as much with the transformation of individuals' sense of self and civic identities as with the economy. At the same time, in relation to the economy, those aspects of government that welfare construed as political responsibilities are transformed into commodified forms and regulated by market principles (Miller and Rose 2008). Neoliberalism positions all subjects as active individuals eager to better themselves in the market. Active entrepreneurship, in which individuals are urged to optimise their own quality of life and that of their families, is juxtaposed to what is perceived to be the inertia and dependency of responsible solidarity. Obligations to others outside the immediate family become peripheral within neoliberal agendas. Rather, there has been the steady growth in 'amoral familism' (Rodger 2003), the tendency to feel accountable only for yourself and those in your immediate circle.

When we focus specifically on the impact of neoliberalism within the field of education, we are faced with the centrality of targets, marketisation and the 'choice and voice' of enterprising individuals (Justesen 2002; Miliband 2006). Neoliberal policy creates a 'market' in which there is competition between schools, and the most significant indicator of market position is the percentage of higher-level examination passes at the end of compulsory schooling. Some 'consumers' take this at face-value, reading off impressions of educational quality or even using the information to make some estimate of the chances of their own children achieving certain academic credentials. Others view the picture as too simplistic, instead reading into the situation a much more complex engagement. In the case of the counter-intuitive choosers in our study, there is relative confidence that their own children are likely to do well, coupled with the widespread rejection of league tables as indicating anything useful about the quality of a school. This situation is inherently more complex than neoliberal accounts allow.

It has been argued that it is the middle-classes who provide the ideal individual for neoliberal times, the person for whom life can be a conscious reflexive project of the self and to whom it may seem plausible that, barring accidents, the individual is primarily the author of what befalls them. As Levitas put it, capitalism continually undermines equality, and those with relative advantage, with more capital (of any kind) are always in the best position to gain (Levitas 2005). Work by Robertson and Lauder (2001), Gewirtz (2001) and Ball (2003) illustrate, in different but overlapping ways, how the process of selecting and applying to schools 'favors middle-class families' (Hursh 2005 p. 8).

As we admitted in the introduction, we started out wondering (perhaps a little naively) if counter-intuitive school choices might be explained at the level of families as a political project, as a form of opposition to the well-embedded neoliberal assumptions underpinning an individualised subject as consumer of education. We wondered if there were community orientations that put the interests of the collective on a par with those of the individual. Similarly, we wondered if there were attempts at a personal level to try to reverse the shift noted by Hursh (2005) away from shared interests in respect of schooling in the United States and England.

Such questions meant it was important to find out about the families' ability to 'think otherwise' in civic terms, in particular, how the 125 families positioned themselves in relation to discourses of communitarianism. There were indeed some who drew on a strongly communitarian discourse characterised by a commitment to social justice and opposition to the marketisation of education. These parents would not contemplate selective or private schooling in any circumstances, expressed a total aversion to 'playing the market', and were strongly community orientated to relation to schooling and locality. For Etzioni (1993) a central underpinning of communitarianism is the balancing of self-advancement with investment in one's community and such a balance was prioritised by these families. However, a majority of the parents drew on weaker discourses of communitarianism, which, whilst supportive of comprehensive schooling, did not intrude on the securing and maintaining of advantage. For these parents commitment to comprehensives is conditional on ensuring their children's educational success. They may not be classic neoliberal subjects but like their more exclusivity-oriented middle-class counterparts choosing high-performing selective state or private schools, they are active agents seeking to maximise their own advantage with little consideration of the costs to less-advantaged others. In a contemporary culture in which education is subject to processes of commodification and economising, schools are increasingly seen in terms of risky investments, even by the left leaning parents in our sample. They become the educational equivalent of stocks and shares. And like the stock market they require vigilance and careful monitoring in order to maintain their value and ensure a profit. There is always the risk that their value may plummet, necessitating middle-class parents to pull out and find a safer educational investment that will still generate profits in terms of exam results.

The impossibility of cross-class community

We have discussed social mix more generally in Chapter 7. Here we explore social mix in relation to parents' desires for their children to be educated with children from different cultures, as part of a communitarian impulse. As we have seen in Chapter 3, it was common for parents in all three locales to draw on discourses of 'community' and multiculturalism when asked about their motivations for choosing the local comprehensive school. Many of the parents felt passionate about the need to produce well-rounded, tolerant individuals and they saw urban comprehensive schooling as making an important contribution to this process. They stressed a social and cultural fluency in which an active engagement with difference is signalled as a highly valued attribute:

> Part of why we chose the school was for social reasons. I think Guy's going to get a far better education going to the local comprehensive where he is going to be meeting and dealing with a complete range of children.
>
> (Gill Harrison, Riverton)

This positive value in comprehensive schooling emerges strongly in what Gavin and Deirdre say below. We also glimpse in their words more communitarian impulses, both a view of schools as central to community building (Etzioni 1993) and the desire to contribute something positive to the local school:

> If sending our kids to the local school can help that school continue its improvement and development and attract more middle class people to send their kids, then their kids can get a more rounded experience of where other kids come from and what their experiences are like and just a greater social mix.
>
> (Gavin Featherstone, Riverton)

> The school gives them this wonderful bond of popular culture that unites them you know for getting on with all types of people in all ways in the future. I don't think I could have given him a better education.
>
> (Deirdre Johansson, London)

This valuing of comprehensive education, particularly in the London context, is closely tied to a valorisation of multiculturalism. The parents are seeking schools with a wide social mix because they see value in their children being educated with children from different cultures. Attending comprehensives has a compensatory value, providing multicultural experiences that home life cannot. As Fred Drummond, a Norton parent explains:

> Because our local community isn't multiethnic, it's not part of our normal existence to be achieving the kind of intercultural mingling

that we should be doing. That, you know, would make the world a better place, whereas at The Park [the local comprehensive] it is.

Again we see in Fred's words a strong communitarian urge 'to make the world a better place'. But for many of the parents such communitarian impulses are in constant tension with neoliberal appropriating tendencies to better and enhance the self and generate a profit through contact with the other. As we have argued in Chapter 5, diversity, and ethnic diversity in particular, is viewed as a valuable asset. Relatedly, socially diverse comprehensives are seen as contributing an education that is much broader than the National Curriculum, one that gives children experiences of, and the ability to deal with, 'the wider world'.

For a majority of the parents, commitment to comprehensives is complicated. It is more than the straightforward enactment of communitarian principles because they also anticipate gains in terms of their children's cultural knowledge and social skills. The imperatives for self-advancement too often override 'a responsibility for the material and moral well-being of others' (Etzioni 1993 p. 264). As Burbules (2000 p. 256) argues:

> The framework within which multiculturalism often takes shape, a broad (and sometimes patronizing) 'tolerance' for difference, leaves dominant beliefs and values largely unquestioned – indeed even insulated from challenge and change – because they are shielded within the comforting self-conception of openness and inclusivity.

The children, attending socially mixed comprehensive schooling, are seen by their parents to be developing key citizenship skills of tolerance and understanding difference that are perceived to be increasingly vital in a global society. At the same time, a powerful theme, of the gains to be made from urban comprehensive schooling, also emerged from the interviews. This is hinted at in Deirdre's assertion of 'the marvellous advantage' accruing to her son from attending schools that, in Lorraine's words, make 'our kids more real'. In contrast to the 'solidary individualism' among the liberal middle-classes described by Berking (1996 p. 195), these parents seem to be pursuing 'an individualistic solidarity'. Neoliberalism may be configured slightly differently in their and their children's identity formation but it still seeps into the soul. While there is a strong commitment to (and valorisation of) multiculturalism across the families, this was underpinned by a strong sense of the benefits for their own children; of the gains to be made in encountering rich cultural diversity. And these benefits were primarily seen to come through contact with ethnic rather than classed others. Despite valuing a particular 'other' there is still enormous ambivalence about children connecting with or become allied with the working-class majority in the comprehensive schools they attend (Reay et al. 2007). As Ravaeud and van Zanten (2007 p. 117) found, while it appears unacceptable to attribute negative educational effects to the presence of minority ethnic children there are no such strictures on criticism directed at the working-classes. The paradox that Binnie et al. (2006) articulate between simultaneously embracing certain forms of difference whilst devalorising others is evident in the distinction many of the parents made between the desired ethnic and the feared working-class other (Reay et al. 2007). One consequence is a semi-detachedness from the working-classes despite sending their children to school with them. This was evident in what we saw Ross describing in Chapter 6 about the contrast between his comprehensive and the far more middle-class sixth form he moved on to.

In fact when these white middle-classes talked about the working-classes, rather than expressing empathy, they often conveyed an instrumentalising impulse; that to know about their classed 'other' was a useful resource for later life. Neoliberal appropriation is still powerfully in evidence. As we saw in Chapter 2, Audrey comments that her son's friends were exclusively white and middle-class, and goes on to assert in relation to the working-class children in his comprehensive school:

> He doesn't bring these children home but he knows they are there and he meets them in school and I know when he grows up and he's going to be a lawyer or a teacher or whatever at least he'll know where these people have come from.
>
> (Audrey Caisey, Norton)

Audrey echoes the semi-detachedness expressed by Ross. The 'at least' that Audrey qualifies her comment with is telling. The aim appears not to befriend and mix as equals with working-class others but rather to know them in appropriating ways that resource the self.

Despite an enthusiasm for comprehensive schooling among the families there was often ambivalence and anxiety about too close contact with working-class others:

> I have to say for me as great a fear was that my son would get in with the scrap metal dealer's son who was given everything from this age

and that he would think he should have that lifestyle as well when we wanted it to be balanced and even.

(Sheila Moss, Norton)

Although most parents did not display such overt feelings of fear of contamination, almost half referred to attending comprehensives as 'a toughening experience', the opportunity for their children to develop resilience and become 'worldly-wise'. These parents rationalise their choice of urban comprehensive as, in part, a matter of ensuring their children become used to operating in an unequal society. Clearly, this is a somewhat different concern to that of actually opposing inequalities. Rather, the ambition is more that children are to become inured to, and learn to cope with a socially unjust world.

So for the parents comprehensives are one of the best ways of preparing children for the 'real world', and here the contrast with private and selective schooling is apposite. In Chapter 2 we discussed the importance of private and selective schooling in family history, and how this could continue to function as a point of departure in current school choices. But for many of the parents, we also see strong contemporary aspirations for their children to acquire the type of appropriating knowledge that enables a process of capitalising on contact with the other, rather than prioritising empathetic connections. This is a clear case of neoliberal impulses trumping those of communitarianism. Their children are learning to know of and about the working-classes rather than to know them in a companionable, reciprocal way.

Invigorating democracy? A minority within a minority

Yet, as we have touched on at the beginning of this chapter there was also a countervailing discourse of public engagement. If we look firstly at contact with school governance, parental involvement was both complex and contradictory, and the parents' rationales reveal some of the ambiguities and ambivalences embedded in these families' relationships to their locality, and in particular, local schooling (Ball and Vincent 2007). For a majority becoming a school governor was as much an issue of developing insider knowledge as a desire to make a civic contribution. They thought they could intervene more effectively by becoming involved in their children's schooling:

I just thought a way to be attached to a school and know what is going on is to become a governor.

(Sandra Hayes, London)

Secondary schools tend to keep the parents at a distance, which again is why I've become a governor so I could actually find out a bit more what was going on.

(Jane Taylor, Riverton)

So I got to know the school very well and obviously got insider knowledge.

(Victoria Williamson, London)

For a majority of the parents then school governance became an additional way of managing the risks in sending children to inner city state schooling (Vincent 2000), a way of subjecting the school to surveillance as well as a means of supporting it. As Savage et al. (2005 p. 65) point out, such narratives of support have 'an edge of instrumentalism'. This 'edge of instrumentalism' is particularly powerful in Linda Quercy's account of being a school governor:

Well I thought if they're going to go there I need to find out what its like, I need to make a really informed decision so I became a governor, and I'm still a governor now I'm in my second term, erm and I was chair of governors and now vice chair... so I decided that I would get involved and become involved in their education. And I am now the ultimate busy body. I know almost every teacher in the school, I know exactly what's going on, erm I'm always in e-mail contact with the teachers like today for example I've e-mailed the head of Spanish. Hazel erm got a grade B in her mock and was predicted a grade B but she's only two marks away from an A so I'm saying can you please explain to me why you didn't predict her an A. Not saying 'how dare you' but I just want to know why. You know because she's now thinking about applying for De Veres school in Westborough, you have to have 6 As and so that A's gonna make a difference to her.

(Linda Quercy, London)

Here Linda makes explicit the individualised gains to be made from formal participation in governance of schooling.

However, as we pointed out earlier in the chapter, 16 of the white middle-class families possessed a strong 'vocabulary of association' (Jordan et al. 1994 p. 43). These families had a commitment to a local community that was broader than 'people like them' and expressed strong views that it should be the focus of civic responsibility with local schooling as a key community project:

We have each got the responsibility to get the best for our own children but not at the expense of abdicating the responsibility for the local community that we are a part of or whatever.

(David Johnson, London)

Going to the local comprehensive makes us part of the community and that is a slightly yucky thing but in a way I feel we are contributing to the community rather than withdrawing our children. I mean it's part of our general philosophy I'd definitely try to move them away from thinking they want jobs that have good money to jobs that have a benefit to society. Both Bill and I think it's important to put something back... or at least not harming people, I suppose.

(Sally Rouse, London)

We should all have equal access to good education and good health. I believe in that and I think that's what any government should be trying to do and not be trying to create areas or sort of separate, either wittingly or unwittingly, people in society, so that some people have better opportunities than others, or that you end up with situations where schools do end up on sort of tiers and you do end up with stupid league tables reflecting that, because some schools aren't getting a cross section of the community. Because people are being encouraged to think that they should choose something better, because what's there in the community isn't better, and it's a mindset. And I just feel that principles are important and that we should support things for the benefit of everyone as a whole. And I suppose they're the basic Socialist principles or whatever and I sometimes think perhaps we're terribly naïve and other times I think, no we're not, I think we're just really trying to hang on to a really good idea that has been beaten to death by successive policies over the years.

(Alice Featherstone, Riverton)

It gave me an opportunity to explain to her about life, about putting into the community that you are living in, not just getting the best for yourself and bugger everyone else. But actually giving and not just taking from society. That there is some value in trying to be a good person and part of that is giving back to the community you are part of and that includes your school and where you live and on both counts my kids are very privileged compared to other kids so it's even more important for them. Everything we believe in is about putting into your community and not taking from it, this encompasses everything we believe.

(Yvonne Scott, London)

If we explore how community is being envisaged in these four extracts, we can see ideas that emphasise notions of group solidarity, collective action and responsibility, all concepts that Burke and MacFarlane (2001 p. 71) argue lie at the 'root of socialism'. Such socialist values of community, solidarity and collective responsibility are further reinforced in Sally and Yvonne's priorities around 'giving back'. We are presented with a discourse that concentrates on citizenship obligation and the public good and we would argue notions of social justice that attempt to connect it to a coherent vision of the good society. The social practices these families endorse are those that contribute to community and benefit society. All the parents in these 16 families made strong statements about the imperative to invest in local state schooling. All expressed the view that education is fundamental to the sort of adults that children turn into. While only Patricia stated explicitly that 'if you pull the middle-classes out of state schooling society as a whole loses out', it was clear that there was a vital link between individual investment in inner city state schooling and collective gains. As Ian asserted, 'if your local school isn't good you bloody well make sure it's good'. In a similar vein the most upper-class parent in the sample (with parents firmly located in the aristocracy) commented, 'I just don't think you can talk about a real democracy if everybody is, almost secretly, is being educated according to their class background.' Perhaps the greatest contrast between these 16 families and the other 109 was that they held powerful political commitments grounded in a conception of 'the common good' (Etzioni 1993 p. 259) as an objective that still held value. We saw in Chapter 4 how Laura Franklin (Riverton) argued that 'comprehensive education truly only works if you close down your private education and everybody sends their child to the local catchment school.' Louise Naylor makes a similar point:

Everybody is only concerned with their own child, but if you could see the bigger picture, it doesn't work like that. If you're concerned about your own child, somebody else is disadvantaged.

(Louise Naylor, London)

The orientation here is one where a 'principle' is clearly articulated and fastidiously applied.

Threaded through the narratives of these families' relationships with their locality and local schooling is a powerful language of democracy and civic engagement. The possessive individualism is muted and in its place there is a rhetoric of community responsibility. We gain a strong sense of public values and a collectivist repertoire (Jordan et al. 1994) in which these parents attempt to link their choice of comprehensive schooling with discourses of democratic participation and active citizenship. Yet, even in these white middle-class narratives that profess the strongest commitment to the 'public' and civic values, we glimpse the same contradictions and confusion over how to translate social democratic discourses of collectivism and community into effective action as citizens that Jordan et al. (1994) found. Within those families with the strongest commitment to comprehensive education and community, children still mixed in almost exclusively middle-class, predominantly white social networks. Although all these parents were resolutely opposed to choice and markets within education and often asserted that real choice was a myth for most parents, they continued to accept 'the dominant principles of vision and division' (Bourdieu 2000 p. 143) within society. In fact it all seems even more difficult 15 years on from the period Jordan et al. were writing about. In a twenty-first-century society increasingly devoid of languages for creating visions of egalitarianism, civic and community responsibilities and 'giving back' (Reay 2002), even those white middle-class who combine the resources with the will to invigorate democracy seem to have little if any deliberate involvement in actions that would benefit less-advantaged others, despite sending their children to school with them. While most of the parents in the study were trying to act ethically or in accordance with a range of political beliefs normally associated with the Left (or for a few, Socialism), as we saw in Chapter 4, they nevertheless often presented a distinction between 'politics' and 'what is right for your child'. In this view 'politics' is positioned as superficial, while 'what is right for your child' is positioned as a more authentic expression of interest or concern. In this respect even this group of parents, despite their left-leaning, welfarist orientations and their strongly stated commitments, speak the neoliberal language of individualism and self-interest. As Andrew Sayer pessimistically concludes:

> Even actions which are not driven by struggle for advantage over others, indeed, even those that have egalitarian motives, are likely to be twisted by the field of class forces in ways which reproduce class hierarchy.
>
> (Sayer 2005 p. 169)

Yet, it is parents, such as the ones in our study, who offer a real prospect for a fairer educational system. As Richard Webber, director of a large statistical survey of school performance, argues, 'the best educational achievement for the largest number of pupils will be achieved by having a broad social mix of pupils in as many schools as possible' (Taylor 2006 pp. 1–2). Although our data and analysis show it is important not to confuse 'social mix' with 'social mixing', it remains the case that there are important democratic and communitarian possibilities of comprehensive schooling, where children of different class and ethnic cultures may actually mix and become friends. In Avril Smart's words:

> I think it is an understanding of others you can only have if you are sort of with them all the time. It is something to learn of other cultures, but to actually learn with other cultures, of other cultures, it is a completely different thing...and that can only come through comprehensive schooling.

Avril articulates strong democratic aspirations for her children and the possibilities of achieving these through comprehensive schooling. However, practices of attending the same schools as class and ethnic others whilst maintaining a safe distance from them amounts to a rather weak form of openness to difference. Common practices of setting and streaming as well as Gifted and Talented schemes enable the white middle-classes to cultivate distinction and maintain social distance from classed others even when they attend the same schools.

Conclusion

According to Kahlenberg, middle-class parents are particularly powerful advocates for, and assets to, state schools:

> Educated middle-class parents are more likely to be involved in their children's schools, to insist on high standards, to rid the school of bad teachers, and to ensure adequate resources (both public and private) -in effect to promote effective schools for their children.
>
> (Kahlenberg, 2001 p. 62)

He goes to argue that 'when parents volunteer in the classroom and participate in school activities, they raise the average achievement of all children in the school' (2001 p. 63). In other words, the benefits of a parent's involvement reach beyond her own child to benefit the *school and students as a whole.* Of course we found a few parents whose involvement fitted the model Kahlenberg describes. For example, Yvonne Scott and her husband John, both accomplished in drama and dance, worked every year with an entire year group to put on an end-of-year school play. However, such parents were a rarity. More often parents were engaged in practices of parental involvement similar to those Brantlinger (2003) and McGrath and Kuriloff (1999) describe in the US context. Both studies found white middle-class mothers tended to exclude parents from lower classes and tried to ensure that their children were involved in schemes that benefited them at the expense of other children.

There is a key distinction between the domain of the ethic of care (Fraser 1997) obtaining in relation to people who have a strong personal attachment or dependence and the domain of social justice. It is perfectly natural and understandable to make a distinction between the welfare of one's own children and those of others. In Honneth's terms (1995) they involve different kinds of recognition. It is important to acknowledge this care–justice distinction as legitimate and to distinguish it from the differential treatment of one's own class from other classes. However, this distinction (between the welfare of one's own children and that of others) is over-determined for most of the parents by attitudes and behaviours that make additional distinctions on class grounds.

Contemporary research examining middle-class relationships to the public sector indicates that normative middle-class practices are increasingly underpinned by elite separatism rather than public welfarism. Under neoliberalism a selfish individualism has become hegemonic among the white middle-classes, exacerbated by growing privatisation, consumerism and the market culture (Ball 2003; Brantlinger 2003). Our research focuses on those middle-classes who think and act otherwise in order to uncover some of the commitments and investments that might make for a renewed and reinvigorated democratic citizenry. The parents in the study stand out against normative white middle-class practices because, for the most part, they do not choose 'the best' schools for their children. Rather, they choose schools they feel are 'good enough'. It is this acceptance of 'good enough' that marks out these families from those who 'play the market'. They are choosing not to use their privilege as much as they might.

Yet, the data also reveal painful contradictions. The parents were caught within impossible tensions between being 'good neoliberal individualists' and their communitarian impulses. These two competing pressures work against each other discursively within wider society but also psychically within individuals as we have explored in Chapter 6. And just as neoliberalism has triumphed over socialist and more communitarian ways of living and relating in the United Kingdom and globally so, its hold on the individual, even those who struggle against its grip, remains powerful and dominant.

As a consequence, attempting to live and even foster egalitarian lifestyles in a society, which valorises competitive individualism, is both difficult, conflictual and tension laden (Sayer 2005). It is vital to recognise the relations of distance, power and conflict that living with difference is embedded in. As Anne-Marie Fortier (2007 p. 111) argues, 'the illusion of tolerance with multicultural intimacy is that power relations and conflicts will be somehow suspended through intimacy, and that the distance and hierarchy between those who tolerate and those who are tolerated will dissolve.' As our research demonstrates, living in the same neighbourhoods and going to school with class and ethnic others rarely dissolves distance and hierarchy. While a significant minority of the parents feel passionately about local community and comprehensive schooling with a strong sense (as one father asserted, those who are more privileged should be engaged in 'the giving back side of things'), giving back and a concern with civic renewal were not on the agenda of most of these white middle-class parents. While we have found a great deal of commitment we also found more troubling aspects of white middle-class investments in inner city comprehensives. There was more self-interest than altruism, and more superficial endorsement of social mix rather than commitment to social mixing. Like Stephen Ball (2003 p. 142) we found that 'there are lines to be drawn within social diversity and there are limits to community and social mixing'. Although this is far removed from the elitist and narrow version of citizenship of the socially isolationist, exclusive and excluding white middle-classes that both Butler and Giddens have written about, it is also a great distance from egalitarian notions of democratic citizenry.

Conclusion

What do we learn from these white middle-class parents? Clearly, there are partially realised goals, undercurrents of provisionality and surges of anxiety associated with against-the-grain choices of secondary school. But looking at the often pragmatic, sometimes conflictual aspirations of most of the parents in the sample, we also learn a great deal about the narrowness of mainstream white middle-class aspirations under neoliberalism, the failures, ignorance and short-falls of privilege. Despite their left-leaning, 'radical' inclinations, they, like the majority of middle-class parents, are motivated by the desire 'to make the most of the child' (Ball 2003 p. 25), and view them in terms of investments in and for the future. Theirs is a carefully monitored investment of human capital in educational stock that many of their middle-class peers have rejected as too risky. But the differences between mainstream middle-class practices and those of most of our sample are fairly superficial, and when we strip them away to focus on what lies beneath, the processes at play are similar. These parents are also playing the educational market, and capitalising on educational investments. While most would claim that they want a good education for all children, their actual social practices in the educational arena are still primarily about competition and trying to generate a greater profit than other parents. This paucity of aspiration comes as something of a surprise. The irony here is that it has traditionally been the white working-classes who have been judged for a paucity of aspirations: perhaps it is just that the circumscribed range of aspirations differs for different classes.

What the parents tell us appears particularly apposite in the aftermath of a series of scandals of sleaze and greed (in the United Kingdom in 2010). It has become increasingly evident that our political and economic elites are often ignorant of the lives and desires of ordinary people, perhaps whom they see as too ordinary to be worth knowing and understanding; their calculating and cynical self-interest is testimony to the long hegemony of the neoliberal moral vision (Marquand 2009; Hutton 2010). In contrast the parents in our study have a social reflexivity that their political 'betters' seem to lack. However, it remains one infused with difficult contradictions, in particular between a self-interested desire to know of their class and ethnic others that is in tension with a communitarian impulse to reach out and understand them. The political climate with an emphasis on individualism and competitiveness promotes a fear of falling (see for example Ehrenreich 1990) and serves to deter any such intentions. There is evidence of parents displaying a lack of knowledge of how to operationalise their 'communitarian impulses'. Some parents clearly stated that they wanted their children to mix with 'diverse' groups because they themselves had never done so and did not know how to do so. At the same time there is a constant concern of the impact of getting too close and embracing the Other. As we have argued this represents on the one hand an appropriating desire for control and advantage, and on the other an open receptivity that promises greater equality and valuing. The result is a profound paradox that lies at the heart of liberal white middle-class identity, in which, as Savage and his colleagues found (2005 p. 43), 'The celebration of diversity figures as a means of self-reinforcement, a form of self-congratulation for avoiding the narrowness of fixed lifestyles.'

In order to understand why even these parents, those who profess strong egalitarian commitments, still are not able to make equal and sustaining connections with, in particular, their class others, we have drawn on Lynn Layton's (2009) psychosocial account of the failure of accountability and empathy within American society. Layton argues that across American society there is a pervasive and profound failure. Firstly, a failure to take responsibility for things that individuals should be personally responsible for; secondly a failure in regard to societal responsibility. There are hints of this in the suggestions of some UK commentators that the recent public outrage at Members of Parliament's greed and self-interest in claiming expenses they were not entitled to might stem, in some measure, from a denial and dis-identification with their own self-interested acquisitiveness.

While in some ways these families reveal the long reach of the neoliberal tentacles, holding even these pro-welfare, left-leaning individuals largely in its sway, they also provide a glimmer of hope for a more complex and nuanced moral economy. Their narratives hold in tension difficult, contradictory strands, but we would argue that there is also evidence here of a burgeoning challenge to the neoliberal model of the unhindered, rationally calculated, pursuit of individual self-interest in free competitive markets. There is a strong recognition that many people are seriously disadvantaged by this model, though as we have already argued, there is little by way of articulation of what might be done about it (although see Hutton 2010).

The janus middle-classes

Our middle-class sample then are those middle-classes looking both ways; defensively inwards, to varying degrees deploying strategies for protecting their investments of capital and their children's futures, but also looking outwards, towards otherness, tentatively recognising a value in difference that is more than just tokenistic. It is the second of these effects where hope for the future might lie. Consistently both Conservative and Labour Governments have foregrounded the role of parents in relation to schools in terms of implementing their respective market policies, by monitoring teachers as well as the children (see for example Crozier 1998). Also as we have reported here schools liked (and as could be argued, needed) middle-class parents. Such parents tend to bring with them forms of social, cultural and economic capital that help the children achieve within the status quo; thereby boosting the schools' league-table indicators. But despite (or perhaps because) of this, as soon as the middle-classes are involved, in whatever capacity, they do seem to dominate, and through their advantageous position they acquire more advantage, in this case for their children. This is a conundrum for policy aiming to address equality of opportunity, and for critical sociologists like ourselves. But just as the involvement of the middle-classes can have these negative effects on those less advantaged, their power and influence could be put to good use with a more equitable purpose. There are examples in our findings of a minority of parents organising and intervening to bring about school change for the good of all. There are others whose main concern was to improve a curriculum area such as music or art for their own children's benefit, but whose actions in effect benefitted a range of children. Such initiatives could be harnessed and more consciously exploited by schools and those concerned with their character.

Although the focus of our research was not on the schools themselves, it does appear to us that the schools have to take some responsibility in trying to balance the equality scales between parents. This responsibility could be realised through a number of positive action measures, which could include greater subtlety in decisions about which children bene-fit from the extra resources and opportunities presented by the Gifted and Talented Scheme. It could also include seeking school governors from a diverse range of backgrounds and introducing support strategies to increase familiarity with educational processes and to bolster confi-dence amongst some parents. Schools could choose to depart from the now ubiquitous but problematic subject setting that goes on in all sec-ondary schools for at least the core subjects of Mathematics, English and Science. Many schools could do more to utilise the skills, knowledge and other capitals of middle-class parents, as well as the funds of knowledge of all parents (Moll et al. 1992) in order to make that work for all of the children. Moreover, teachers are in a position to notice something of the lack of mixing in their schools, and it is possible that this knowledge could be used in finding ways to address class antagonisms.

This brings us back to the issues relating to citizenship which we have alluded to rather than developed throughout the book. We recognise that whilst we have referred to most of the parents as cosmopoli-tans in the sense presented by Beck (2000), we have not addressed the complexity of 'cosmopolitanism'. As many of the parents indi-cated, they see themselves as global citizens who embrace difference and diversity and more importantly desire these life enhancing, con-temporary experiences for their children. Consequently these parents travel internationally, taking holidays in exotic places and accumulat-ing the experiences of the more tangible aspects of diverse cultures (such as food, music, dress). This type of international cultural capital is increasingly important – perhaps essential – for the credibility of the cos-mopolitan. There are though different views on cosmopolitanism and globalisation and different values attached to both. Processes of glob-alisation have created a range of opportunities for some people, whilst reducing opportunities for others, throughout the world. Yet whether globalisation and cosmopolitanism are seen as a threat to national iden-tity or an enhancement of self-identity, neither can yet be associated with liberating oppressed and discriminated peoples. Likewise the cos-mopolitan citizen tends to be a privileged citizen. Beck describes it as an 'idea', but it is an idea which as we have seen people like to be associated with and embody. In this sense it becomes part of white middle-class identity. By contrast the white and black working-class par-ents and children – those hidden others in our study who attend the same schools as the white middle-class children – live in 'global' com-munities and engage and interact with the effects of globalisation on a daily basis. We do not think these experiences endow them with the same kind of symbolic capital that cosmopolitan citizenry probably does for the middle-classes.

Finally, conducting this research, and the analysis and writing that followed, has been a difficult, sometimes painful process. Many of the research team could be described as white, urban-dwelling first-generation middle-class. Researching the white middle-classes was often like holding up a mirror to the self. We were confronted with our own culpability, failings, conceits and self-deceptions. If, at times, the analysis appears too harsh a criticism of a social group who, to all intents and purposes, are making an effort to reach out across social differences when many are not, that is because we have had to engage simultaneously in a process of self-interrogation. In this project they (the left-wing, pro-welfare white middle-classes) are not 'the other', they are ourselves with all that brings in terms of desires, defendedness and attempts at dis-identification. We have come to see that the challenge for us as well as the middle-classes more generally is to create positive 'complexity and mutual attachment in cities that tend to difference rather than alterity, cities in which people withdraw behind the walls of difference' (Sennett 2005 p. 121). We too have turned inwards, spurning activism (although we would justify this by saying we were too busy – as do some of the sample of parents), and instead investing heavily in our own families. Our social circles, although not primarily academic ones, are still largely white and middle-class. Just as much as the participants in the research, we are stumbling, rather than moving purposefully, towards a different moral vision, a different way of being and relating. Conducting this research has illustrated the power and subtlety of education's role in the generation of social inequality, even where actions are motivated or justified by a desire to contest, oppose or mitigate such effects. Recognising our own centrality within the research has helped to reveal the overwhelming need for a different collective, moral vision, one rooted in reciprocity, care, mutual accountability and empathy.

Appendix 1
Methods and Methodology

The book is based on an analysis of data arising from an interpretative qualitative 30-month study which took place during 2004–2007. The study, entitled *Identities, Educational Choice and the White Urban Middle-Classes*, was funded by the Economic and Social Research Council (ESRC) (UK) (grant ref. RES-148-25-0023) and was part of the ESRC Identities and Social Action Programme directed by Professor Margaret Wetherell at the Open University (www.identities.org.uk/). The research took place in three cities in three different geographical areas. These were London, Riverton in the South West and Norton in the North East of England. 'Riverton' and 'Norton' are pseudonyms. Strictly speaking, Norton data are not confined to one city as we involved a few participants from beyond the city limits. We interviewed at least one parent from 125 white middle-class households who had chosen inner city comprehensive schooling: 181 parent interviews in total. In most cases we also gathered outline information about the remaining 69 parents. There were: 63 families in London, 30 in Riverton and 32 in Norton. We aimed to capture the diversity of middle-class identities and the consequences of these differences for dilemmas of choice. Therefore, those middle-class parents who 'work the educational system' by choosing and getting high-status comprehensive schools at the top of league tables (Ball 2003), a majority in both Ball's (2003) and Butler with Robson's (2003) samples, are only a small minority in our sample. Our main target group were middle-class parents who were seemingly committed to comprehensive schooling as an educational principle; those who deliberately eschewed a conventional 'working the system to their advantage'. Our main target group were middle-class parents who were seemingly committed to comprehensive schooling as an educational principle; those who deliberately eschewed a conventional 'working the system to their advantage'. At the time we carried out the fieldwork 80 per cent of the comprehensives the London families sent their children to were performing at or below the national average, while comparable figures were 83 per cent in Riverton and 50 per cent in Norton. However, these figures offer a conservative indication because they refer to the period in which we conducted our interviews, and many of the young people had left school by this time. Several of the schools had 'improved' over recent years in terms of where they sat on the indices that are conventionally used to compare them.

We interviewed 68 middle-class young people (39 young women and 29 young men) from our 125 households – 28 in London, 20 in Norton and 20 in Riverton. Forty-one of the young people were 18 or over at the time of the interview. They were interviewed in order to explore their identities and identifications and the extent to which these are constructed in accord with or against the orientations, commitments and dispositions of their parents.

We also collected rigorous demographic data. This was important because we were interested in exploring the extent to which the main sample could be mapped on to existing models of intra-middle-class differentiation (Savage et al. 1992; Power et al. 2003).

The data analysis drew on a number of conceptual approaches, including: contemporary adaptations of Bourdieu's social theory (Skeggs 1997, 2004; Grenfell and James 1998; Charlesworth 2000; Savage 2001; Ball 2003; Butler with Robson 2003; Reay et al. 2005); contemporary theorising on the experiential, moral and ethical dimensions of social class, in particular Andrew Sayer's (2005) work; and psycho-social approaches (Hollway and Jefferson 2000) that allow for an analysis of how anxieties are defended against by white middle-class parents investing in a different notion of 'the best' for their child to that of majority middle-class opinion. We also employed an approach to qualitative data analysis that was informed by grounded theory (e.g. Strauss and Corbin 1990) and by critique of grounded theory (e.g. Thomas and James 2006). An important aspect of the data analysis was that it was for the most part a collective process allowing refinement through constant comparison of examples. The issues, themes and patterns we have illustrated in this book are all products of this joint process.

The aims of the study were:

1. To contribute to contemporary theorising on social class that is extending the scope and analytical framework of social class through a close investigation of interests and identities.
2. To examine the identity work of white middle-class parents dealing with dilemmas of ethical choice, and the part played by gender and ethnicity in such identity work.
3. To investigate the impact on children's identities and identifications of parents appearing to act against self-interest and how their perspectives relate back to parents' self-perceptions.
4. To investigate the extent to which such identity work is related to a wider sense of identity and identification that transgresses contemporary notions of the middle-class self through an exploration of the psycho-social basis of principled choices.
5. To examine ethnographically tensions and affinities between familial and wider social interests and ideas of community and the common good among the middle-classes.

We used the Registrar General classification scheme (ONS/Rose and O'Reilly 2000) together with educational credentials (virtually all of our sample have at least one higher education qualification as detailed in Chapter 2) to identify households as middle-class. In addition, all members of our parental sample self-identified as middle-class. In London, access to just over half of our sample came through parents responding to a Guardian newspaper article about the research project which specified that its focus was the white middle-classes. In Riverton, six families contacted the team having seen the national press article. A further 12 responded to an approach via letters from schools, and the remaining 12 came through snowballing and personal contacts. As in Riverton, six of the Norton families contacted us after the national press article (plus a local press variant).

The remainder of the Norton sample came through one particular urban comprehensive school that sent out letters on our behalf (11), via personal contacts (7) and through snowballing (8). The families contacted through snowballing included a high proportion of medical professionals. It is worth mentioning that our approaches to several head teachers of 'low-performing' schools in Riverton and Norton, seeking their help in sending letters inviting participation, resulted in them telling us that their schools did not have any middle-class pupils.

We strove to include a number of fathers as well as mothers in our sample and we also ensured that there was a balance between families with daughters and those with sons. We wanted to explore the impact of gender on principled choices. While most interviews were conducted with one parent and this was most often the mother (64), five were with fathers alone, and 56 were conducted with both parents together. The children and young people were interviewed on their own or with a sibling.

We utilised a semi-structured in-depth interview technique, and the majority of interviews were conducted in the family home. The interviews covered the following areas:

Parents' interviews

- their own biography
- educational/career trajectory
- the choice-making process
- their children's experience of both primary and secondary school
- aspirations for their children
- values and opinions on education, the welfare state and politics

Children's interviews

- primary and secondary school experience
- the choice-making process
- friendships
- aspirations and values

Ethnographic interviewing practices (Brewer 2000) that allow for a mix of open-ended questioning and careful prompting and probing enabled us to elicit rich and reflexive data. Of particular importance were the educational biographies, not only because of the insights that the past can shed on the present, but also because they would help us to examine how far narratives of self and family accorded with collectivist commitments. Dilemmas of choice and ethical commitments are difficult, abstract areas to research that are also highly emotive which our methodology was designed to take into account. We followed, therefore, an adaptation of the biographical interpretative method outlined in Hollway and Jefferson (2000 p. 53) in order to elicit significant personal meanings and narratives of identity. The emphasis was thus on understanding participant meanings (Spradley 1979) but unlike Hollway and Jefferson we did use the 'why' question, albeit in a subtle and non-confrontational manner.

Gaining trust and establishing rapport are key elements in the qualitative interview process. The former is an obvious requirement with any type of research, but it is particularly important in personal experience research and when dealing with a topic that is emotive and which involves questions about personal histories and the revelation of political perspectives and personal values. The efficacy of this questioning placed great emphasis on us establishing rapport and empathy. According to Fontana and Frey (2000), 'the researcher must be able to take the role of the respondents and attempt to see the situation from their viewpoint rather than superimpose his or her world of academia and preconceptions upon them' (p. 655). At the same time it was important for us not to over identify with them and get drawn in to imposing our own views on to the research and the respondents.

As we had three research sites, much of the work was carried in three sub-groupings of the research team. In London, Diane worked with two half-time research assistants; David in Riverton and Gill in Norton both worked with a half-time research assistant each. All but one of the team members was white; all except one were women, though age and positions within universities varied. Also five of the team were parents: three with grown-up children; one with a child who was entering secondary school around the start of the project; and one with primary aged children. Two of the team had mixed-race children. All members of the research team can be described as middle-class, though with different types and degrees of class inheritance. Presentation of self in the interview situation is important and no doubt we each did this slightly differently depending on the circumstances but also our individual dispositions. Basically however, through adopting a feminist approach to interviewing and approaching the respondent as a subject, an individual, rather than an object (Reinharz 1992), we aimed to create an experience that was conducive to accessing the participants' stories. As Oakley (1981) has indicated, 'There is no intimacy without reciprocity' (p. 49). With respect to the parents they mostly seemed to identify with us as middle-class people – as people like them – who had empathy with their school choice decisions and would understand their dilemmas and at times difficulties. We used, perhaps at times unconsciously, the 'same' language and established shared meanings. We also followed and responded to respondents' ordering and phrasing (Hollway and Jefferson 2000) all of which facilitated the development of a trusting and comfortable relationship. Although accessing this section of middle-class parents was challenging, once we had made contact with our participants they were very helpful and accommodating with some people agreeing to be interviewed after a long day at work. Also in almost all cases they were happy for the interview to be recorded. It is worth noting that as with other aspects of the research process, we shared early interview transcripts in team meetings and acted as critical friends to weigh up the strengths and areas for further development in data collection. We also devoted team meeting time to refining aspects of the analysis.

Interviewing the children was in some cases characterised by a slightly more constrained relationship than that we were able to form with parents. However, as the transcripts testify, the young people were generally very self-confident and forthcoming. The majority of the interviews took place in the family home and whilst the parents were not in the room, we made sure that at least one parent was present nearby in the house. These interviews were also tape-recorded and transcribed.

All names of people, places and institutions have been anonymised and disguised where necessary and as much as possible. We use pseudonyms for everything except for London boroughs and London itself, where this would be less effective as a strategy.

Subsequently, some of us 'bumped into' a number of our participants at conferences where we were presenting our findings from this project and others contacted us on reading press reports of hearing mention of the research on media programmes of which there were several. These encounters were not always easy as some parents felt their intentions had been misrepresented, albeit unintentionally. Where it was requested or desired we sent them the complete research report so that they could get a better sense of our findings and contextualise the often-fragmented sound bites represented in the media. For most of us this kind of reaction from research participants was new, and it speaks of different power relations to those experienced in researching disadvantaged groups. It gave us further indications of the nature and extent of the kinds of social and cultural capital the families held and the confidence this inspired them with.

Undertaking personal experience research of this kind comes with significant responsibilities to the participants, to the research community and also to the funding body. It is of paramount importance that the data are handled with respect, ethically and productively. In this project the parents had entrusted their stories to us. It was our responsibility to achieve something useful from the research and hopefully make a contribution to positive change in some way (Crozier 2003). Whilst we utilise the parents' and young people's voices drawing on representative quotations from their transcripts, we do not use a 'tell it as it is approach' (Hollway and Jefferson 2000). Rather we have employed a robust interpretative approach to our analysis informed by the theoretical frameworks and the emerging themes grounded in the data set. We analysed the data within and between our three research teams, both vertically and horizontally within and across each family, each geographical location and across all three geographical areas. The purpose was to contextualise emerging issues and themes and to triangulate the data and test out emerging hypotheses (Strauss and Corbin 1990).

As interpretativists we reject the notion of objectivity and absolute truths. But through our systematic analyses we have arrived at as rigorous and reliable an account as we believe possible at this point in time. That is to say we recognise there could and no doubt will be other interpretations that could be made of our data, and we recognise the influence of our own perspectives and experiences upon the analysis. However, the strength of the analysis is evidenced by the process of triangulation of data and also the fact that the seven different researchers engaged critically in this challenging process. Each of us had to defend to each other our analysis/interpretation of the data. In terms of replicability in the traditional sense, we would argue that this does not apply to our research given its uniqueness in terms of the individual perspectives and experiences.

This brings us finally to the issue of generalisability, which is sometimes raised as a criticism of interpretive research. Notwithstanding our epistemological position outlined above, we also recognise and address in our analysis the situatedness of the personal within the policy and wider structural context and the impact of the structural on individual and collective actions. We also agree with Giddens (1976) that social and subjective action contributes to the reproduction of structures which in turn enable and constrain individual and collective action. In our analysis we develop theoretical ideas around white middle-class actions and behaviours and identity formations. Our participants are not representative of all white middle-class families, as we have demonstrated they are an unusual fraction of the white middle-classes in terms of their school choice practices and also demonstrate different class-related histories within that subset. Whilst our data set is quite substantial and located in three very different geographical areas, it is difficult to claim generalisability of this group of families as a type. Nevertheless, we believe there are concepts that have arisen from our findings that can probably be attributed in general terms to white middle-class families. One example would be our findings in relation to the white middle-class anxiety about the white working-class Other and the investment in processes which position the ethnic minorities as a symbolic buffer between themselves and the pathologised white working-classes.

Appendix 2
Parental Occupations and Sector

The data are shown as far as possible in mother/father pairs. Sector shown as 'Public', 'Private' or 'Third'.

Mother's occupation	Sector	Father's occupation	Sector
LONDON			
University Senior Lecturer	Public	University Principal Lecturer	Public
University Senior Lecturer	Public	Businessman	Private
Novelist	Public	Banker	Private
University Senior Lecturer	Private	Barrister	Private
Senior Civil Servant	Public	Barrister	Private
University Lecturer	Public	University Lecturer	Public
Data Analyst, Research Company	Private	Housing Officer	Public
Writer/Journalist	Private	Policy Analyst	Private
Consultant	Private	Banker	Private
Dancer/Choreographer	Private	Actor	Private
Teacher	Private	Trade Union Official	Public
Politician	Public	University Lecturer	Public
Teacher	Public	CSV Organiser & Teacher	Third
Primary Teacher	Public	Director of Special Needs Education	Public
Teacher	Public	Teacher	Public
Under-Fives Worker	Public	Shop Manager	Private
Educational Advisor	Public	Local Gov Worker	Public
Local Gov Officer	Public	Senior Master Independent School	Private
Further Education Lecturer	Public	Small business (translation & publishing)	Private
Solicitor for Consumer Council	Public	Government Solicitor	Public
School Bursar	Private	Investment Banker	Private
Freelance Special Needs Teacher	Public	Architect	Private
Journalist	Public	Journalist	Private
University Academic/TV producer	Private	(not known)	

School Librarian	Public	Photographer	Private
Freelance Translator	Public	Retired Accountant	Private
TV Producer	Private	Musician	Private
Senior Civil Servant	Public	Middle Manager	Private
Senior Civil Servant	Public	Charity Manager	Third
Teacher	Public	Local Government Manager	Public
Special Needs Teacher	Public	(not known)	
Journalist	Private	Media Business Director	Public
Nursery School Teacher	Public	Primary Teacher	Public
PA for Media Managing Director	Private	Media	Private
PhD Student & University Researcher	Public	Transport Planner	Public
Trade Union Organiser	Public	Trades Union Accountant	Public
Psychotherapist	Private	Computer Systems Consultant	Private
University Lecturer	Public	Television Repair Engineer	Private
Further Education Lecturer	Public	Solicitor	Private
University Researcher	Public	Self-Employed Web Designer	Private
Book Trade Administrator	Private	Director of IT, Health Service	Public
University Research Fellow	Public	Deputy Head Teacher	Public
Housing Association Employee	Public	Accountant	Private
PA for a political party	Public	Head of Public Affairs, Trades Union	Public
Sure Start/Home Start Co-ordinator	Public	University Lecturer	Public
PA for an engineering company	Private	Projects Manager Nat. charity	Third
University Administrator	Public	Retired Theatre Manager	Private
Librarian	Public	TV Journalist & Correspondent	Private
Psychotherapist	Private	Media Executive	Public
Director, NGO	Public	Investment Manager	Private
Librarian	Public	Bank Manager	Private
Picture Editor	Private	Senior Arts Manager	Public
Community Development Worker	Public	(not known)	
Social Worker	Public	Arts Journalist	Private
Project Manager for Social Enterprise	Third	Sports Journalist	Private
Financial Consultant	Private	Teacher	Public

(Continued)

Mother's occupation	Sector	Father's occupation	Sector
International Banking	Private	Fundraising Business Advisor	Private
Charity Worker	Third	Financial Journalist	Private
Clinical psychologist	Private	Journalist & Magazine Editor	Private
Accountant Local Government	Public	Management Consultant	Private
Head Teacher (retired) Primary	Public	Actor	Private
Director of NGO	Public	Photographer	Private
NORTON			
Primary Teacher	Public	General Practitioner	Public
University Academic	Public	Welfare Rights Officer	Public
Health Service Manager	Public	Manager, Electricity Company	Private
Mature Student		General Practitioner	Public
Manager Local Authority	Public	Owner of small business	Private
Mkt Research Manager in a University	Public	Teacher	Public
General Practitioner	Public	Teacher	Public
General Practitioner	Public	Arts Director	Public
General Practitioner	Public	University Academic	Public
Former Legal Secretary – not in paid employment		Lawyer PRIV	Private
University Academic	Public	Generalist Advice Worker	Public
Not in paid employment		Dentist	Public
Social Worker	Public	Manager Gov agency	Public
Not in paid employment		University Academic	Public
Health Worker	Public	Quant Surveyor	Private
Clinical Psychologist	Public	University Academic	Public
Accountant	Private	Manager Gov agency	Public
Nurse/Midwife/Volunteer	Third	Senior Health Researcher	Public
General Practitioner	Public	Not known	
Secondary Teacher	Public	Secondary Teacher	Public
Civil Service Manager	Public	Manager Local Authority	Public
Senior Clinician	Public	Senior Clinician	Public
Speech Therapist	Public	Civil Engineer	Private
Clinical Psychologist	Public	Clinical Psychologist	Public
Secondary Teacher	Public	Freelance Cameraman	Private
Manager Civil Service	Public	Not known	
IT manager, University	Public	University Researcher	Public
University Academic	Public	General Practitioner	Public
General Practitioner	Public	Bank Worker	Private
Arts Administrator	Public	Arts Director	Public

Senior Manager, health	Public	Nurse Tutor	Public
Deputy Head, Primary	Public	IT Technician Local Authority	Public

RIVERTON

Nurse	Public	Computing	Private
Physiotherapist	Public	Probation Officer	Public
Health Worker	Pub/Priv	Buildings Officer	Public
Teacher (early years)	Public	Non-professional in NHS	Public
Health Worker	Public	Freelance media	Pub/Priv
Teacher	Public	Teacher	Public
Practice Manager GP surgery	Public	Machine Operator	Private
Care Worker	Third	Teacher	Third
Bookkeeper	Private	Accountant	Private
Middle Manager in gov agency	Public	CEO for charity	Third
Health Worker	Public	Teacher	Public
Pharmacist	Private	Financial Consultant	Private
IT Manager	Private	Teacher	Public
Health Service Manager	Public	CEO, educational charity	Third
Primary Head	Public	Landscape Architect	Public
SEN specialist	Public	Not known	
University Academic	Public	University Academic	Public
Freelance Artist	Private	Training Consultant	Third
Local Authority (housing)	Public	University Academic	Public
(not known)		Television Producer/ Manager	Public
Primary Teacher	Public	Nurse	Public
FE College Schools Liaison Officer	Public	Connexions Manager	Public
Manager	Public	University Academic	Public
Middle Manager, health service	Public	Not known	
Education-out-of-school Service Manager	Public	Secondary Head	Public
Finance Manager	Public	University Academic	Public
Insurance Manager	Private	Teacher	Public
Not working		Prof Musician & Teacher	Priv/Third
Executive	Third	Not known	
University Marketing Manager	Public	Area Housing Manager	Public

Appendix 3
The Sample Families in Terms of ACORN Categories

Acorn Category	'RED' CATEGORIES						'ORANGE' CATEGORIES								'GREEN' CATEGORIES					Unknown
	1	9	13	14	15	16	6	7	18	19	20	25	21	39	37	38	45	55	56	
Norton N = 32	3	5	7				2				3		4	3			1			4
Percentage	9%	16%	19%				6%				9%		13%	6%			3%			13%
London N = 63		2	9	2	15	4			10	1	1		11	1	1	1		1	1	3
Percentage		3%	14%	3%	24%	6%			16%	2%	2%		17%	2%	2%	2%		2%	2%	5%
Riverton N = 30	1	1	10		2	1		1			1	11		2						
Percentage	3%	3%	33%		6%	3%		3%			3%	37%		6%						
Totals N = 125	4	8	26	2	17	5	2	1	10	1	5	11	15	6	1	1	1	1	1	7
Percentage (rounded up)	3%	6%	21%	2%	14%	4%	2%	1%	8%	1%	4%	9%	12%	5%	1%	1%	1%	1%	1%	6%
Grouped numbers and percentages	N = 62. (49.6%)						N = 51. (40.8%)								N = 5. (4%)					N = 7. (5.6%)

Note: Acorn Categories as described on the Acorn website: www.caci.co.uk. The categories provide indications of types of housing and demographic information about the residents.

'RED' categories

1. Very high income and education qualifications. High knowledge of current affairs and high number of couples with children. This type of postcode encompasses some of the most affluent people in the United Kingdom. They live in wealthy, high-status suburban and semi-rural neighbourhoods, particularly in the Home Counties. Most are highly qualified professionals, senior executives and business owners, often in their 40s and 50s. They tend to live in large detached houses with four or more bedrooms, many of which are owned outright.

9. High income, very high education, very high number of couples with children. Professionals often with older children. Homes are typically semi-detached.

13. Very high income, very high level education, very high number of couples with children. Well-off professionals and managerial occupations, large houses and converted flats. Some young singles starting their careers and some students.

14. High income; well-educated; professional and managerial. A mixture of couples, families and singles; more retired people than the national average. Low number of children. Suburban houses and apartments; prosperous neighbourhood.

15. Very high income, very high level of education and knowledge of current affairs current affairs. Low numbers of couples with children. Affluent urban professionals. They work in professional and senior managerial occupations. These people live in affluent urban areas, where large attractive houses have often been converted into flats. Whilst many do own their home, the proportion of rented accommodation is relatively high, where large attractive houses have often been converted into flats. Most residents are either young singles or couples. There are very few children and those there are tend to be under five, which suggests that young families move on from these areas.

16. Very high income and education. Low numbers of children. Prosperous professionals and managers. High levels of younger people (25–29). These young people live in urban areas in purpose built and converted flats. They are very highly qualified, and are making their way up the career ladder in the professions and managerial roles. Forty per cent of people live alone. There are also high numbers sharing larger properties. They are typically renting rather than buying, which reflects the more transient nature of these communities.

'ORANGE' categories

6. Medium income, very high level education and high numbers of couples with children. People tend to be older with older children. Houses are large and detached.

7. Medium income. High level of education. Medium income. Medium number of couples with children. Most households are older couples, although the number of single pensioners is also relatively high. Residents who do work tend to be in well-paid senior management and professional occupations, or work in agriculture. These people live in prosperous areas, often where tourism is important and holiday homes are popular. These are affluent people and they tend to live in detached homes with three or four bedrooms.

18. Young multi-ethnic communities found mainly in London. Medium income and good education. Most are professionals or in managerial jobs. Most people are between 20 and 30 years old and developing their Category careers. Very few children. Most are in rented accommodation. However, the area is very diverse and there are those living in Housing Association accommodation and some are unemployed.

19. Well-educated and with incomes well above average. A mixture of private renting and home ownership. Mainly younger people developing their careers.

20. Medium income. High levels of education. Low number of couples with children. Cosmopolitan professionals; shared accommodation or students. These are cosmopolitan areas of shared flats and bed-sits.

   Households tend to be young single people renting small one or two bedroom flats, which may be purpose built or converted. Around a third are student households. This is a fast changing environment with a high turnover of occupancy.

21. Medium income. Very high levels of education. Medium number of children. Singles and shared accommodation. Inner London and outer Metropolitan areas. White collar with high concentration of Minority Ethnic groups. High number of public sector workers.

25. Medium income. High levels of education. Low number of children. Often, many of the people who live in this sort of postcode will be white-collar singles or sharers living in terraces and flats. This type is a mixture of young professionals and students in prosperous provincial towns and cities.

39. Medium income and education. High number of children. Often, many of the people who live in this sort of postcode will be skilled older families living in terraces.

'GREEN' categories

37. Low income; characterised by high numbers of Asian families living in terraced housing and students sharing and first-time buyers. Tendency to overcrowded accommodation. Low levels of education and high unemployment.

38. Low-income Asian families and other minority ethnic groups. Also a minority of students. Low levels of education qualifications. High proportion of single (mainly mothers) parents.

45. Low income. Very low level of education qualifications. Medium number of children.

55. Low income. Densely populated characterised by young multi-ethnic population. Purpose built local authority housing estates and housing association property. Almost a quarter of African Caribbean families in this type of housing and also white low-income families. High numbers of single people including single pensioners, young people and single parents. A small proportion of students.

56. High percentage of purpose built blocks of flats. Large proportion of young multi-ethnic families. Large numbers of children many of whom live in single-parent households. High unemployment. Large numbers of students.

Notes

3   Habitus as a Sense of Place

1. ACORN is a website (www.caci.co.uk) which provides geodemographic information of the United Kingdom's population. It segments small neighbourhoods, postcodes or consumer households into 5 categories, 17 groups and 56
   types.
2. In the case of Norton when we accessed schools the only available data were
   2004; for Riverton and London the data relate to 2005.
3. For example, in 2004, 90 per cent of pupils at Mountvale Primary achieved the
   expected level 4 in English, 89 per cent in maths and 95 per cent in science.

7   Young People and the Urban Comprehensive: Remaking Cosmopolitan Citizens or Reproducing Hegemonic White Middle-Class Values?

1. We were unable to access more precise data regarding ethnic minority pupil
   intake either from the local authority or from the school itself. These details
   referred to here were indicated on the school website in the OFSTED report.

References

ACORN (2006) www.caci.co.uk (accessed August 2010).

Adams, M. (2006) 'Hybridizing habitus and reflexivity: Towards an understanding of contemporary identity', *Sociology* 40 (3): 511–528.

Adkins, L. (2003) 'Reflexivity: Freedom or habit of gender?', *Theory, Culture and Society* 20 (6): 21–42.

Ainscow, M., Crow, M., Dyson, A., Goldrick, S., Kerr, K., Lennie, C., Miles, S., Muijs, D. and Skyrme, J. (2007) *Equity in Education: New Directions*. Manchester: Centre for Equity in Education.

Allatt, P. (1996) 'Consuming schooling: Choice, commodity, gift and systems of exchange', in S. Edgell, K. Hetherington and A. Warde (eds), *Consumption Matters: The Production and Experience of Consumption*. Oxford: Blackwell.

Apple, M. (2003) 'Creating difference: Neo-liberalism, neo-conservatism and the politics of educational reform', in J. Freeman-Moir and A. Scott (eds), *Yesterday's Dreams: International and Critical Perspectives on Education and Social Class*. Christchurch, New Zealand: Canterbury University Press.

Apple, M. (2010) 'Global crises, social justice and education: An introduction', in M. Apple (ed.), *Global Crises, Social Justice and Education*. New York: Routledge, pp. 1–24.

Applebaum, B. (2005) 'In the name of morality: Moral responsibility, whiteness and social justice education', *Journal of Moral Education* 34 (3): 277–290.

Avineri, S. (1968) *The Social and Political Thought of Karl Marx*. Cambridge: Cambridge University Press.

Back, L. (2002) 'Guess who's coming to dinner? The political morality of investigating whiteness in the gray zone', in V. Ware and L. Back (eds), *Out of Whiteness: Color, Politics, and Culture*. Chicago, IL: The University of Chicago Press, pp. 33–59.

Bagguley, P. (1995) 'Middle class radicalism revisted', in T. Butler and M. Savage (eds), *Social Change and the Middle Classes*. London: Routledge, pp. 293–312.

Baker, S. and Brown, B. (2008) 'Habitus and homeland: Educational aspirations, family life and culture in autobiographical narratives of educational experience in rural Wales', *Sociologia Ruralis* 48 (1): 57–72.

Ball, S. J. (2003) *Class Strategies and the Educational Market: The Middle-Classes and Social Advantage*. London: RoutledgeFalmer.

Ball, S. J. (2008) *The Education Debate*. Bristol: The Policy Press.

Ball, S. J. and Vincent, C. (1998) 'I heard it on the grapevine: Hot knowledge and school choice', *British Journal of Sociology of Education* 19 (3): 377–400.

Ball, S. J. and Vincent, C. (2007) 'Education, class fractions and the local rules of spatial relations', *Urban Studies: Special Issue on the Geography of Education* 44 (7): 1175–1189.

Ball, S. J., Bowe, R. and Gewirtz, S. (1995) 'Circuits of schooling: A sociological exploration of parental choice of school in social class contexts', *Sociological Review* 43 (1): 52–78.

Ball, S. J., Bowe, R. and Gewirtz, S. (1996) 'School choice, social class and distinction: The realisation of social advantage in education', *Journal of Education Policy* 11 (1): 89–112.

Bamfield, L. and Horton, T. (2009) *Understanding Attitudes to Tackling Economic Inequality.* London: The Fabian Society with Joseph Rowntree.

Baumann, Z. (2001) *The Individualised Society.* Cambridge: Polity Press.

BBC (2008) 'More Parents Lie to Get Schools' *BBC News* online, 19 March 2008, Available at: http://news.bbc.co.uk/1/hi/education/7304588.stm (accessed June 2009).

Beck, U. (1992) *The Risk Society.* London: Sage.

Beck, U. (2000) 'The cosmopolitan perspective. Sociology in the second age of modernity', *British Journal of Sociology* 151: 79–106.

Beck, U. (2006) *Cosmopolitan Vision.* Cambridge: Polity Press.

Behreandt, D. (2007) 'Losing our way: Once the heart and soul of America, the middle class has recently endured mounting job losses and declining standards of living', *The New American* 25 June 2007, pp. 1–2.

Ben-Ner, A. and Putterman, L. (1998) 'Values and institutions in economic analyses', in A. Ben-Ner and L. Putterman (eds), *Economics, Values and Organizations.* Cambridge: Cambridge University Press, pp. 3–72.

Bennett, T., Savage, M., Silva, E., Warde, A., Gayo-Cal, M. and Wright, D. (2009) *Culture, Class, Distinction.* London: Routledge.

Berking, H. (1996) 'Solitary individualism: The moral impact of cultural modernisation in late modernity', in S. Lash, B. Szerszynski and B. Wynne (eds), *Risk, Environment and Modernity.* London: Routledge, pp. 189–202.

Bernstein, B. (1977) 'Class and pedagogies: Visible and invisible', in J. Karabel and A. H. Halsey (eds), *Power and Ideology in Education.* Oxford: Oxford University Press.

Bernstein, B. (1996) *Pedagogy, Symbolic Control and Identity.* London: Taylor and Francis.

Binnie, J., Holloway, J., Millington, S. and Young, C. (eds) (2006) *Cosmopolitan Urbanism.* London: Routledge.

Blanden, J. and Machin, S. (2007) *Recent Changes in Intergenerational Mobility in Britain.* London: School of Economics and The Sutton Trust.

Blanden, J., Gregg, P. and Machin, S. (2007) *Intergenerational Mobility in Europe and North America.* London: London School of Economics and The Sutton Trust.

Bollas, C. (1995) *Being a Character: Psychoanalysis and Personal Experience.* London: Routledge.

Bondi, L. and Laurie, N. (2005) 'Introduction: Working the spaces of neoliberal subjectivity', *Antipode* 37 (3): 401–494.

Bonnett, A. (1998) 'How the British working class became white: The symbolic (re)formation of racialised capitalism', *Journal of Historical Sociology* 11: 316–340.

Bottero, W. (2004) 'Class identities and the identity of class', *Sociology* 38 (5): 985–1003.

Boulton, P. and Coldron, J. (1996) 'Does the rhetoric work? Parental responses to new right policy assumptions', *British Journal of Education Studies* 44 (3): 296–306.

Bourdieu, P. (1977) *Outline of a Theory of Practice* (Nice, R. trans.). Cambridge: Cambidge University Press.

Bourdieu, P. (1984) *Distinction: A Social Critique of the Judgement of Taste*. London: Routledge.

Bourdieu, P. (1988) *Homo Academicus*. Cambridge: Polity Press.

Bourdieu, P. (1990) *The Logic of Practice*. Cambridge: Polity press.

Bourdieu, P. (1998) *Acts of Resistance: Against the New Myths of Our Time*. Cambridge: Polity Press.

Bourdieu, P. (1999) 'The contradictions of inheritance', in P. Bourdieu Alain Accardo et al. (eds), *Weight of the World: Social Suffering in Contemporary Society*. Cambridge: Polity Press, pp. 507–513.

Bourdieu, P. (2000) *Pascalian Meditations*. Cambridge: Polity Press.

Bourdieu, P. (2005) 'Habitus', in J. Hillier and E. Rooksby (eds), *Habitus: A Sense of Place*. Aldershot & Burlington: Ashgate Publishing.

Bourdieu, P. (2007) *Sketch for a Self-Analysis*. Cambridge: Polity Press.

Bourdieu, P. and Boltanski, L. (2000) 'Changes in social structure and changes in demand for education', in S. J. Ball (ed.), *Sociology of Education: Major Themes Volume 2*. London: RoutledgeFalmer.

Bradley, H. (2010) *State of Confusion: A Nation of In-deciders*, Report for CAKE and Confused.com.

Brantlinger, E. (2003) *Dividing Classes: How the Middle Class Negotiate and Rationalize School Advantage*. New York: RoutledgeFalmer.

Brewer, J. (2000) *Ethnography*. Buckingham: Open University Press.

Bridge, G. (2006) 'Perspectives on cultural capital and the neighbourhood', *Urban Studies* 43 (4): 719–730.

Brint, S. (1984) ' "New Class" and cumulative trends explanation of liberal political attitudes of professionals', *American Journal of Sociology* 11: 389–414.

Brodken, K. (2001) 'Comments on discourses of whiteness', *Journal of Linguistic Anthropology* 11 (1): 23–41.

Bruce-Biggs, B. (1979) 'An introduction to the idea of the new class', in B. Bruce-Biggs (ed.), *The New Class?* New York: Transaction Books, pp. 1–18.

Burbules, N. (2000) 'The limits of dialogue as a critical pedagogy', in P. Trifonas (ed.), *Revolutionary Pedagogies*. New York: Routledge.

Burke, M. and MacFarlane, R. (2001) 'Communities', in R. Pain, M. Burke, D. Fuller, J. Gough and R. MacFarlane (eds), *Introducing Social Geographies*. London: Arnold.

Butler, J. (1997) *The Psychic Life of Power*. Stanford, CA: Stanford University Press.

Butler, T. (1997) *Gentrification and the Middle Classes*. Aldershot: Ashgate.

Butler, T. and Hamnett, C. (2007) 'The geography of education: An introduction', *Urban Studies: Special Issue on the Geography of Education* 44 (7): 1161–1174.

Butler, T. and Hamnett, C. (2010) *Ethnicity, Class and Aspiration: Understanding London's New Eastend*. Cambridge: Polity Press.

Butler, T. with Robson, G. (2003) *London Calling: The Middle Classes and the Remaking of Inner London*. Oxford: Berg.

Byrne, B. (2006) *White Lives*. London: Routledge.

Caldeira, T. (2005) 'Fortified enclaves: The new urban segregation', in J. Lin and C. Mele (eds), *The Urban Sociology Reader*. London: Routledge.

Carey, J. (1992) *The Intellectuals and the Masses*. London: Faber and Faber.

Charlesworth, S. J. (2000) *A Phenomenology of Working Class Experience*. Cambridge: Cambridge University Press.

Chen, Y. (2004) *The Negotiation of Equality of Opportunity for Emergent Bilingual Children in English Mainstream Classes,* Unpublished PhD thesis Goldsmiths College, London.

Coleman, J. S., Campbell, E. Q., Hobson, C. J., McPartland, J., Mood, A. M. and Weinfeld, F. D. (1966) *Equality of Educational Opportunity.* Washington, D.C.: US Government Printing Office.

Collins, R. (1977) 'Functional and conflict theories in educational stratification', in J. Karabel and A. H. Halsey (eds), *Power and Ideology in Education.* Oxford and New York: Oxford University Press.

Connell, R. (2007) *Southern Theory: The Global Dynamics of Knowledge in Social Science.* Cambridge: Polity Press.

Cooper, A. (2000) 'The state of mind we are in', *Soundings* 15 (2–3): 118–138.

Crosland, A. (1956) *The Future of Socialism.* London: Jonathan Cape Ltd.

Crosland, A. (1962) *The Conservative Enemy.* London: Cape.

Crow, G. (2002) *Social Solidarities: Theories, Identities and Social Change.* Buckingham: Open University Press.

Crozier, G. (1998) 'Parents and schools: Partnership or surveillance?', *Journal of Educational Policy* 13 (1): 185–195.

Crozier, G. (2000) *Parents and Schools. Partners or Protagonists?* Stoke-on-Trent & Sterling, VA: Trentham Books.

Crozier, G. (2003) 'Researching black parents: Making sense of the role of the research and researcher', *Qualitative Researcher* 3 (1): 79–94.

Crozier, G., Reay, D. and James, D. (2007) White Middle Class Parents and Working Class Schools: Making It Work for their Children – the use and transmission of privilege. Paper presented at the European Research Network About Parents (ERNAPE) Conference, Nicosia, Cyprus August.

Crozier, G., Reay, D., James, D., Jamieson, F., Beedell, P., Hollingworth, S. and Williams, K. (2008) 'White middle class parents, identities, educational choice and the urban comprehensive school: Dilemmas, ambivalence and moral ambiguity', *British Journal of Sociology of Education* 29 (3): 261–272.

Cucchiara, M. and Horvat, E. (2009) 'Perils and promises: Middle-class parental involvement in urban schools', *American Educational Research Journal* 46: 974–1004.

Curry-Stevens, A. (2008) 'Building the case for the study of the middle class: Shifting our gaze from margins to center', *International Journal of Social Welfare* 17 (4): 379–389.

De Certeau, M. (1984) *The Practice of Everyday Life.* Berkeley & LA: University of California Press.

Dobbernack, J. (2010) 'Things fall apart: Social imaginaries and the politics of social cohesion', *Critical Policy Studies* 4 (2): 146–163.

Dowling, R. (2009) 'Geographies of identity: Landscapes of class', *Progress in Human Geography* 1: 1–7.

Du Bois-Raymond, M. (1998) ' "I don't want to commit myself yet": Young people's life concepts', *Journal of Youth Studies* 1 (1): 63–79.

Duncan, J. S. and Duncan, N. G. (2004) *Landscapes of Privilege: The Politics of the Aesthetic in an American Suburb.* New York: Routledge.

Duncan, N. (1999) *Sexual Bullying.* London: Routledge.

Dunleavy, P. (1980) *Urban Political Analysis: The Politics of Collective Consumption.* London: Macmillan.

Edwards, T., Fitz, J. and Whitty, G. (1989) *The State and Private Education: An Evaluation of the Assisted Places Scheme.* Basingstoke: Falmer Press.

Elliott, A. (2004) *Social Theory Since Freud: Traversing Social Imaginaries.* London: Routledge.

Elliott, A. and Lemert, C. (2006) *The New Individualism: The Emotional Costs of Globalisation.* London: Routledge.

Ehrenreich, B. (1990) *Fear of Falling: The Inner Life of the Middle Classes.* New York: HarperPerennial.

Erickson, B. (1996) 'Culture, class and connections', *American Journal of Sociology* 102: 217–251.

Etzioni, A. (1993) *The Spirit of Community: Rights, Responsibilities and the Communitarian Agenda.* New York: Crown Publishers.

Fontana, A. and Frey, J. H. (2000) 'The interview: From structured questions to negotiated text', in N. K. Denzin and Y. S. Lincoln (eds), *Handbook of Qualitative Research.* Second edition. London, Thousand Oaks & Delhi: Sage Publications.

Forsey, M., Davies, S. and Walford, G. (2008) 'The globalisation of school choice? An introduction to key issues and concerns', in M. Forsey, S. Davies and G. Walford (eds), *The Globalisation of School Choice?* Oxford: Symposium Books, pp. 9–25.

Fortier, A.-M. (2007) 'Too close for comfort: Loving thy neighbour and the management of multicultural intimacies', *Environment and Planning D: Society and Space* 25 (1): 104–119.

Foster, J. and Wolfson, M. (2010) 'Polarisation and the decline of the middle class: Canada and the US', *Journal of Economic Inequality* 8 (2): 247–273.

Francis, B. and Skelton, S. (2005) *Reassessing Gender and Achievement. Questioning Contemporary Key Debates.* Abingdon, Oxon and New York: Routledge.

Frankenberg, R. (ed.) (1997) *Displacing Whiteness: Essays in Social and Cultural Criticism.* Durham, NC: Duke University Press.

Fraser, N. (1997) *Justice Interruptus: Critical Reflections on the 'Postsocialist' Condition.* New York: Routledge.

Fraser, N. (2000) 'Rethinking recognition', *New Left Review* 3: 107–121.

Freeman-Moir, J. and Scott, A. (eds) (2003) *Yesterday's Dreams: International and Critical Perspectives on Education and Social Class.* Christchurch, New Zealand: Canterbury University Press.

Freud, S. (1940) *An Outline of Psychoanalysis. The Standard Edition of the Complete Psychological Works of Sigmund Freud*, Volume XXIII. New York: W. W. Norton & Co., Inc.

Gerwirtz, S., Ball, S. J. and Bowe, R. (1995) *Markets, Choice and Equity in Education.* Buckingham: Open University Press.

Gewirtz, S. (2001) 'Cloning the Blairs: New labour's programme for the re-socialization of working-class parents', *Journal of Education Policy* 16 (4): 365–378.

Gibbons, M. (2002) 'White trash: A class relevant scapegoat for the cultural elite', *Journal of Mundane Behaviour* 5 (1): 1–27.

Giddens, A. (1976) *New Rules of Sociological Method.* London: Hutchinson.

Giddens, A. (1991) *Modernity and Self-Identity.* Stanford: Stanford University Press.

Giddens, A. (1998) *The Third Way. The Renewal of Social Democracy.* Cambridge: Polity Press.

Giddens, A. (2000) *Runaway World: How Globalisation Is Reshaping Our Lives.* London: Routledge.

Giroux, H. A. (1999). 'Rewriting the discourse of racial identity: Toward a pedagogy and politics of whiteness', in C. Clark and J. O'Donnell (eds), *Becoming and Unbecoming White: Owning and Disowning a Racial Identity.* Westport, CT: Bergin & Garvey, pp. 224–252.

Goldthorpe, J. (2007) *On Sociology, Vol 2: Illustration and Retrospect.* Stanford: Stanford University Press.

Gouldner, A. (1979) *The Future of Intellectuals and the Rise of the Ruling Class.* London: Macmillan.

Grenfell, M. and James, D. (1998) *Bourdieu and Education: Acts of Practical Theory.* London: Falmer Press.

Gunn, S. and Bell, R. (2002) *Middle Classes: Their Rise and Sprawl.* London: Cassell & Co.

Hacker, J. S. (2006) *The Great Risk Shift.* New York: Oxford University Press.

Hage, G. (1998) *White Nation: Fantasies of White Supremacy in a Multicultural Society.* West Wickham: Pluto Press.

Hall, S. (1996) 'Who needs identity'?, in S. Hall and P. Du Gay (eds), *Questions of Cultural Identity.* London: Sage, pp. 1–17.

Halsey, A. H., Heath, A. F. and Ridge, J. M. (1980) *Origins and Destinations: Family, Class, and Education in Modern Britain.* London: Clarendon Press.

Hargreaves, D. (2009) 'Labouring to lead', in C. Chapman and H. Gunter (eds), *Radical Reforms: Perspectives on an Era of Educational Change.* London and New York: Routledge, pp. 14–27.

Harker, R. K. (1984) 'On reproduction, habitus and education', *British Journal of Sociology of Education* 5 (2): 117–127.

Harker, R. K. (1992) 'Cultural capital, education and power in New Zealand: An agenda for research', *New Zealand Sociology* 7 (1): 1–19.

Harker, R. K. and May, S. A. (1993) 'Code and habitus: Comparing the accounts of Bernstein and Bourdieu', *British Journal of Sociology of Education* 14 (2): 169–178.

Harvey, D. (1989) *The Condition of Postmodernity: An Enquiry into the Origins of Cultural Change.* Oxford: Basil Blackwell.

Harvey, D. (1993) 'From space to place and back again: Reflections on the condition of postmodernity', in J. Bird, J. Curtis, T. Putnam, G. Robertson and L. Ticker (eds), *Mapping the Futures: Local Cultures, Global Change.* London: Routledge, pp. 3–29.

Harvey, D. (2005) *A Brief History of Neoliberalism.* Oxford: Oxford University Press.

Harvey, M. (2008) 'Parents who cheat at school', *The Times* 29 April 2008. Available at: http://women.timesonline.co.uk/tol/life_and_style/women/families/article3840412.ece (accessed 10 June 2008).

Haylett, C. (2001) 'Illegitimate subjects? Abject whites, neoliberal modernisation and middle-class multiculturalism', *Environment and Planning D: Society and Space* 19 (3): 351–370.

Hey, H., Leonard, D., Daniels, H. and Smith, M. (1998) 'Boys' underachievement, special needs practices and questions of equity', in D. Epstein, J. Elwood, V. Hey, J. Maw (eds), *Failing Boys? Issues in Gender and Achievement.* London: Taylor and Francis.

Hill, M. (2004) *After Whiteness: Unmaking an American Majority.* New York: New York University Press.

Hillier, J. and Rooksby, E. (eds) (2005) *Habitus: A Sense of Place*. Aldershot & Burlington: Ashgate Publishing.

Hoggett, P. (2000) *Emotional Life and the Politics of Welfare*. London: Macmillan.

Hollway, W. (ed.) (2004) 'Psycho-social research', editorial. Special issue of *International Journal of Critical Psychology* 10: 1–4.

Hollway, W. and Jefferson, T. (2000) *Doing Qualitative Research Differently*. London: Sage.

Holt, M. and Griffin, C. (2005) 'Students versus locals: Young adults' constructions of the working-class other', *British Journal of Social Psychology* 44 (2) June: 241–267.

Honneth, A. (1995) *The Struggle for Recognition: The Moral Grammar of Social Conflicts*. Cambridge: Polity Press.

hooks, b. (1992) 'Representations of whiteness', in b. hooks (ed.), *Black Looks: Race and Representation*. London: Turnaround books.

hooks, b. (2000) *Where We Stand: Class Matters*. New York: Routledge.

House of Commons (1999) *A Century of Change: Trends in UK Statistics Since 1900* Research Paper 99/111, 21 December 1999, available at http://www.parliament. uk/commons/lib/research/rp99/rp99-111.pdf (accessed February 2010).

Hughes, C. (2007) 'The equality of social envies', *Sociology* 41 (2): 347–363.

Hursh, D. (2005) 'Neo-liberalism, markets and accountability: Transforming education and underpinning democracy in the US and England', *Policy Futures in Education* 3 (1): 3–15.

Hutton, W. (2010) *Them and Us: Changing Britain – Why We Need a Fair Society*. London: Little Brown.

James, D. and Beedell, P. (2009) 'Transgression for transition? White urban middle class families making and managing "against the grain" school choices', in K. Ecclestone, G. Biesta and M. Hughes (eds), *Transitions and Learning through the Lifecourse*. London and New York: Routledge, pp. 32–46.

James, D. and Biesta, G. J. J. (2007) *Improving Learning Cultures in Further Education*. London and New York: Routledge.

James, D. and Diment, K. (2003) 'Going underground? Learning and assessment in an ambiguous space', *Journal of Vocational Education and Training* [special issue on TLC project] 55 (4): 407–422.

James, D., Crozier, G., Reay, D., Beedell, P., Jamieson, F., Williams, K. and Hollingworth, S. (2009) 'White middle-class identity-work through "Against the Grain" school choices', in M. Wetherell (ed.), *Identity in the 21st Century: New Trends in Changing Times*. Basingstoke: Palgrave Macmillan.

James, D., Crozier, G., Reay, D., Beedell, P., Jamieson, F., Williams, K. and Hollingworth, S. (2010) 'Neoliberal policy and the meaning of counter-intuitive middle class school choices', *Current Sociology* 58 (4): 623–641.

James, O. (2008) *The Selfish Capitalist: Origins of Affluenza*. London: Vermillion.

Jenkins, R. (1992/2002) *Pierre Bourdieu*. London: Routledge.

Jordan, B., Redley, M. and James, S. (1994) *Putting the Family First*. London: University College Press.

Justesen, M. K. (2002) *Learning from Europe – the Dutch and Danish School Systems* London, Adam Smith Research Trust (accessed January 2006 – http/www. adamsmith.org/publications).

Kahlenberg, R. (2001) *All Together Now: Creating Middle Class Schools through Public School Choice*. New York: Brookings Institution Press.

Kalleberg, A. (2009) 'Precarious work, insecure workers: Employment relations in transition', *American Sociological Review* 7: 1–22.

Knox, P. (2005) 'Vulgaria: The re-enchantment of suburbia', *Opolis: An International Journal of Suburban and Metropolitan Studies* 1 (2): 33–46.

Lamont, M. (1987) *Money, Morals and Manners: The Culture of the French and American Upper Middle Class*. Chicago, IL: The University of Chicago Press.

Lansley, S. (2009) 'The unreported cause of the financial crisis is shrinking wages', *The Independent* Thursday, 12 November 2009.

Lareau, A. (2003) *Unequal Childhoods: Class, Race and Family Life*. Berkeley, CA: University of California Press.

Lasch, C. (1978) *Haven in a Heartless World: The Family Beseiged*. New York: Basic Books.

Lash, S. and Urry, J. (1987) *The End of Organised Capital*. Cambridge: Polity Books.

Lawler, S. (2005) 'Disgusted subjects: The making of middle-class identities', *Sociological Review* 3 (3): 429–446.

Layard, R. and Dunn, J. (2009) *A Good Childhood: Searching for Values in a Competitive Age*. London: Penguin.

Layton, L. (2004) 'A fork in the royal road: On "Defining" the unconscious and its stakes for social theory', *Psychoanalysis, Culture & Society* 9 (1): 33–51.

Layton, L. (2008) 'What divides the subject? Psychoanalytic reflections on subjectivity, subjection and resistance', *Subjectivity* 22: 60–72.

Layton, L. (2009) 'Who's responsible? Our mutual implication in each other's suffering', *Psychoanalytic Dialogues* 19 (2): 105–120.

Lee, D. and Newby, H. (1983) *The Problem of Sociology: An Introduction to the Discipline*. London: Hutchinson.

Leonardo, Z. (2004) 'The souls of white folks', in D. Gillborn and G. Ladson-Billings (eds), *Multicultural Education*. London and New York: RoutledgeFalmer.

Levitas, R. (2005) *The Inclusive Society? Social Exclusion and New Labour*. Basingstoke: Palgrave Macmillan.

Ley, D. (1996) *The New Middle Class and the Remaking of the Central City*. Oxford: Oxford University Press.

Lipsitz, G. (1998) *The Possessive Investment in Whiteness: How White People Profit from Identity Politics*. Philadelphia, PA: Temple University Press.

Lockwood, D. (1995) 'Marking out the middle class(es)', in T. Butler and M. Savage (eds), *Social Change and the Middle Classes*. London: Routledge, pp. 1–14.

Lucey, H., Melody, J. and Walkerdine, V. (2003) 'Developing a psycho-social method in one longitudinal study', *International Journal of Social Research Methodology* 6 (3): 279–284.

Mahony, P. (1998) 'Girls will be girls and boys will be first', in J. Elwood, D. Epstein, V. Hey and J. Maw (eds), *Failing Boys? Issues in Gender and Achievement*. Buckingham: Open University Press.

Mansell, W. and Curtis, P. (2009) 'Segregation in schools fuelled by "white flight"', *The Guardian* Friday 10 July 2009.

Marquand, D. (2009) 'The moral economy can't be righted until we accept our own culpability', *The Guardian* 26 May 2009.

Martin, A. (2010) 'One pupil in five is given paid tuition as competitive parents fork out', *Daily Mail* 21 June 2010.

Massey, D. (1994) *Space, Place and Gender*. Cambridge: Polity Press.

Maxwell, C. and Aggleton, P. (2010) 'The bubble of privilege. Young, privately educated women talk about social class', *British Journal of Sociology of Education* 31 (1): 3–15.

May, J. (1996) 'Globalization and the politics of place: Place and identity in an inner London neighbourhood', *Transactions of the Institute of British Geographers* 21 (1): 194–215.

Mayer, J. (1975) 'The lower middle class as historical problem', *Journal of Modern History* 47 (3): 409–436.

McLeod, J. and Yates, L. (2006) *Making Modern Lives: Subjectivity, Schooling and Social Change.* Albany, NY: State University of New York Press.

McGrath, D. and Kuriloff, P. (1999) ' "They're going to tear the doors off this place" upper middle class parental school involvement and the educational opportunities of other people's children', *Educational Policy* 13 (6): 603–629.

McLeod, J. and Yates, L. (2008) 'Class and the middle: Schooling, subjectivity and social formation', in L. Weis (ed.), *The Way Class Works: Readings on School, Family and the Economy.* New York: Routledge, pp. 347–362.

McNay, L. (2000) *Gender and Agency: Reconfiguring the Subject in Feminist and Social Theory.* Cambridge: Polity Press.

MacWhirter, I. (2008) 'Everything you want to know about the banking crisis', *The New Statesman* 1 May 2008.

Melucci, A. (1996) *Challenging Codes: Collective Action in the Information Age.* Cambridge: Cambridge University Press.

Miliband, D. (2006) 'Public services and public goods: Lessons for reform', Speech by the Rt Hon David Miliband MP at the National School of Governance conference, Queen Elizabeth II Conference Centre, London, 6 June 2006. See http://www.defra.gov.uk/corporate/ministers/speeches/david-miliband/dm060606.htm (accessed July 2006).

Miller, T. (1993) *The Well-Tempered Self: Citizenship, Culture and the Postmodern Self.* Baltimore, MD: Johns Hopkins University Press.

Miller, P. and Rose, N. (2008) *Governing the Present.* Cambridge: Polity Press.

Mills, C. (2008) 'Reproduction and transformation of inequalities in schooling: The transformative potential of the theoretical constructs of Bourdieu', *British Journal of Sociology of Education* 29 (1): 79–89.

Mishel, L., Bernstein, J. and Shierholz, H. (2009) *The State of Working America 2008/2009.* Ithaca, NY: ILR/Cornell University Press.

Moll, L., Amanti, C., Neff, D. and Gonzales, N. (1992) 'Funds of knowledge for teaching: Using a qualitative approach to connect homes and schools', *Theory into Practice* 31 (2): 131–141.

Mongon, D. and Chapman, C. (2009) 'New provisions of schooling', in C. Chapman and H. Gunter (eds), *Radical Reforms: Perspectives on an Era of Educational Change.* London and New York: Routledge.

Moore, R. (2004) *Education and Society.* Cambridge: Polity Press.

Mouffe, C. (2005) 'Which kind of public space for a democratic habitus?', in J. Hillier and E. Rooksby (eds), *Habitus: A Sense of Place.* Aldershot: Ashgate.

Nakayama, T. K. and Martin, J. (eds) (1997) *Whiteness: The Communication of Social Identity.* London: Sage Publications Ltd.

Nayak, A. (2003) *Race, Place and Globalization. Youth Cultures in a Changing World.* Oxford & New York: BERG.

Nayak, A. (2006) 'Displaced masculinities: Chavs, youth and class in post-industrial city', *Sociology* 40 (5): 813–831.

New York Times (2010) Barack Obama: An overview 2 September 2010 http://www.nytimes.com/info/presidency-of-barack-obama/.

Oakley, A. (1981) 'Interviewing women: A contradiction in terms', in H. Roberts (ed.), *Doing Feminist Research.* London: Routledge, pp. 30–61.

OECD (1994) *School: A Matter of Choice.* Paris: Organisation for Economic Cooperation and Development.

Olssen, M. (2004) 'Neoliberalism, globalisation, democracy: Challenges for education', *Globalisation, Societies and Education* 2 (2): 231–275.

Oria, A., Cardini, A., Stamou, E., Kolookitha, M., Vertigan, S., Ball, S. and Flores-Moreno, C. (2007) 'Urban education, the middle classes and their dilemmas of school choice', *Journal of Education Policy* 22 (1): 91–106.

Page, R. (2007) ' "Without a Song in Their Heart": New labour, the welfare state and the retreat from democratic socialism', *Journal of Social Policy* 36 (1): 19–37.

Parkin, F. (1968) *Middle Class Radicalism.* Manchester: Manchester University Press.

Parkin, F. (1979) *Marxism and Class Theory: A Bourgeois Critique.* London: Tavistock.

Pearmain, A. (2008) 'England and the national-popular', *Soundings* 15 (38): 89–103.

Perkin, H. (1989) *The Rise of Professional Society: England since 1880.* London: Routledge.

Perry, P. (2002) *Shades of White: White Kids and Racial Identities in High School.* Durham, NC: Duke University Press.

Peterson, R. and Kern, R. (1996) 'Changing highbrow taste: From snob to omnivore', *American Sociological Review* 61: 900–907.

Plank, D. N. and Sykes, G. (eds) (2003) *Choosing Choice: School Choice in International Perspective.* New York and London: Teachers College Press.

Platt, L. (2005) *Migration and Social Mobility: The Life Chances of Britain's Minority Ethnic Communities.* Joseph Rowntree Foundation.

Power, S. (2000) 'Educational pathways into the middle class(es)', *British Journal of Sociology of Education* 21 (2): 133–146.

Power, S., Edwards, T., Whitty, G. and Wigfall, V. (2003) *Education and the Middle Class.* Buckinghamshire: Open University Press.

Prout, A. (2000) 'Children's participation: Control and self-realisation in late modernity', *Children and Society* 14 (4): 304–315.

Putnam, R. D. (2000) *Bowling Alone: The Collapse and Revival of American Community.* London: Simon and Schuster.

Raisborough, J. and Adams, M. (2008) 'Mockery and morality in popular cultural representations of the white, working class', *Sociological Research Online.* Available at http://www.socresonline.org.uk/13/6/2.html (accessed 2 February 2010).

Raveaud, M. and van Zanten, A. (2007) 'Choosing the local school: Middle class parents' values and social and ethnic mix in London and Paris', *Journal of Education Policy* 2 (1): 107–124.

Razack, S. (ed.) (2002) *Race, Space and the Law: Unmapping a White Settler Society.* Toronto, ON: Between the Lines.

Reay, D. (1998a) 'Rethinking social class: Qualitative perspectives on gender and social class', *Sociology* 32 (2): 259–275.

Reay, D. (1998b) *Class Work: Mothers' Involvement in Their Children's Primary Schooling*. London: University College Press.

Reay, D. (2002) 'Class, authenticity and the transition to higher education for mature students', *Sociological Review* 50 (3): 396–416.

Reay, D. (2004) ' "Mostly Roughs and Toughs": Social class, race and representation in inner city schooling', *Sociology* 35 (4): 1005–1023.

Reay, D. (2005) 'Beyond consciousness?: The psychic landscape of social class', *Sociology* (special issue on social class) 39 (5): 911–928.

Reay, D. (2006) 'The zombie stalking English schools: Social class and educational inequality', *British Journal of Educational Studies* 54 (3): 288–307.

Reay, D. (2008) 'Psycho-social aspects of white middle-class identities: Desiring and defending against the class and ethnic "other" in urban multiethnic schooling', *Sociology* 42 (6): 1072–1088.

Reay, D. and Ball, S. (1998) ' "Making their minds up": Family dynamics of school choice', *British Educational Research Journal* 24 (4): 431–448.

Reay, D., David, M. E. and Ball, S. (2005) *Degrees of Choice: Social Class, Race and Gender in Higher Education*. Stoke-on-Trent: Trentham Books.

Reay, D., Hollingworth, S., Williams, K., Crozier, G., Jamieson, F., James, D. and Beedell, P. (2007) 'A darker shade of pale: Whiteness, the middle classes and multi-ethnic inner city schooling', *Sociology* 41 (6): 1041–1060.

Reinharz, S. (with L. Daidman) (1992) *Feminist Methods in Social Research*. Oxford: Oxford University Press.

Revill, G. (1993) 'Reading Rosehill: Community, identity and inner-city Derby', in M. Keith and S. Pile (eds), *Place and the Politics of Identity*. London: Routledge.

Ridge, M. (2005) 'Ethnic minority youngsters getting better jobs', *The Guardian* 14 November 2005, p. 13.

Robbins, D. (2006) *On Bourdieu, Education and Society*. Oxford: Bardwell Press.

Robertson, S. and Lauder, H. (2001) 'Restructuring the education/social class relation: A class choice?', in J. Furlong and R. Phillips (eds), *Education, Reform and the State: Twenty Five Years of Politics, Policy and Practice*. London: RoutledgeFalmer, pp. 222–236.

Rodger, J. (2003) 'Social solidarity, welfarism and post-emotionalism', *Journal of Social Policy* 32 (3): 403–421.

Roediger, D. (1994) *Towards the Abolition of Whiteness*. London: Verso.

Rose, D. and O'Reilly, K. (2000) *The ESRC Review of Government Social Classifications*. London: Office for National Statistics, and Swindon: Economic and Social Research Council.

Rose, N. (1989) *Governing the Soul: The Shaping of the Private Self*. London: Routledge.

Rose, N. (1998) *Inventing Our Selves: Psychology, Power and Personhood*. Cambridge: Cambridge University Press.

Rutherford, J. (2008) 'The culture of capitalism', *Soundings* 38: 8–18.

Ryan, J. (2006) 'Class in you: An exploration of some social class issues in psychotherapeutic work', *British Journal of Psychotherapy* 23 (1): 49–62.

Savage, M. (2000) *Class Analysis and Social Transformation*. Milton Keynes: Open University Press.

Savage, M. (2001) 'Ordinary, ambivalent and defensive: Class identities in the northwest of England', *Sociology* 35 (4): 875–892.

Savage, M. (2003) 'A new class paradigm?', *British Journal of Sociology of Education* 24 (4): 535–541.

Savage, M. (2010) 'The politics of elective belonging', Seminar paper presented to the Centre for Research and Intersectionalities, Roehampton University, 27 January.

Savage, M., Bagnall, G. and Longhurst, B. (2005) *Globalisation and Belonging*. London: Sage Publications Ltd.

Savage, M., Barlow, J., Dickens, P. and Fielding, A. J. (1992) *Property, Bureaucracy and Culture: Middle Class Formations in Contemporary Britain*. London: Routledge.

Sayer, A. (2005) *The Moral Significance of Class*. Cambridge: Cambridge University Press.

Seager, A. and Milner, M. (2006) 'Gap between the richest and poorest workers widens', *The Guardian* 3 October 2009, pp. 26–27.

Seed, J. (1992) 'From "middling sort" to middle class in late eighteenth and early nineteenth century England', in M. Bush (ed.), *Social Orders and Social Classes in Europe since 1500*. London: Longmans.

Sen, A. (1977) 'Rational fools: A critique of the behavioural foundations of economic theory', *Philosophy and Public Affairs* 6 (4): 317–344.

Sennett, R. (2005) 'Capitalism and the city: Globalisation, flexibility and indifference', in Y. Kazepov (ed.), *Cities of Europe, Changing Contexts, Local Arrangements and the Challenge to Urban Cohesion*. Oxford: Blackwell.

Sennett, R. and Cobb, J. (1973) *The Hidden Injuries of Class*. New York: Alfred A. Knopf.

Sibley, D. (1995) *Geographies of Exclusion*. London & New York: Routledge.

Skeggs, B. (1997) *Formations of Class and Gender*. London: Sage.

Skeggs, B. (2004) *Class, Self, Culture*. London: Routledge.

Skeggs, B. (2005) 'The making of class through visualising moral subject formation', *Sociology* 39 (5): 965–982.

Smith, S. (1981) 'A London suburb', in J. Barbera and W. McBrien (eds), *Me Again: Uncollected Writings of Stevie Smith*. London: Virago Press, 100–104.

Southerton, D. (2002) 'Boundaries of "Us" and "Them": Class, mobility and identification in a new town', *Sociology* 36 (1): 171–193.

Spradley, J. (1979) *The Ethnographic Interview*. New York: Holt, Rinehart and Winston.

Stallybrass, P. and White, A. (1986) *The Politics and Poetics of Transgression*. London: Methuen & Co.

Steinmetz, G. (2006) 'Bourdieu's disavowal of lacan: Psychoanalytic theory and the concepts of "Habitus" and "Symbolic Capital"', *Constellations* 13 (4): 445–464.

Stevenson, N. (2008) 'Living in "X Factor" Britain: Neo-liberalism and "Educated" Publics', *Soundings Class and Culture Debate* http://www.lwbooks.co.uk/journals/soundings/class_and_culture/stevenson.html (accessed 8 August 2010).

Strauss, A. and Corbin, J. (1990) *Basics of Qualitative Research, Grounded Theory Procedures and Techniques*. California and London: Sage Publications.

Szreter, S. (2006) *Health and Wealth: Studies in History and Policy.* New York: University of Rochester Press.

Tabb, W. (2002) *Unequal Partners: A Primer on Globalisation.* New York: The New Press.

Taunton Commission (1886) Report of the Royal Commission known as the *Schools Inquiry Report* Vol 1, London.

Tawney, R. (1931) *Equality.* London: Allen and Unwin.

Taylor, M. (2006) 'It's official: Class matters', *The Education Guardian* 28 February 2006, p. 2.

Thomas, G. and James, D. (2006) 'Reinventing grounded theory: Some questions about theory, ground and discovery', *British Educational Research Journal* 32 (6): 767–795.

Thompson, A. (2003) 'Tiffany, friend of people of colour: White investments in anti-racism', *International Journal of Qualitative Studies in Education* 16 (1): 7–29.

Thompson, F. (1982) *The Rise of Suburbia.* Leicester: Leicester University Press.

Thompson, J. B. (1991) 'Editor's introduction', in P. Bourdieu (ed.), *Language and Symbolic Power.* Cambridge: Polity, pp. 1–31.

Thrupp, M. (1999) *Schools Making a Difference: Let's be Realistic.* Buckingham: Open University Press.

Tomlinson, S. (2005a) 'Race, ethnicity and education under new labour', *Oxford Review of Education* 31 (1): 153–171.

Tomlinson, S. (2005b) *Education in a Post-Welfare Society.* Maidenhead: Open University Press.

Van Galen, J. (2007) 'Introduction', in J. Van Galen and G. Noblit (eds), *Late to Class: Social Class and Schooling in the New Economy.* New York: State University of New York Press, pp. 1–18.

Van Zanten, A. (2003) 'Middle-class parents and social mix in French urban schools: Reproduction and transformation of class relations in education', *International Studies in Sociology of Education* 13 (2): 107–123.

Vincent, C. (2000) *Including Parents? Education, Citizenship and Parental Agency.* Buckingham: Open University Press.

Vincent, C. and Ball, S. (2006) *Childcare Choice and Class Practices: Middle Class Parents and their Children.* London: Routledge.

Vincent, C. and Martin, J. (2002) 'Class, culture and agency: Researching parental voice', *Discourse: Studies in the Cultural Politics of Education* 23 (1): 108–127.

Vincent, C., Ball, S. and Kemp, S. (2004) 'The social geography of childcare: Making up the middle class child', *British Journal of Sociology of Education* 25 (2): 229–244.

Vincent, C., Braun, A., and Ball, S. J. (2008) 'Childcare, choice and social class', *Critical Social Policy* 28 (1): 5–26.

Walkerdine, V. and Lucey, H. (1989) *Democracy in the Kitchen.* London: Virago.

Wallace, M. and Hoyle, E. (2005) 'Towards effective management of a reformed teaching profession', paper presented to ESRC Teaching and Learning Research Programme thematic seminar series *Changing Teacher Roles, Identities and Professionalism*, Kings College, London, July. Available at http://www.kcl.ac.uk/content/1/c6/01/41/66/paper-wallace.pdf (accessed September 2006).

Warde, A., Tomlinson, M. and McMeekin, A. (2000) *Expanding Tastes? Cultural Omnivorousness and Social Change in the UK.* Manchester CRIC: University of Manchester.

Ware, V. and Back, L. (eds) (2002) *Out of Whiteness: Color, Politics, and Culture.* Chicago, IL: The University of Chicago Press.

Warren, J. and Twine, F. (1997) 'White Americans, the new minority?: Non-Blacks and the ever-expanding boundaries of Whiteness', *Journal of Black Studies* 28 (2): 200–218.

Watt, P. (2009) 'Living in an Oasis: Middle-class disaffiliation and selective belonging in an English suburb', *Environment and Planning A* 41: 2874–2892.

Webber, R. and Butler, T. (2007) 'Classifying pupils by where they live: How well does this predict variations in their GCSE results?', *Urban Studies* 44 (7): 1229–1254.

Weis, L. (1990) *Working Class Without Work: High School Students in a De-industrialising Economy.* New York: Routledge.

Weis, L. (2004) *Class Reunion: The Remaking of the American White Working Class.* New York: Routledge.

Weis, L. (ed.) (2008) *The Way Class Works: Readings on School, Family, and the Economy.* New York: Routledge.

West, A. and Varlaam, A. (1991) 'Choosing a secondary school: Parents of junior school children', *Educational Research* 33 (1): 22–30.

Wetherell, M. (ed.) (2009a) *Identity in the 21st Century: New Trends in Changing Times.* Basingstoke: Palgrave Macmillan.

Wetherell, M. (ed.) (2009b) *Theorizing Identities and Social Action.* Basingstoke: Palgrave Macmillan.

Wetherell, M. (2010) 'The field of identity studies', in M. Wetherell and C. T. Mohanty (eds), *The Sage Handbook of Identities.* London: Sage, 3–26.

Williams, K., Jamieson, F. and Hollingworth, S. (2008) ' "He was a bit of a delicate thing": White middle-class boys, gender, school choice and parental anxiety', *Gender and Education* 20 (4): 399–408.

Williams, R. (1976) *Keywords.* London: Fontana.

Willis, P. (1977) *Learning to Labour.* Farnborough: Saxon House.

Willmott, P. and Young, M. (1967) *Family and Class in a London Suburb.* NEL: Mentor.

Wood, A. W. (1990) *Hegel's Ethical Thought.* Cambridge: Cambridge University Press.

Young, I. M. (1997) 'Asymmetrical reciprocity: On mutual respect, wonder, and enlarged thought', *Constellations* 3 (3): 340–363.

Zizek, S. (2006) *The Parallax View.* Cambridge, Massachusetts: The MIT Press.

Index

CPSIA information can be obtained at www.ICGtesting.com
Printed in the USA
BVOW03s0006251013

334603BV00006B/47/P